SCIENCE
Formative
Assessment

This book is dedicated to Francis Eberle. In 1996, you opened the door for me to pursue my vision, goals, and ideas with the MMSA, and that door has been opening wider ever since. I will always be grateful for your unwavering support, integrity, kindness, and respect for people and their ideas.

SCIENCE
Formative Assessment

75 Practical Strategies for Linking Assessment, Instruction, and Learning

Page Keeley

A Joint Publication

CORWIN PRESS
A SAGE Company
Thousand Oaks, CA 91320

National Science Teachers Association

For information:

Corwin Press
A SAGE Company
2455 Teller Road
Thousand Oaks, California 91320
www.corwinpress.com

SAGE Ltd.
1 Oliver's Yard
55 City Road
London EC1Y 1SP
United Kingdom

SAGE India Pvt. Ltd.
B 1/I 1 Mohan Cooperative
   Industrial Area
Mathura Road, New Delhi 110 044
India

SAGE Asia-Pacific Pte. Ltd.
33 Pekin Street #02-01
Far East Square
Singapore 048763

Printed in the United States of America.

Library of Congress Cataloging-in-Publication Data

Keeley, Page.
Science formative assessment: 75 practical strategies for linking assessment, instruction, and learning/Page Keeley.
    p. cm.
"A joint publication with the National Science Teachers Association."
Includes bibliographical references and index.
ISBN 978-1-4129-4179-2 (cloth: acid-free paper)
ISBN 978-1-4129-4180-8 (pbk.: acid-free paper)
   1. Science—Study and teaching—Evaluation. 2. Interaction analysis in education.
3. Creative ability in science. 4. Effective teaching. 5. Curriculum planning.
I. National Science Teachers Association. II. Title.

Q181.K247 2008
507.1—dc22   2007043276

This book is printed on acid-free paper.

        11   12   10   9   8

Acquisitions Editor:	Cathy Hernandez
Editorial Assistant:	Ena Rosen
Production Editor:	Libby Larson
Copy Editor:	Gillian Dickens
Typesetter:	C&M Digitals (P) Ltd.
Proofreader:	Caryne Brown
Indexer:	Maria Sosnowski
Cover Designer:	Monique Hahn
Graphic Designer:	Lisa Riley

Contents

Preface

The most important single factor influencing learning is what the learner already knows. Ascertain this and teach him accordingly.

—Ausubel, Novak, and Hanesian (1978)

FORMATIVE ASSESSMENT IN SCIENCE

Science educators agree that good assessment practices are integral to informing teaching and learning, as well as measuring and documenting student achievement. In the current climate of high-stakes testing and accountability, the balance of time, resources, and emphasis on students' scores related to assessment have been tilted considerably toward the summative side. Unfortunately, this imbalance has led to a cycle of even more standardized testing of students and "mile wide, inch deep" instruction, often with only marginal gains in achievement. When science test scores fail to improve significantly, often the knee-jerk reaction is to increase the cycle of testing and test preparation, covering large amounts of content in a superficial way. This tension between assessment for accountability and assessment to inform teaching reduces the amount of time teachers spend on understanding what their students think prior to instruction and using that information to design learning opportunities that help students develop deeper conceptual understanding.

This book addresses the need to balance opportunity to learn, which includes assessment *for* learning (Black, Harrison, Lee, Marshall, & Wiliam, 2003), with assessment *of* learning. Optimal opportunities to learn exist when science teachers are aware of the variety of different ideas students are likely to bring to their learning, see the connections between students' thinking and the specific ideas targeted by state and national standards, and provide learning experiences that build a bridge between their students' thinking and the accepted scientific ideas. What is effective for one purpose—external accountability—may not effectively serve the purpose of informing instructional planning and decision making, which is what ultimately affects student learning. A rich repertoire of formative assessment techniques provides the ongoing feedback and stimulus for deep thinking that a high-stakes test once or twice a year cannot provide in time to inform instruction and affect learning.

Teachers are the most important link in the chain that connects assessment, instruction, and learning. The need for a varied repertoire of purposeful techniques that weave assessment throughout instruction and learning is what led to this book. I hope you can turn the insights and ideas gleaned from this book into practical actions that will transform teaching and learning in your classroom.

PURPOSE AND NEED

A substantive body of research indicates that formative assessment can significantly improve student learning. Yet this same research shows that the features of formative assessment that affect student achievement are, sadly, missing from many classrooms (Black et al., 2003). The purpose of this book is to provide teachers with guidance, suggestions, and techniques for using formative assessment to improve teaching and learning in the science classroom. A wide variety of assessment books and resources available to science educators provide the theoretical rationale for formative assessment and its implications for teaching and learning. This book expands on the current literature by identifying and describing practical techniques teachers can use to build a rich repertoire of formative assessment strategies for the science classroom.

The acronym, FACT, is used to label the 75 techniques included in this book. FACT stands for formative assessment classroom technique. Through the varied use of FACTs, explicitly tied to a purpose for gathering information about or promoting students' thinking and learning, teachers can focus on what works best for learning and design or modify lessons to fit the needs of the students.

AUDIENCE

The primary audience for this book is K–12 science teachers. However, many of the techniques described can be used in other disciplines such as mathematics, social studies, language arts, fine arts, health, and foreign language and are thus noted in each of the FACT descriptions. University faculty may also find the FACTs useful with college students. In addition, professional developers can use several of the FACTs to design and monitor learning experiences for adult learners, including teachers.

ORGANIZATION

Chapter 1 provides an introduction to formative assessment in the science classroom. It describes the inextricable link between assessment, instruction, and learning. It describes what a FACT is and the cognitive research that supports the use of FACTs. It describes the learning environments that support assessment, instruction, and learning. It examines the relationship between teaching and learning and describes new roles and implications for a formative assessment-centered classroom.

Chapter 2 focuses on the use of FACTs to integrate assessment, instruction, and learning. It examines the connection between assessment and instruction and describes a learning cycle model in science (SAIL cycle) that integrates assessment with instruction and learning and provides a framework for using FACTs. It describes how formative assessment promotes learning in the science classroom, including the role of metacognition, self-assessment, and reflection. It provides suggestions for strengthening the link between assessment, instruction, and learning.

Chapter 3 addresses considerations for selecting, implementing, and using the data from science formative assessment. It includes a matrix for matching FACTs with their primary purposes in teaching and learning.

Chapter 4 is the heart of the book. It includes a collection of 75 different FACTs. The FACTs are arranged in alphabetical order so that teachers can locate them by name. They are also numbered on the matrix in Figure 3.4 (starting on page 42) in Chapter 3. Each FACT uses a common format that provides a description, how it promotes student learning, how it informs instruction, considerations for design and administration, modifications that can be made to a FACT for different types of students or purposes, caveats for using a particular technique, general attributes, and uses in other disciplines besides science. Where appropriate, each FACT includes an example that shows or describes how the FACT is used in science. Space is provided after each FACT to record your notes on how it worked in your classroom and any modifications or suggestions for further use.

The Appendix contains annotated resources referenced in Chapter 4. These resources also contain additional material that a teacher would find useful for expanding his or her knowledge of formative assessment and building a repertoire of strategies.

Acknowledgments

M ost of the ideas and techniques in this book are not new or unique. They have been drawn from formative assessment techniques used by classroom teachers, professional developers, researchers, and the author's experiences as a former middle and high school science teacher. Several of the FACTs are so commonly used that it is hard to trace back the original source. In some cases, a new name and a new twist have been added to an old technique.

I am indebted to the teachers I have had the honor and pleasure to work with in various projects both in Maine and nationally, who have shared their repertoire of strategies with me, tried out new as well as variations of existing strategies, and helped me to understand which FACTs work best in different contexts. In particular, I would like to thank Beth Chagrasulis for her inspirational ideas on formative assessment and all the teachers in the NNECN, EMSS, and SC4 projects for giving me a window into your use of formative assessment strategies. Thank you to all the teachers who have inspired me through your dedication to the continuous improvement of teaching practice and your keen insights into student learning.

I especially wish to acknowledge my dear friend and colleague Joyce Tugel. Oh, the places we have gone and the professional development we have designed and led—it wouldn't be half as rewarding without you! Many thanks go to my colleagues at the Maine Mathematic and Science Alliance (MMSA) who have joined me on this exciting journey into formative assessment: Francis Eberle, Lynn Farrin, Joyce Tugel, Chad Dorsey, Nancy Chesley, Mary Dunn, Brianne Van Den Bossche, Meghan Southworth, and Cheryl Rose. There are too many to mention here, but I especially want to acknowledge Bev Cox, Bonnie Mizell, Joan Walker, Molly Malloy, Takumi Sato, Jean May-Brett, Brenda Nixon, Pam Pelletier, Marilyn Decker, Pat Shane, Jackie Menasco, Susan German, Carolyn Landel, Kathy DiRanna, Karen Cerwin, Susan Mundry, Susan Hodges, Linda Lacy, Felicia Roher, Jane Voth-Palisi, and Ray Barber for spreading our formative assessment work to new audiences.

I gratefully acknowledge my new Corwin Press editor, Cathy Hernandez, for her positive enthusiasm and ability to keep me on track, along with kudos for the outstanding support the staff at Corwin Press provides their authors. My deep appreciation also goes to the NSTA Press—David Beacom, Claire Reinburg, Judy Cusick, and Robin Allan—for the opportunity to further extend this work to the science education community.

Publisher's Acknowledgments

Corwin Press gratefully acknowledges the contributions of the following reviewers:

Beverly Cox, Elementary Science Resource Teacher, Orange County Public Schools, Orlando, FL

Sandra K. Enger, Associate Professor of Science Education, UAH Institute for Science Education, Huntsville, AL

Darleen Horton, Science Teacher, Chenoweth Elementary School, Prospect, KY

Susan B. Koba, Science Education Consultant, Omaha, NE

Jackie Menasco, Professional Development Coordinator in Science Education, Center for Science Teaching and Learning, Northern Arizona University, Flagstaff, AZ

Bill Nave, Research & Evaluation Consultant, Winthrop, ME

About the Author

 **Page Keeley** is the Senior Science Program Director at the Maine Mathematics and Science Alliance (MMSA). She directs projects in the areas of leadership, professional development, formative assessment, mentoring and coaching, and standards and research-based teaching and learning. She consults nationally with schools and organizations throughout the United States and serves on several national advisory boards for science education. She has been a Principal Investigator on three National Science Foundation Projects and a National Semiconductor Foundation–supported Science and Literacy Project, as well as a Co-Principal Investigator on two state Math-Science Partnership Projects and an NOAA Environmental Literacy Grant. She is the author of five nationally published books, including the *Curriculum Topic Study* series (2005 and 2006) and the *Uncovering Student Ideas in Science* series (2006, 2007, 2008), as well as several journal articles. She has served as an adjunct instructor in inquiry science at the University of Maine and is a Fellow in the National Academy for Science and Mathematics Education Leadership. She was elected the 63rd President of the National Science Teachers Association (NSTA) for the 2008–2009 term.

Prior to working at the MMSA, she taught middle and high school science for 15 years. During that time, she received several distinguished awards for teaching, including the Presidential Award for Excellence in Secondary Science Teaching in 1992 and the Milken National Distinguished Educator Award in 1993. Prior to teaching, she was a research assistant in immunodeficiency diseases at the Jackson Laboratory of Mammalian Genetics in Bar Harbor, Maine. She received her undergraduate degree in life sciences from the University of New Hampshire and her master's degree in science education from the University of Maine.

An Introduction to Formative Assessment Classroom Techniques (FACTs)

WHAT DOES A FORMATIVE ASSESSMENT-CENTERED CLASSROOM LOOK LIKE?

In a primary classroom, students are having a "science talk" to decide which organisms illustrated on a set of cards are called "animals." After using a *Card Sort* strategy to group the cards as "animals" and "not animals," the teacher encourages the students to develop a rule that could be used to decide whether an organism is an animal. The students share their ideas, openly agreeing or disagreeing with their peers. The teacher records the ideas that are most common among students and notes the reasoning students use. She notices many students think animals must have fur or legs and that humans are not animals and makes note of this to address in the next lesson. She then gives students an opportunity to regroup their cards, using the rule they developed as a class. She listens carefully as students explain their reasoning based on the "animal rule" they developed. The teacher adds new cards to the *Card Sort*. Some students decide they need to revise the rule to fit the new cards. The teacher probes deeper to find out why some students revised their thinking.

In an intermediate classroom, students use a *P-E-O Probe* to predict and explain whether the mass of an ice cube in a sealed ziplock bag will increase, decrease, or stay the same after it melts. Using the *Human Scatterplots* technique, the teacher quickly sees that students differ in their predictions and confidence in their answer. She then provides them with an opportunity to discuss their prediction and the justification for it in small groups. The teacher listens carefully and notes the preconceptions students bring to the problem, particularly concepts they may have encountered previously, such as ice floating, that seem to muddle their understanding of the conservation-of-matter phenomenon of ice melting. After students have had an opportunity to explain their thinking about what would happen to the mass of the ice cube after it melts, the teacher provides an opportunity for students to test their ideas by observing and recording the mass of an ice cube in a sealed ziplock bag before and after it melts. She notices how some students are starting to rethink their ideas. The class then comes together to discuss and reconcile their findings with their original predictions and ideas. The students use *Scientists' Ideas Comparison* to examine their new thinking and compare how closely their current ideas match the scientific explanation.

In a middle school classroom, the teacher uses a *Familiar Phenomenon Probe* to uncover students' explanations for the phases of the moon. Using the *Sticky Bars* strategy to anonymously display students' ideas, the teacher and the class could instantly see that most students believed the phases of the moon were caused by the shadow of the Earth on the moon. Knowing that this would be a difficult idea to change, the teacher designs a lesson that involves the students in constructing a model to visually see for themselves how the position of the moon in relation to the Earth and the sun results in the different moon phases. After students experience the model, they revisit their original explanations and have an opportunity to revise them. The next day, students are given a task of researching lunar eclipses. They work in small groups with *Whiteboards* to illustrate and explain the difference between an eclipse and a new moon. Students share their *Whiteboard* ideas and get feedback from the class and teacher regarding the differences in representing the two sun-Earth-moon phenomena. At the end of the lesson, students use *I Used to Think . . . But Now I Know* to reflect on their original explanation for the phases of the moon and describe how comparing the model of an eclipse with the model of a moon phase helped them better understand both phenomena.

In a high school chemistry class, small groups of students are using *A & D Statements* to discuss and reconcile their different ideas about the claim, "The mass of an iron object decreases as it rusts." One student who agrees with the claim is trying to persuade her classmates to consider her idea that rust is like a mold that eats and breaks down iron, causing it to lose mass. Another student who disagrees with the claim argues that the air is combined with the iron to make rust, which would add mass. Each group is trying to come up with a consensus idea and explanation to share with the class along with a method to test its idea. The teacher circulates among groups, probing further and encouraging argumentation. Students write a *Two-Minute Paper* at the end of class to share their thinking with the teacher and describe what they need to do next to test their ideas. The teacher uses this information to prepare for student inquiry the next day.

What do all of these classroom snapshots have in common? Each of these examples combines formative assessment techniques with instruction for a specific teaching and learning purpose. Often it is hard to tell whether a particular technique or strategy serves an instructional, assessment, or learning purpose since they are so intertwined. Students are learning while at the same time the teacher is gathering valuable information about their thinking that will inform instruction and provide feedback to students on their learning.

Each of these snapshots gives a brief glimpse into the different techniques teachers use to promote student thinking, uncover students' ideas, and use information about their students' progress in learning to improve their instruction. The teaching strategies in these snapshots are just a few of the 75 formative assessment classroom techniques (FACTs) described in Chapter 4, along with the underpinnings described in Chapters 1 through 3, that will help you understand and effectively use formative assessment. While you may be tempted to skip ahead and go directly to Chapter 4 to find FACTs you can use in your classroom, you are encouraged to read the preceding chapters. By having a firm knowledge base about the purposes and uses of formative assessment, as well as considerations for their use before you select a FACT, the image and implementation of formative assessment in your classroom will be sharper and more deliberately focused.

WHY USE FACTS?

Every day, science teachers are asking questions, listening carefully to students as they explain their ideas, observing students as they work in groups, examining student writing and drawings, and orchestrating classroom discourse that promotes the public sharing of ideas. These purposeful, planned, and often spontaneous teacher-to-student, student-to-teacher, and student-to-student verbal and written interactions involve a variety of assessment techniques. These techniques are used to engage students in thinking deeply about their ideas in science, uncover the preexisting ideas students bring to their learning that can be used as starting points to build upon during instruction, and help teachers and students determine how well individuals and the class are progressing toward developing scientific understanding.

"Assessment for learning is any assessment for which the first priority in its design and practice is to serve the purpose of promoting pupils' learning. It thus differs from assessment designed primarily to serve the purposes of accountability, or of ranking, or of certifying competence" (Black & Harrison, 2004).

The 75 science formative assessment classroom techniques, FACTs, described in this book are inextricably linked to assessment, instruction, and learning. The interconnected nature of formative assessment clearly differentiates the types of assessments we call assessments *for* learning from assessments *of* learning—the summative assessments used to measure and document student achievement. Although it is important to recognize that summative assessments can also be used formatively, they tend to be more formal in nature, tend to be given at an endpoint of instruction, and usually involve grading or other means of determining proficiency. Figure 1.1 describes the different types and purposes of assessment in the science classroom. Note that diagnostic assessment becomes formative assessment when the information is used by the teacher to improve teaching and learning. For example, a teacher can collect data in response to a probing question in order to identify the commonly held ideas students have about a phenomenon. But, if the data are not used to inform teaching and learning, then it is merely a diagnosis without action. In a medical context, this would be analogous to the sick patient who goes to the doctor and is diagnosed with a medical condition. To go beyond the diagnosis, the doctor would use the information collected diagnostically to design the best course of treatment so that the patient's health would improve.

Each FACT described in Chapter 4 is a type of question, process, or activity that helps to provide teachers and students with information about their factual, conceptual, and procedural understandings in science. These formative assessment techniques inform teaching by allowing the teacher to continuously gather information on student thinking and learning in order to make data-informed decisions to plan for or adjust instructional activities, monitor the pace of instruction, identify potential

Figure 1.1   Types and Purposes of Assessment

Diagnostic—To identify preconceptions, lines of reasoning, and learning difficulties.

Formative—To inform instruction and provide feedback to students on their learning.

Summative—To measure and document the extent to which students have achieved a learning target.

NOTE: Diagnostic assessment becomes formative when the assessment data are used to inform instruction.

misconceptions that can be barriers as well as springboards for learning, and spend more time on ideas that students struggle with. Formative assessment is also used to provide feedback to students, engaging them in the assessment of their own and their peers' thinking and learning. In addition to informing instruction and providing feedback, many of the formative assessment techniques included in this book initiate the use of metacognitive skills and promote deeper student thinking.

The FACTs described in this book are designed to be easily embedded into classroom instruction. They are primarily used to assess *before and throughout* the learning process, rather than at an endpoint of instruction (except for reflection). Their main purpose is to improve student learning and opportunities to learn through carefully designed instruction. They are not used for the summative purpose of accountability—measuring and reporting student achievement. The versatility of the techniques described accommodates a range of learning styles and can be used to differentiate instruction and assessment for individuals and groups of students. FACTs can be used to spark students' interest, surface ideas, initiate an inquiry, and encourage classroom discourse—all assessment strategies that promote learning rather than measure and report learning. A rich repertoire of FACTs enables learners to interact with assessment in multiple ways—through writing, drawing, speaking, listening, physically moving, and designing and carrying out investigations. Figure 1.2 lists a variety of purposes for using FACTs in the science classroom.

"When data are used by teachers to make decisions about next steps for a student or group of students, to plan instruction, and to improve their own practice, they help *inform* as well as *form* practice; this is *formative assessment.* When data are collected at certain planned intervals, and are used to show what students have achieved to date, they provide a *summary* of progress and are *summative assessment*" (Carlson, Humphrey, & Reinhardt, 2003, p. 4).

Regardless of geographic area, type of school, diversity of student population, science discipline, and grade level science teachers teach in, every teacher shares the same goal. That goal is to provide the highest quality instruction that will ensure that all students have opportunities to learn the concepts and skills that will help them become science-literate students and adults. Formative assessment provides ongoing opportunities for teachers to elicit students' prior knowledge; identify the ideas they struggle with, accommodate, or develop as they engage in the process of learning; and determine the extent to which students are moving toward or have reached scientific understanding at an appropriate developmental level. FACTs help teachers continuously examine how students' ideas form and change over time as well as how students respond to particular teaching approaches. This information is constantly used to adjust instruction and refocus learning to support each student's intellectual growth in science.

Figure 1.2   Twenty Purposes for Using FACTs

- Activate thinking and engage students in learning
- Make students' ideas explicit to themselves and the teacher
- Challenge students' existing ideas and encourage intellectual curiosity
- Encourage continuous reflection on teaching and learning
- Help students consider alternative viewpoints
- Provide a stimulus for discussion and scientific argumentation
- Help students recognize when they have learned or not learned something
- Encourage students to ask better questions and provide thoughtful responses
- Provide starting points for student investigations and idea exploration
- Aid formal concept development and transfer
- Determine if students can apply scientific ideas to new situations
- Differentiate instruction for individuals or groups of students
- Promote the use of academic language in science learning
- Evaluate the effectiveness of a lesson
- Help students develop self-assessment and peer assessment skills
- Give and use feedback (student to student, teacher to student, and student to teacher)
- Encourage social construction of ideas in science
- Inform immediate or later adjustments to instruction
- Encourage and include participation of all learners
- Increase comfort in making one's own ideas public

HOW DOES RESEARCH SUPPORT THE USE OF FACTS?

The seminal report from the National Research Council, *How People Learn: Brain, Mind, Experience, and School* (Bransford, Brown, & Cocking, 1999), has significantly contributed to our understanding of how students learn science. This understanding has implications for what is taught in science, how science is taught, how science learning is assessed, and how to promote deeper understanding in science. Three core principles from this report strongly support the use of FACTs in the science classroom.

> **Principle 1:** If their [students'] initial understanding is not engaged, they may fail to grasp new concepts and information presented in the classroom, or they may learn them for purposes of a test but revert to their preconceptions (Bransford et al., 1999, p. 14).

This principle supports the use of FACTs as a way to elicit the prior ideas students bring to the classroom, making their thinking visible to themselves, their peers, and the teacher. Students do not begin science learning as blank slates waiting to be filled with knowledge. By knowing in advance the ideas students have already formed in their minds, teachers can design targeted instruction and create conditions for learning that take into account and build upon students' preconceived ideas. Students' own ideas and the instructional opportunities that use them as springboards provide a foundation on which formal concepts and skills in science can be developed. As students engage in learning experiences designed to help them develop scientific understandings, teachers keep their fingers on the pulse of students' learning, determining when instruction is effective in helping students revise or refine their ideas and make midcourse corrections as needed.

> **Principle 2:** To develop competence in an area of inquiry, students must (a) have a deep foundation of factual knowledge, (b) understand facts and ideas in the context of a conceptual framework, and (c) organize knowledge in ways that facilitate retrieval and application (Bransford et al., 1999, p. 16).

This principle points out the importance of factual knowledge but cautions that knowledge of a large set of disconnected facts is not sufficient to support conceptual understanding. Several of the FACTs described in Chapter 4 not only provide strategies for teachers to assess students' knowledge of facts and understanding of concepts but actually promote thinking that supports understanding. This thinking and the feedback students receive during the learning process help support the development of a conceptual framework of ideas. Teachers use the information on students' thinking to design opportunities that will help move students from novice learners to deeper, conceptual learners who can draw upon and retrieve information from their framework. As concept development is monitored, reinforced, and solidified, formative assessment techniques are also used to determine how well students can transfer their new knowledge and skills from one context to another.

> **Principle 3:** A "metacognitive" approach to instruction can help students learn to take control of their own learning by defining learning goals and monitoring their progress in achieving them (Bransford et al., 1999, p. 18).

John Flavel, a Stanford University psychologist, coined the term *metacognition* in the late 1970s to name the process of thinking about one's own thinking and learning. Since then, cognitive science has focused considerable attention on this phenomenon (Walsh & Sattes, 2005). Several FACTs described in this book promote the use of metacognitive strategies for self-regulation of learning. These strategies help students monitor their own learning by helping them predict outcomes, explain ideas to themselves, note areas where they have difficulty understanding scientific concepts, activate prior knowledge and background information, and recognize experiences that help or hinder their learning. White and Frederickson (1998) suggest that metacognitive strategies not be taught generically but rather be embedded into the subject matter that students are learning. The FACTs that support metacognition are designed to be seamlessly embedded into the science learning experiences that target students' ideas and thinking in science. They provide opportunities for students to have an internal dialogue that mentally verbalizes their thinking, which can then be shared with others.

Evidence from the research studies described in *How People Learn* (Bransford et al., 1999) indicates that when these three principles are incorporated into instruction, assessment, and learning, student achievement improves. This research is further supported by the metastudy described in *Assessment for Learning* (Black et al., 2003), which makes a strong case, supported with quantitative evidence, for the use of formative assessment to improve learning, particularly to raise the achievement levels of students who have typically been described as low performers.

CLASSROOM ENVIRONMENTS THAT SUPPORT FORMATIVE ASSESSMENT

In addition to contributing to our understanding of how students learn science, *How People Learn* (Bransford et al., 1999) has changed our view of how classroom environments should be designed that support teaching and learning. These characteristics relate directly to classroom climates and cultures where the use of FACTs is an integral part of teaching and learning. These environments include the following:

Learner-Centered Environment. In a learner-centered environment, teachers pay careful attention to the knowledge, beliefs, attitudes, and skills students bring to the classroom (Bransford et al., 1999, p. 23). In a learner-centered classroom, teachers use FACTs before and throughout instruction, pay careful attention to the progress of each student, and know at all times where their students are in their thinking and learning. All ideas, whether they are right or wrong, are valued in a learner-centered environment. Learners come to value their ideas, knowing that their existing conceptions that surface through the use of FACTs provide the beginning of a pathway to new understandings.

Knowledge-Centered Environment. In a knowledge-centered environment, teachers know what the goals for learning are, the key concepts and ideas that make up the goals, the prerequisites upon which prior and later understandings are built, the types of experiences that support conceptual learning, and the assessments that will provide information about student learning. In addition, these goals, key concepts and ideas, and prerequisite learnings can be made explicit to students as well so they can monitor their progress toward achieving understanding (Bransford et al., 1999, p. 24). The knowledge-centered environment uses FACTs to understand students' thinking in order to provide the necessary depth of experience students need to develop conceptual understanding. It looks beyond student engagement and how well students enjoy their science activities. There are important differences between science activities that are "fun" and those that encourage learning with understanding. FACTs support a knowledge-centered environment by promoting and monitoring learning with understanding.

Assessment-Centered Environment. Assessment-centered environments provide opportunities for students to surface, examine, and revise their thinking (Bransford et al., 1999, p. 24). The ongoing use of FACTs makes students' thinking visible to both teachers and students and provides students with opportunities to revise and improve their thinking and monitor their own learning progress. In a formative assessment-centered environment, teachers identify problem learning areas to focus on. They encourage students to examine how their ideas

> "An important feature of the assessment-centered classroom is assessment that supports learning by providing students with opportunities to revise and improve their thinking" (Donovan & Bransford, 2005, p. 16).

have changed over the course of a unit of study. Having an opportunity to examine their own ideas and share how and why they have changed is a powerful moment that connects the student to the teaching and learning process.

Community-Centered Environment. A community-centered environment is a place where students learn from each other and continually strive to improve their learning. It is a place where social norms are valued in the search for understanding, and both teachers and students believe that everyone can learn (Bransford et al., 1999, p. 25). Within this environment, FACTs are used to promote intellectual camaraderie around discussing and learning ideas in science. A science community-centered environment that uses FACTs encourages the following:

- Public sharing of all ideas, not just the "right answers"
- Safety in academic risk taking
- Shared revision of ideas and reflection
- Questioning and clarification of explanations
- Discussions with peers and use of norms of scientific argumentation
- Group and individual feedback on teaching and learning

A classroom "ecosystem" with these four overlapping environments is a place where students and teachers both feel part of an intellectual learning community that is continuously improving opportunities to teach and learn. It is a place where students and teachers thrive. It is a place where the connections between assessment, teaching, and learning are inseparable.

CONNECTING TEACHING AND LEARNING

Imagine the following scenario. Two friends are talking about their pets. One friend says that he taught his dog how to ride a skateboard. The other friend pulls out his skateboard and waits for the dog to ride it. After encouraging the dog to ride the skateboard with no luck, his friend says, "I said I taught him how to ride a skateboard. I didn't say he learned it." Without the effective use of formative assessment, teaching science to children can be like teaching your dog to ride a skateboard.

"Learning can and often does take place without the benefit of teaching—and sometimes even in spite of it—but there is no such thing as effective teaching in the absence of learning" (Angelo & Cross, 1993, p. 3).

Teaching without learning can happen in science classrooms. The unfortunate truth is, even with what one perceives as his or her most engaging activity or best teaching moments, instruction can result in little or no gain in conceptual understanding if the time is not taken to find out students' initial preconceptions, ascertain their readiness to learn, monitor their learning to uncover any conceptual difficulties that can be addressed during instruction, and provide opportunities for feedback and reflection.

Even our brightest students can "learn" science for the purpose of passing a test but then quickly revert back to their misconceptions. Gaps often exist between what was taught and what students actually learned. Frequently, these gaps do not show up until after students have been summatively assessed through end-of-unit, district, or state assessments. At that point, it is often too late to go back and modify the lessons, particularly when assessments given months and even years later point out the gaps in student learning.

To stop this inefficient cycle of backfilling the gaps, teachers need better ways of determining where their students are in their thinking and understanding prior to and throughout the instructional process. Students need to be actively involved in the assessment process so that they are learning through assessment as well as providing useful feedback to the teacher and other students. Good formative assessment practices raise the quality of classroom instruction and promote deeper conceptual learning. Formative assessment ultimately empowers both the teacher and the student to make the best possible decisions regarding teaching and learning.

Linking assessment, instruction, and learning does not merely involve adding some new techniques to teachers' repertoire of strategies. The purposeful use of FACTs, on a continuous basis, provides much more—it organizes the entire classroom around learning and informs ways teachers can provide more effective learning experiences based on how their own students think and learn. Formative assessment can be used formally or informally, but it is always purposeful. The FACTs teachers use and the actions they take based on the information they have gained can be immediate, the next day, over the course of a unit, or even shared with and used by teachers who will have the same students the next

"Formative assessment isn't just about strategies to ascertain current knowledge—formative happens after the finding out has taken place. It's about furthering student learning during the learning process" (Clarke, 2005, p. 1).

year. If information about student learning is collected but not used as feedback for the teacher or student to take action on that will improve teaching or learning, then it is not formative. It becomes information for information's sake. For example, using a FACT to find out if students have misconceptions similar to the commonly held ideas noted in the research literature is interesting and important in and of itself. However, just knowing students have these ideas does not make this a formative assessment activity. It is the collecting of this information and the decisions made as a result of carefully examining the data that gives it the distinction of formative assessment and connects teaching to learning.

MAKING THE SHIFT TO A FORMATIVE ASSESSMENT-CENTERED CLASSROOM

Formative assessment requires a fundamental shift in our beliefs about the role of a teacher. In a formative assessment-centered classroom, teachers interact more frequently and effectively with students on a day-to-day basis, promoting their learning (Black & Harrison, 2004). This interaction requires the teacher to step back from the traditional role of information provider and corrector of misconceptions in order to listen to and encourage a range of ideas among students. The teacher takes all ideas seriously, whether they are right or wrong, while helping students talk through their ideas and consider evidence that supports or challenges their thinking. During such interactions, the teacher is continuously thinking about how to shape instruction to meet the learning needs of their students and

"Even though teachers routinely gather assessment information through homework, quizzes, and tests, from the students' perspective, this type of information is often collected too late to affect their learning. It is very difficult to 'de-program' students who are used to turning in homework, quizzes, and tests, getting grades back, and considering it 'over and done with'" (Angelo & Cross, 1993, p. 7).

build a bridge between their initial ideas and the scientific understandings all students need to achieve.

The teacher also plays a pivotal role in connecting assessment to students' opportunities to understand how science is conducted in the real world. Providing opportunities for students to make discoveries through their own investigations and authentic testing of ideas often surfaces new ideas and scientific ways of thinking. The provision of opportunities to speak, write about, and draw to organize thinking about such discoveries helps give rise to the students' view of science as an enterprise that values curiosity and personally meaningful insight (Shapiro, 1994).

Traditionally, science teachers were considered the providers of content that students then learned—teachers teach content and, as a result, students learn. The role of the teacher in a formative assessment-centered classroom is more of a facilitator and monitor of content learning. The teacher's role expands to helping students use strategies to understand how well they are learning. As a result, students become more conscious of the learning process itself and take greater responsibility for their own learning.

In a formative assessment-centered classroom, students learn to play an active role in the process of learning. They learn that their role is not only to actively engage in their own learning but to support the learning of others as well. They come to realize that learning has to be done *by* them—it cannot be done *for* them. They learn to use various FACTs that help them take charge of their own learning and assess where they stand in relation to identified learning goals. When they know what the learning target is, they use metacognitive skills along with peer and self-assessment strategies that enable them to steer their own learning in the right direction so they can take responsibility for it (Black & Harrison, 2004).

"The role of the learner is not to passively receive information, but to actively participate in the construction of new meaning" (Shapiro, 1994, p. 8).

Standards and learning goals have a significant impact on what teachers teach and students learn. Developing content knowledge that includes important scientific facts, conceptual ideas, skills of science, and habits of mind is at the center of science teaching and learning. As a result, teaching, assessing, and learning must take place with a clear target in mind. Standards should not become a checklist of content to be taught and assessed. Rather, they inform thinking about content as an interconnected cluster of learning goals that develop over time. By clarifying the specific ideas and skills described in the standards and articulated as learning goals, teachers are in a better position to uncover the gap between students' existing knowledge or skill and the knowledge or skill described in the learning goal. As a result, they are better able to monitor that gap as it closes (Black et al., 2003). While a particular FACT may determine the approach that teachers take to uncover students' ideas and modify instruction accordingly, the fundamental ideas and skills students need to learn remain the same. The focus of teaching and learning is on meeting goal-oriented learning needs rather than delivering a set of curricula at an established pace or teaching a favorite activity that does little to promote conceptual understanding.

Identifying and targeting learning goals is not the sole purview of the teacher. In a formative assessment-centered classroom, teachers share learning goals with students. This may involve breaking them down into the key ideas students will learn. Awareness of the goals and key ideas for learning helps students see the bigger picture of learning and make connections to what they already know about science concepts.

Another major shift that happens in a formative assessment-centered classroom is the recognition of the importance of students' ideas. Traditional instruction involved the passing on of information from the teacher or the instructional materials, with little thought given to building on students' existing conceptions. Students form many of their ideas in science before they ever formally encounter them in the classroom. These ideas come from previous school and life experiences and often conflict with the science understandings teachers are trying to develop. These preformed ideas are referred to in a variety of ways, including naive ideas, misconceptions, facets of understanding, partial understandings, commonly held ideas, or alternative conceptions. In this book, they will be referred to generically as *misconceptions*, although the term does not necessarily imply that the idea is completely incorrect. In some cases, misconceptions include partially formed correct ideas, but they are not yet put together in a way that is scientifically correct. It is important to recognize that these misconceptions have the following general characteristics (Connor, 1990):

> Putting one's ideas forward allows an opportunity for students to experience uncertainty and cognitive dissonance—the first step in building a bridge between students' ideas and scientific knowledge.

They form early, often before school begins, and continue lifelong.

They are subtle and can easily be missed by teachers who are unaware of them.

They are separable. Students retain their personal ideas even though they might give "school answers."

They are persistent, even after being disproved.

They are highly personal—each student sees experiences or draws conclusions from his or her point of view and constructs a personal meaning.

They appear to be incoherent to the teacher but make a lot of sense to the student.

A constructivist approach to teaching and learning posits that students' existing ideas make a difference to their future learning, so effective teaching needs to take these existing ideas into account. Research indicates that misconceptions held by students persist into adulthood if they are left unconfronted and unchallenged (Carre, 1993). However, this does not simply imply that misconceptions are a bad thing and must be confronted on the spot as "wrong ideas." Rather than immediately correcting misconceptions when they surface, teachers should gather information that may reveal how misconceptions can be used as starting points for instruction. Starting with students' ideas and monitoring their progress as they are guided through activities that help them recognize when their ideas no longer work for them and need to be modified or changed is the essence of an idea-focused, formative assessment classroom that promotes conceptual change.

As you gain a deeper understanding of the purposes and uses of formative assessment, you may find yourself reshaping techniques or developing new ones. You might find that some techniques work better than others depending on the scientific idea being assessed or the nature of the learners in your classroom. Many of the FACTs described in Chapter 4 may be new to you; others may be ones you use routinely. Regardless of how you use the FACTs or your familiarity with them, one important implication for the science classroom stands out—formative assessment provides an effective way for teachers to create classrooms that reflect current research on learning and provide greater opportunities for all students to achieve deeper levels of learning.

2

Integrating FACTs
With Instruction
and Learning

I taught a great lesson but the wrong class came.

—Anonymous

INTEGRATING ASSESSMENT
AND INSTRUCTION

Formative assessment classroom techniques (FACTs) are rooted in good teaching practice. They offer a variety of ways to seamlessly integrate assessment and instruction that help teachers learn more about what students need in order to be successful learners of science. Teachers who use FACTs start their lessons where their students' ideas are, identifying, charting, and monitoring learning paths that will eventually lead students to discover, understand, and use the important ideas and processes of science. Adapting teaching practice to align with the emerging research on formative assessment and how students learn has a reciprocal effect on teaching and learning. As teachers incorporate more FACTs into their practice, their understanding of student learning increases, which in turn improves the quality of their teaching and raises student achievement.

Consider how one first-grade teacher who studied her own assessment practices reflected on the link between assessment and her teaching:

> Assessment is best if embedded within instruction. Authentic assessment does not aim to assign a child a grade but to determine what children know and where to go next. . . . I need to embed more assessment tools within the curriculum. I need to also consider a variety of assessment tools to make certain that I am actually assessing science knowledge and not another curriculum area such as writing. I need to choose tools that allow students comfort to reveal their knowledge of science. (Cox-Peterson & Olson, 2002, p. 106)

The above reflection clearly notes the need to select the right tool or technique for the right instructional purpose. With 75 FACTs described in Chapter 4 to choose from, it is important to keep in mind that FACTs are not intended to be used as strategies picked at random. To be effectively integrated into one's teaching practice, FACTs must be thoughtfully selected to match the appropriate stage and purpose of instruction.

"The quality of student learning is directly, although not exclusively, related to the quality of teaching. Therefore, one of the most promising ways to improve learning is to improve teaching" Angelo & Cross, 1993, p. 7).

The teacher's reflection in the above quote indicates that the purpose of formative assessment is to guide teaching rather than assign a grade to students. While some of the FACTs described in Chapter 4 can be graded for summative purposes, their primary purpose is to inform and guide teaching and learning. This requires the teacher to shift instructional approaches from the "deliverer of content" and "assigner of grades" to careful gatherer and analyzer of student thinking and learning data that provide the teacher with information that can be used to make the content of a lesson more accessible to learners. This requires teachers to keep their fingers on the pulse of student learning by constantly being aware of, supporting, and monitoring students' questions, comments, ideas, feedback, and reflections. When used throughout instruction, formative assessment helps build the type of deeper conceptual knowledge that leads to enduring understanding.

ASSESSMENT THAT PROMOTES THINKING AND LEARNING

Formative assessment enhances the daily interactions between students and between students and teachers by providing varied opportunities to surface, examine, work through, and reflect on scientific ideas. While

FACTs provide valuable information to the teacher to use for making instructional decisions, they also activate, encourage, and deepen student thinking. Students use their existing ideas and build on them to understand and explain everyday objects, processes, and phenomena. FACTs encourage the use of thinking skills such as predicting, hypothesizing, using analogies, evaluating evidence, asking questions, and justifying ideas. Through the act of thinking about their ideas that surface through formative assessment, students actively engage in the process of constructing, modifying, or deepening their knowledge. Therefore, assessment not only serves the purpose of finding out what students are learning but also promotes learning.

> "Learning is a consequence of thinking. Retention, understanding, and the active use of knowledge can be brought about by learning experiences in which learners think about and think with what they are learning . . . knowledge comes on the coattails of thinking" (Perkins, 1992).

Metacognition is a key component of assessment that promotes learning. Metacognition involves thinking about one's thinking, including knowledge about one's self as a processor of concepts and ideas. Figure 2.1 lists several indicators of metacognition.

Appropriate kinds of self-monitoring through metacognitive techniques and reflection have been demonstrated to support learning with understanding in a variety of areas. Helping students become more metacognitive about their own thinking and learning is closely tied to instructional practices that encourage feedback and self-assessment. However, it is important to point out that responding to feedback provided by the teacher or other students is different from students' actively seeking feedback from the teacher or other students in order to assess their current thinking and level of understanding (Donovan & Bransford, 2005).

> "An assessment activity can help learning if it provides information to be used as feedback by teachers, and by their students in assessing themselves and each other, to modify the teaching and learning activities in which they are engaged. Such assessment becomes *formative assessment* when the evidence is used to adapt the teaching work to meet learning needs" (Black et al., 2003, p. 2).

Figure 2.1   Indicators of Metacognition

Students engaged in metacognitive processes . . .

- know what they or the teacher needs to do in order for them to learn effectively,
- monitor their current understanding and recognize the basis for their ideas,
- recognize how new knowledge relates to or challenges their existing conceptions,
- know what questions to ask to further one's understanding,
- are able to evaluate claims and ideas of others, and/or
- can monitor the extent to which they are able to contribute to others' learning.

"Supporting students to become aware of and engaged in their own learning will serve them well in all learning endeavors" (Donovan & Bransford, 2005, p. 12).

Providing support for metacognition and peer and self-assessment is an important use of several of the FACTs described in Chapter 4. FACTs can provide opportunities for students to analyze and evaluate their own ideas and the ideas of their peers. Awareness of one's thinking includes knowing when new knowledge relates to or challenges what one already knows or believes and leads to questions that stimulate further inquiry. Opportunities to test out ideas after making predictions confront students with the challenge of deciding if their ideas need to be revised, based on their new observations. Small-group and class discussions provide a forum for students to express their ideas, make their thinking visible to themselves and others, and explore ideas that seem to make the most sense. Graphic organizers help students organize their thinking.

To be effective in promoting thinking and learning, metacognitive and reflection strategies should be explicitly taught in the science classroom. FACTs that incorporate these strategies should be taught in the context of the content students are learning. Teaching FACTs apart from the content of a lesson is like teaching science process skills separate from authentic content-based science inquiry.

LINKING ASSESSMENT, INSTRUCTION, AND LEARNING: THE SCIENCE ASSESSMENT, INSTRUCTION, AND LEARNING CYCLE (SAIL CYCLE)

A continuous assessment, instruction, and learning cycle model for science that can be used with the FACTs in Chapter 4 is the science assessment,

"The notion of teaching for conceptual change has gone hand in hand with considerations of learning as conceptual change" (Hewson, 1992, p. 2).

instruction, and learning (SAIL) cycle shown in Figure 2.2. This instructional model can help guide science teachers in selecting an appropriate FACT to match the purpose and stage in the instructional or learning process and reinforces the inextricable link between assessment, instruction, and learning. The circular diagram illustrates the cyclic nature of the SAIL cycle, while instruction can loop back and repeat different stages as needed. Self-assessment and reflection are the centerpiece that promotes metacognition and is connected to each stage in the cycle.

In the early 1960s, J. Myron Atkin and Robert Karplus formulated a constructivist instructional model of guided discovery designed to be similar to the way scientists invent and use new concepts to explain the natural world. This instructional model, called the learning cycle, was

Figure 2.2   The Science Assessment, Instruction, and Learning (SAIL) Cycle

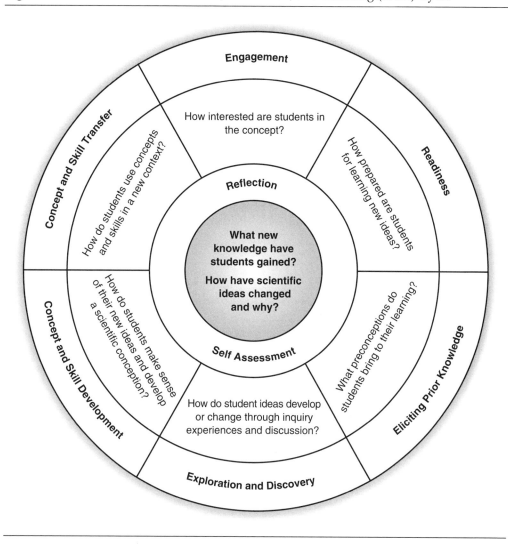

designed to allow students an opportunity to surface and examine their prior conceptions. Once ideas are revealed, students have an opportunity to explore their ideas, arguing about and testing them in the process. When students see that their existing ideas do not fully match their findings, a disequilibrium results that opens the door to the construction of new scientific ideas. When students reach the stage where they develop the formal scientific understandings and patterns of reasoning that help them make sense of phenomena, they are encouraged to extend their learning and apply their ideas to a new situation or context.

Throughout the various stages of a learning cycle, teachers design and monitor instruction so that students become increasingly conscious of their own and others' ideas. They gain confidence in their ability to learn, apply concepts to new situations, and construct evidence-based arguments (Lawson, 2002). Teachers orchestrate student learning in different ways at different stages, encouraging a classroom climate where ideas are openly generated and sufficient time is allowed for sense making and construction of new knowledge. All the while they are facilitating students' construction of new ideas, teachers are formatively assessing by monitoring students' changing conceptions and adapting their teaching and assessment techniques to match their students' needs.

The original learning cycle has undergone several adaptations, including the popular 5E model (Bybee, 1997), the conceptual change model (CCM) (Posner, Strike, Hewson, & Gertzog, 1982; Stepans, 2003), and the SAIL cycle described in this book. Figure 2.3 shows the similarities between the various stages of these three adaptations of the Karplus learning cycle.

STAGES IN THE SAIL CYCLE

The FACTs described in Chapter 4 can be used with any instructional model. The advantage to linking the FACTs to the SAIL cycle is that it helps provide a framework for seamlessly integrating assessment, teaching, and learning. Each of the stages in the SAIL cycle has an explicit purpose connected to assessment, instruction, and learning, as shown in Figure 2.4 and described below. Figure 2.5 shows the different types of assessment used in each stage of the cycle.

ENGAGEMENT AND READINESS

FACTs can provide an opportunity to activate student thinking, develop curiosity, and stimulate interest in the content of a lesson. One widely accepted role of any teacher is that of student motivator (Osborne & Freyberg, 1985). Several of the FACTs involve interesting situations that capture students' attention and trigger their thinking. Most students come to school ready to learn but with different social, cultural, educational, and real-life experiences. Various FACTs can reveal information about students' diverse backgrounds that affect their readiness to learn. The information is used by the teacher to determine supports and provisions that may be necessary to help students succeed in their classroom learning environment. Examples from Chapter 4: *Familiar Phenomenon Probes*, *Interest Scale*, or *Learning Goals Inventory*.

ELICITING PRIOR KNOWLEDGE

Drawing out the initial ideas students have developed through their prior experiences, intuition, and encounters with familiar phenomena provides

Figure 2.3   Related Versions of the Learning Cycle

5E Learning Cycle (R. Bybee)	Conceptual Change Model (CCM) (G. Posner et al.)	Science Assessment Instruction and Learning Cycle (SAIL Cycle) (P. Keeley)
Engage—provides an opportunity to capture interest in the topic, motivate students, and identify students' existing conceptions (including misconceptions)

Explore—provides students with an opportunity to test out their ideas as well as compare their ideas to the ideas of their peers

Explain—provides an opportunity for resolving misconceptions, sense making, and developing formal concept understanding and terminology

Elaborate—provides an opportunity to apply or extend the development of concepts and skills to new contexts and activities

Evaluate—provides an opportunity to determine how well students understand a concept or can apply a skill | **Commit to an Outcome**—provides an opportunity for students to become aware of their own preconceptions by making predictions about the result of an activity

Expose Beliefs—provides an opportunity to share ideas in small groups and then with the whole class

Confront Beliefs—provides an opportunity to test ideas and discuss them in small and large groups

Accommodate the Concept—provides an opportunity to resolve any discrepancies between their existing ideas and their observations or newly acquired information and to develop formal understanding of the concept

Extend the Concept—provides an opportunity to make a connection between their formal understanding of the concept from their class experience and new situations

Go Beyond—provides an opportunity to pursue additional questions or problems related to the concept | **Engagement and Readiness**—provides an opportunity to find out students' interest in the topic and preparation for further learning

Eliciting Prior Knowledge—provides an opportunity to identify the prior ideas and skills students bring to their learning

Exploration and Discovery—provides an opportunity to explore concepts and skills, test out ideas, and discover new findings before formal development of concepts and skills

Concept and Skill Development—provides an opportunity to link ideas developed up to this point with formal development of concept and skills through clarification, sense making, and development of appropriate scientific terminology

Concept and Skill Transfer—provides an opportunity to try out ideas and skills in new contexts and situations

Reflection and Self-Assessment—provides a metacognitive opportunity to think about how ideas have changed and how well one understands the concept and skills |

Figure 2.4 SAIL Cycle Connections to Teaching, Assessing, and Learning

Stage in the SAIL Cycle	Connection to Assessment The teacher . . .	Connection to Instruction The teacher . . .	Connection to Learning The student . . .
Engagement and Readiness	• determines students' interest in the content • gathers information about prerequisite learning goals and students' prior experiences that prepare them to learn new ideas	• interests students in the content and generates curiosity • gets students thinking about what they already know, have previously experienced, and questions they have	• becomes interested in the content and motivated to learn • activates thinking and uses metacognitive strategies • recognizes how prepared he or she is to explore new ideas
Eliciting Prior Knowledge	• elicits and identifies preconceptions students bring to their learning • analyzes students' thinking and reasoning • uses information to design instruction or modify lessons	• gives students an opportunity to identify and voice their preconceived ideas in a nonjudgmental environment • exposes students to others' initial ideas and ways of thinking	• activates own thinking about scientific ideas • surfaces and examines own ideas and prior experiences • considers others' initial ideas and compares them to own
Exploration and Discovery	• observes and listens to students as they interact with the content • asks probing questions • collects evidence of change in or development of students' ideas • monitors students' progress toward developing understandings and redirects when needed • determines need for differentiation of instruction	• challenges students' existing ideas to facilitate learning • provides stimuli for discussion • initiates inquiry and idea exploration • provides sufficient time to allow students to work through or test their ideas and consider new findings • encourages explanations based on observations and discussions • creates a desire to know	• investigates own ideas, including testing of predictions and use of evidence to revisit initial conceptions • uses metacognitive processes to think about own ideas and connect them to observations or discussions • experiences cognitive dissonance that may lead to eventually giving up or modifying his or her ideas

Concept and Skill Development	• monitors students' ideas and thinking for evidence of conceptual change • probes deeper to surface hidden misconceptions • identifies a need for additional lessons if there are discrepancies between students' conceptions and the scientific ideas • assesses student understanding of targeted concepts and skills	• facilitates construction of new knowledge by helping students examine their ideas, argue about them, and put new ideas together in order to make sense of experiences and evidence • encourages students to explain concepts in their own words and justify their ideas with evidence • builds a bridge between students' ideas and the formal ideas accepted by the scientific community	• examines the connection between own ideas and the scientific view that explains one's findings • engages in public sharing, argument, and analysis of ideas • seeks answers to questions, assimilates appropriate terminology and definitions, and clarifies murky understandings • considers alternative explanations
Concept and Skill Transfer	• analyzes how students use their formal scientific ideas and skills to develop a progressively more sophisticated knowledge of the concept or use of a skill and the ability to apply them to different situations • determines the extent to which students can apply concepts and skills to new contexts	• provides further elaboration of the focus concept through additional inquiries or activities • encourages students to build on their previously developed ideas • brings closure to the lessons by having students use the formally developed concepts they have learned in new or novel ways	• develops connections and linkages among ideas • recognizes the explanatory power of relevant phenomena and ideas that are applicable to objects, events, and processes encountered in everyday life • applies knowledge and skills in new or novel situations
Self-Assessment and Reflection	• examines reflections and self-assessments to determine the effectiveness of instruction • provides opportunities for students to give feedback to the teacher on lessons, activities, and instructional strategies that will improve opportunities to learn	• helps students surface what may hinder or support their learning • provides opportunities for students to revisit their initial ideas and skills and compare them to their current use and understandings	• acknowledges own progress in meeting learning goals • identifies areas for improvement or pursuit of new questions • identifies how confident he or she is in ideas and considers what it might take to change thinking

Figure 2.5   SAIL Cycle and General Assessment Types

Stage in the SAIL Cycle	Type of Assessment Used
Engagement and Readiness	Diagnostic Formative
Eliciting Prior Knowledge	Diagnostic Formative
Exploration and Discovery	Formative
Concept and Skill Development	Formative
Concept and Skill Transfer	Formative and Summative
Reflection and Self-Assessment	Formative

a starting point from which the teacher can design instruction that will build from students' ideas. Probing students' thinking allows teachers to determine where and how ideas may have developed and inform the types of instructional experiences that can build a bridge between where the students are in their understanding and the scientific view of the content they are learning. Elicitation strategies promote thinking by safely surfacing ideas in a nonjudgmental way. Discussion that accompanies elicitation allows students to share their thinking with others, which further challenges students' ideas as they consider them in light of their peers' explanations and arguments. Examples from Chapter 4: *Friendly Talk Probes, Commit and Toss,* or *Card Sorts.*

EXPLORATION AND DISCOVERY

The exploration and discovery stage can involve direct experience with physical objects or processes, reading text, or uncovering ideas in discussion with peers. This stage can include FACTs that ask students to make predictions that initiate scientific inquiry. Providing opportunities to justify and test out ideas gives students a body of evidence to use in considering scientific ideas during the concept development stage. This period of exploration and discovery allows the teacher to determine the kinds of understandings and questions students have before developing more structured opportunities for formalizing learning. During this stage, FACTs can also reveal how well students are responding to the activities, considering ideas of others, and whether their original ideas have been challenged based on the evidence gathered during their exploratory experiences. Assessment during this stage gives students a chance to share their developing ideas in a nonjudgmental environment for feedback from the teacher and peers. Selected FACTs expose students to others' ideas and thereby help them reflect on their own thinking, which subsequently informs instruction when shared with the teacher. Examples from Chapter 4: *A&D Statements, P-E-O Probes,* or *Concept Card Mapping.*

CONCEPT AND SKILL DEVELOPMENT

Assessment of conceptual understanding and use of skills during sense making, clarification, and development of formal concepts and processes helps both to reinforce the learning for students and uncover any difficulties in understanding or gaps that might still exist. FACTs used during this stage help teachers determine the extent to which students have grasped a concept, recognized relationships among ideas, or used appropriate terminology. Results inform instruction by identifying the need for additional learning experiences and opportunities to build more solid understandings, indicating readiness to introduce formal terminology, or signaling that students are ready to transfer ideas to a new context. In addition, teacher-to-student and student-to-student feedback further enhances opportunities to build conceptual knowledge and important inquiry skills of science. Examples from Chapter 4: *Refutations, Scientists' Idea Comparison,* or *Odd One Out.*

CONCEPT AND SKILL TRANSFER

Assessment information at this stage is used by the teacher to address impediments that may interfere with transferring learning to a new context or introduce new, related concepts that build more sophisticated understandings. Assessment information is used to modify learning opportunities so that students can use their newly formed or modified ideas in a new situation or novel context. Assessment opportunities provide students with an opportunity to think about how they can use their knowledge and skills in new situations. Examples from Chapter 4: *Justified List, Thought Experiments,* or *Recognizing Exceptions.*

SELF-ASSESSMENT AND REFLECTION

Encouraging reflection and self-assessment helps students develop important metacognitive skills that help them monitor their own thinking and learning. Students learn to *think about learning* as well as *think about thinking.* The distinction here is that self-assessment helps students think about whether the *content makes sense.* Reflection helps them think about how they *make sense of the content.* Students' self-assessments and reflections provide valuable feedback to the teacher to inform how students' ideas have changed or deepened over the course of instruction, how well students are aware of their learning, and the need to further differentiate instruction for individual students. Reflections on learning activities can be used by the teacher to improve an instructional unit or lesson for future classes or inform ways to resurface difficult concepts in subsequent related lessons. Examples from Chapter 4: *First Word–Last Word, I Used to Think . . . But Now I Know,* or *Muddiest Point.*

SELECTING AND USING FACTS TO STRENGTHEN THE LINK BETWEEN ASSESSMENT, INSTRUCTION, AND LEARNING

Selecting a FACT that informs teaching and promotes thinking is a first step in using assessment *for* teaching and learning. The following is a list of suggestions for using FACTs to strengthen the link between assessment, instruction, and learning.

1. **Think like a diagnostician.** Since students' preconceptions have such a powerful influence on their learning, teachers need to continually choose FACTs and devise ways to ascertain students' ideas in such a way that it becomes second nature to the teacher (Osborne & Freyberg, 1985). Teachers need to take advantage of every opportunity in both small groups and whole-class settings to explore students' ideas in depth and analyze their thinking.

2. **Make students' thinking explicit during scientific inquiry.** Use FACTs to draw out students' thinking before and throughout inquiry-based activities. Encourage students to commit to a prediction or outcome, supported by evidence from prior knowledge and experiences, to construct their explanations before testing their ideas. After committing to a justified prediction or outcome, students test their ideas and compare their observations with their initial ideas. When the evidence does not support their original thinking, the dissonance that results is the pivotal point in encouraging students to pursue more information that may help them give up their former ideas in order to accommodate new ones.

3. **Create a classroom culture of ideas, not answers.** Use the FACTs to encourage students to share their ideas, regardless of whether they are right or wrong. Many students have been raised in a classroom culture where they are expected to give the "right answer." Thus they hesitate to share their own ideas when they think they may be "wrong." Hold off on telling students whether they are "right or wrong" and provide time for them to work through their ideas, weighing various viewpoints and evidence, until they are ready to construct a new understanding. The emphasis on testing or discussing ideas and revising one's original

explanations should take precedence over getting the right answer. Getting all ideas out on the table first may be frustrating and take longer, but in the long run, it will develop confidence in reasoning abilities as well as deeper, enduring understandings. In addition, students will be less apt to revert back to their original preconceptions after the lesson or unit of instruction ends.

Vygotsky (1978) established the *zone of proximal development* as the challenge factor in learning—the difference between what students can do independently and what they can accomplish with the support of others. The constructivist model promotes cooperative situations as essential for effective learning, with much classroom talk—between students and teachers and between students together.

4. **Develop a discourse community.** One of the key features of several of the FACTs described in Chapter 4 is the way they promote learning through discussion and argumentation. When students are talking about their science ideas, whether in a whole-class discussion, in small groups, or in pairs, they are using the language of science as well as language that has meaning to them. "Talking the talk is an important part of learning" (Black & Harrison, 2004, p. 4). FACTs that encourage "science talk" not only engage students in activating their own thinking but also provide examples of others' thinking for students to consider.

5. **Encourage students to take risks.** Create a climate where it is acceptable to share an idea without fear of being corrected by or embarrassed in front of the teacher or other students. Students will often hesitate to participate in discussions for fear of being judged by their ideas. Create norms of collaboration in the classroom so that everyone's ideas are respected and acknowledged.

6. **Encourage students to listen carefully.** In a formative assessment classroom, different ideas are surfaced and discussed among pairs of students, small groups, and the whole class. Students need to learn to listen carefully to others' ideas and weigh the evidence that may lead to changing their own ideas. They need to learn not to accept a new idea just because their peers think it is correct. They need to learn how to examine all the ideas, including evidence from investigation and other relevant information sources, before accepting others' ideas or changing a previously held one of their own. Formative assessment encourages students to think rather than just accept ideas as they are presented.

7. **Use a variety of FACTs in a variety of ways.** Although many of the features of effective formative assessment can now be identified, there is no single, simple recipe that teachers can adopt and follow (National Research Council, 2001). Even though FACTs differ from each other in many of the details, a variety of approaches to using formative assessment leads to greater likelihood of success in improving learning. Try out different types of FACTs to promote thinking and learning and inform teaching. Vary the ways they reveal ideas—through writing, drawing, or

speaking. Vary strategies for sharing responses. For example, students can form groups based on the response they selected to discuss their ideas, then jigsaw with other groups to consider alternative explanations. Responses can also be shared anonymously by the teacher, building confidence within the class to discuss and evaluate different explanations without identifying individuals.

8. **Use a variety of grouping configurations.** The social context plays a powerful part in motivation and the effectiveness of learning. Many of the FACTs in this book emphasize the social and community aspects of learning. The social interactions involved when FACTs are used in pairs, small collaborative groups, or whole-class discourse are important for developing and deepening shared understandings. FACTs can provide a context and focal point for the discussion and argumentation that occur between students. Having to provide justification for one's ideas to a partner or others in a group develops deeper understanding in both the justifier and the students engaged in analyzing the justification.

9. **Encourage continuous reflection.** Encourage students to reflect back on their initial ideas in order to note their own evidence of conceptual change or identify areas where they are still struggling with an idea. Understanding is an evolving process. It takes time for students to move toward the accepted scientific view, and students need to understand that there are many steps along the way. Being aware of their own thinking (metacognition) and knowing the learning goal they are striving toward will help students be more accountable for their own learning. Revisiting their initial response to a FACT and comparing it to where they are in their current understanding is a powerful way to recognize and reinforce learning.

Feedback from teachers who have used FACTs to link assessment, instruction, and learning has been overwhelmingly positive. The use of FACTs has considerably elevated teachers' expectations of themselves and their students. The research on the effectiveness of formative assessment in improving learning has been confirmed for teachers through their own empirical observations as they see evidence of their students becoming more engaged and metacognitive in science, increasing their confidence in their ideas, using higher level thinking and response skills, and valuing feedback and reflection. One teacher shared her surprise when her students begged her to use more assessment probes in her science lessons. Her comment—"I can't believe my students were asking for more assessments! They even talk about the assessment probes on their way out the door and continue arguing about their ideas in the hallway"—is indicative of the power of formative assessment on increasing student engagement and eagerness to be learners of science.

All the ingredients are here for you to pay more attention to assessment in the context of effective teaching and learning rather than being distracted by the cloud of coverage and accountability. While coverage and accountability are important, they are achieved appropriately when teachers are truly accountable to students' learning needs and use formative assessment data to continuously inform their teaching so that students will have the knowledge and skills to perform well on summative assessments. When student achievement scores improve and long-term retention and understanding replace the short-term memorization for standardized testing, then you will know you have successfully linked assessment, instruction, and learning!

3

Considerations for Selecting, Implementing, and Using Data From FACTs

SELECTING FACTS

A variety of factors need to be considered before selecting a formative assessment classroom technique (FACT). The FACT needs to be a good match to the specific content targeted, the needs and styles of the teacher, and the types of students in the class.

SELECTING FACTS TO MATCH LEARNING GOALS

Selecting a FACT without a teaching or learning goal in mind because it seems like a fun thing to do in the classroom is analogous to "activitymania"— selecting hands-on science activities that are fun and engaging to students but do not necessarily promote learning. Superficially selecting FACTs can result in "FACTmania" and derail their powerful purpose in teaching and learning.

Formative assessment is not the goal;
it is a means to achieving a teaching
or learning goal.

Before a FACT is selected, identify and clarify the concept, skill, or idea the FACT is intended to provide information about. To best assist students in their science learning, a FACT should attend to one of the many facets of learning, including content understanding, application processes, and reasoning (National Research Council, 2001). There must be a clear match between the FACT and the learning goal it is intended to target. Figure 3.1 includes questions to ask about content and learning goals that can help inform your selection of an appropriate FACT. Using a systematic study process such as curriculum topic study (CTS) can help teachers deeply examine the conceptual and procedural content of the topics they teach through the lens of content standards and research on student learning, which in turn informs the appropriate selection of FACTs (see the Appendix).

SELECTING FACTS TO MATCH TEACHING GOALS

Formative assessment is closely linked to goals teachers have for improving their instruction. Selecting a FACT that matches an instructional goal

Figure 3.1   Content Considerations for Selecting FACTs

Before selecting a FACT, ask yourself these questions:

- How well do I understand the content or skill?
- What is this learning goal about? What is it not about?
- What specific ideas provide meaning for the concept?
- What specific skills are part of the scientific process?
- What content is developmentally appropriate at the level I teach?
- What level of sophistication is appropriate to expect from students at the level I teach?
- What terminology should students understand and use with this idea or skill?
- What types of phenomena can be used to help students understand the idea?
- What types of representations make the content comprehensible to learners?
- What precursor ideas or skills do students need first in order to develop understanding?
- What other ideas or skills contribute to students' understanding and ability to use scientific knowledge and skills?
- What commonly held ideas or difficulties should I anticipate related to the content?

How can answers to the above questions inform the selection of a FACT?

can help teachers become more effective at eliciting students' ideas, promoting thinking and rich discussion in the science classroom, monitoring student learning, and improving all students' opportunity to learn science at high levels of understanding. The extensive body of cognitive research literature on students' conceptions in science has alerted teachers to the fact that even the "brightest" students come to science class with strongly held ideas about the natural world and how it works. Their ideas can differ greatly from the accepted scientific explanations. This recognition of students, not as "blank slates, but filled with ideas about how the world works" (Abel & Volkman, 2006, p. 10), has encouraged teachers to set teaching goals that will help them grow in their own understanding of their students' ideas and the misconceptions that may impede learning while also serving as springboards upon which to build from their students' ideas. Establishing teaching goals and selecting FACTs that match these teaching goals help teachers teach for understanding, monitor meaningful learning over time, and provide a means of assessing the quality of their teaching in relation to gains in student learning. The science assessment, instruction, and learning (SAIL) cycle described in Chapter 2 provides a useful framework on which teachers can overlay their teaching goals and select appropriate FACTs. Figure 3.2 lists questions to ask about teaching goals before selecting a FACT.

> There is no one best FACT or collection of FACTs that can improve teaching. Each FACT must be considered critically in terms of how well it matches goals for improving or enhancing instruction.

Figure 3.2   Considerations for Selecting FACTs to Improve Teaching

Before selecting a FACT to improve or enhance teaching, consider these questions:

- What aspects of instruction and assessment do I need to improve upon?
- What teaching goal will I focus on to advance my students from where they are now to where I want them to be?
- What types of pedagogy embedded in the FACTs are the best match for the content students are learning?
- How will this FACT help me work smarter, not harder?
- How well do I understand the intended purpose of the FACT?
- Which FACTs can produce the best information to inform my teaching?

Each FACT described in Chapter 4 provides descriptions of what it is, how it promotes learning, how it informs instruction, design and administration, modifications, general implementation attributes, and caveats for its use. Each of these should be carefully read over and considered before you select a fact to match a learning or teaching goal. The following suggestions can help you select FACTs that match your instructional context, goals, and style:

- Select a FACT that appropriately matches the science content you are targeting.
- Select a FACT that appropriately matches your teaching or learning purpose and can be easily integrated into the lesson. See the matrix at the end of this chapter that matches each FACT with purposeful uses.
- Choose a FACT that you are comfortable with and that appeals to your professional judgment and teaching style.
- Some FACTs require more time than others and vary with ease of use and cognitive demand. If time, ease of use, and demand on students' thinking are concerns, choose a FACT that has a low rating (see general implementation attributes listed with each FACT description in Chapter 4).
- Some FACTs require advance preparation. Select a FACT in which you can have all the materials prepared in advance or that uses readily available materials.

THE CRITICAL IMPORTANCE OF CLASSROOM CONTEXT IN SELECTING FACTS

Every teacher knows that within each class, individual students are unique. As a whole, they make up a classroom context with its own personality and set of dynamics. Some days you can teach the same lessons and use the same FACTs with different students or different classes of students, and they will feel like very different students or classes. Each class creates an environment that brings diverse cultural backgrounds, developmental readiness, prior experiences, language issues, prior content knowledge and skills, attitudes, learning and social styles, and habits of mind that affect their learning and the interactions that take place between students and between teachers and students. For this reason, teachers are encouraged to *adapt* FACTs, rather than *adopt* them as is (Angelo & Cross, 1993). In essence, selecting a FACT is a first step in differentiating instruction and assessment for diverse students and unique classroom contexts.

> There is no one best FACT or system of FACTs. What works best in one classroom may not work well in another.

The classroom climate has a major impact on how well students engage with the FACTs. To use the FACTs effectively, teachers need to take into account not only the diverse kinds of students who come to their classroom but also the kind of classroom climate the teacher creates that promotes

> "The learning environment which a teacher creates has a profound impact on the success of the assessment strategies used" (Naylor, Keogh, & Goldsworthy, 2004, p. 15).

learning for all students. A classroom climate that values all students' ideas and makes it safe to surface misconceptions promotes creativity in thinking and generating ideas, encourages all students to engage in discussion with other students and the teacher, and values confidence building and collaborative work can significantly affect how well FACTs are used to inform instruction and promote learning.

The following suggestions can help guide your selection of FACTs to match the context of your classroom:

- Be sensitive to the cultural and social backgrounds of your students when selecting a FACT. Set classroom norms that promote respect for and value each others' ideas and the background knowledge and experiences they bring to their learning.
- Select FACTs that accommodate modifications for English-language learners.
- If public sharing of ideas is initially uncomfortable for some students, ease them in by selecting anonymous strategies that do not identify individuals with their response.
- Select FACTs that engage all students in the learning process and do not make it easy for students to "opt out" by letting the most active or vocal students carry the discussions or answer the questions.
- Don't grade FACTs. Use them to provide continuous feedback that raises the confidence level of students and stimulates further thinking and discussion.
- Create a climate where argumentation that combines evidence and explanation is a scientific norm. Choose FACTs that will help all students to feel comfortable debating and defending their ideas, listening to the viewpoints of others, and acknowledging and evaluating alternative explanations.
- Select FACTs that encourage social interaction and collaboration in an emotionally safe environment.
- Select FACTs that provide opportunities for students to interact with diverse types of students and not always with the same classmate.

PLANNING TO USE AND IMPLEMENT FACTS

After a FACT or set of FACTs has been selected, teachers need to consider various factors that support or hinder implementation in the classroom. Chapter 4 provides a description of implementation attributes; considerations for designing and administering a FACT, including modifications; and cautions to be aware of when using a FACT. These considerations and suggestions should be examined carefully before implementing any of the FACTs. In addition, successful implementation requires an understanding of the science content and the way

"A good idea—poorly implemented—is a bad idea" (Ainsworth & Viegut, 2006, p. 109).

science knowledge is structured. Overlooking the critical need to thoroughly understand the content before implementing a FACT can significantly affect its use and impact.

Before using a FACT, it is important to distinguish between two types of formative assessment: *planned formative assessment* and *interactive formative assessment* (Hall & Burke, 2003). Planned formative assessment is a type of formal or semiformal assessment that is planned for ahead of time in order to collect or provide evidence of student thinking and learning. Often it is curriculum driven. Assessment information is gathered through a FACT, interpreted, and acted upon. On the other hand, interactive formative assessment tends to be incidental and unanticipated, and it usually arises out of an instructional activity. It has the potential to occur at any time during student-to-student or student-to-teacher interactions and is more student or teacher driven than curriculum driven. While it is more difficult to plan for interactive formative assessment, one can plan for it insofar as providing opportunities for classroom observation, discussion, and exchange of ideas is concerned. The following considerations will help you plan for and implement the FACTs described in the next chapter:

> "A teacher's interpretation of a student response, question, and action will be related to the teacher's understanding of the concept or skill that is at issue. Thus a solid understanding of the subject matter being taught is essential" (National Research Council, 2001, p. 87).

- Try out some of the FACTs on yourself first to see if they work in the instructional context you have chosen. Make sure you are able to come up with a response or example. If you have difficulty coming up with a response, then you can be sure your students will too.
- Introduce the FACT to students and explain the directions clearly, particularly if it is new to them. Consider modeling it for them the first time it is used.
- If a FACT is new, decide whether to teach the technique first, providing practice and feedback to students in trying out the FACT.
- Decide whether you want students' responses to be anonymous or want to identify them with an individual.
- Modify a FACT for a "teachable moment" or when there is a need to differentiate for particular students or groups of students.
- Vary your use of FACTs. Students can quickly tire of using the same technique repeatedly, and the FACT will lose its effectiveness.
- When using a FACT for the first time, plan on it taking more time than you had anticipated. As with using any new tool or technique, as a FACT becomes more familiar to students and to you, the amount of time it takes to use it well will decrease.

- Let students know why you are using a particular FACT. When the purpose is made explicit to them and they understand how it helps their learning, the quality of responses to a FACT will be higher.
- Elicit students' ideas in a context that is familiar to them when selecting a FACT. Avoid the use of scientific terminology students may be unfamiliar with, particularly during the elicitation phase.
- Be careful that you don't cue or lead students toward the scientific answer too soon after they respond to a FACT. Allowing time for students to ponder and linger in uncertainty can actually promote learning.
- Don't dismiss incorrect ideas. However, refrain from immediately correcting misconceptions when they surface from using a FACT. Research shows students will revert right back to their misconceptions if they haven't worked through them. Use students' ideas as springboards for learning that you can build upon.
- Encourage students to share as many ideas as possible in response to a FACT. Make sure they give reasons or cite evidence for their ideas.
- Provide adequate time for sense making after ideas have been activated and surfaced.
- Involve students. Ask them for their opinions about the FACTs you have used.
- Involve parents. Produce parent-friendly descriptions of the FACTs you are using so that parents are informed and encouraged to further promote student thinking and idea sharing.

STARTING OFF WITH SMALL STEPS

If FACTs are new to you, start small by "dipping your toe into the water" and trying out one or two easy-to-use FACTs. Be sure to record your notes on how it worked in the spaces provided with each FACT description in Chapter 4. After trying out a new technique, thoughtfully reflect on how it worked for you by asking these questions:

- Were your students engaged?
- Were you confident and excited about using the FACT?
- How did use of the FACT affect the student-to-student or student-teacher dynamic?
- Was the information gained useful to you?
- Would you have gotten this information without using the FACT?
- What added value did the FACT bring to teaching and learning?
- Did it cause you to do something differently or think differently about teaching and learning?

MAINTAINING AND EXTENDING IMPLEMENTATION

Formative assessment can make a significant impact on teaching and learning when used purposefully and over time. Dabbling here and there does not produce significant gains in student learning or teacher performance. Instead, it is the purposeful commitment on the part of the teacher to make formative assessment a regular feature of classroom practice that leads to results. In addition, extending the use of formative assessment beyond an individual teacher's classroom and making it part of a schoolwide commitment to improving student learning will lead to gains at a system level.

"The ongoing identification, collection, and use of information in the classroom is a complex business" (Sato, 2003, p. 109).

Formative assessment is an ideal topic on which professional learning communities (PLCs) can base research, study, implementation, observation of others' classrooms, and shared results. Figure 3.3 provides examples of questions science PLCs can use that link to their use of formative assessment.

"Formative assessment is relevant to all school subjects and, although different techniques may be more or less useful in different subjects, all the broad strategies are applicable to all subjects. Provided they are open to new ideas, teachers can learn a great deal by observing good formative assessment practice in other subjects" (Black et al., 2003, p. 74).

This book can serve as a resource that science PLCs can use to improve upon and examine their formative assessment practices as well as PLCs made up of cross-disciplinary teams.

Each of the FACT descriptions in Chapter 4 provides connections to other subject areas, such as mathematics, language arts, social studies, performing arts, health, and foreign languages. The following are suggestions for maintaining the momentum of implementation and extending the impact of formative assessment outward to other teachers in your school:

- Don't go it alone! Work collaboratively with other teachers to try out and evaluate the use of FACTs.
- Encourage schoolwide support of formative assessment. Inform other teachers and administrators about the FACTs in this book. Many of them are applicable to disciplines besides science. Start with a small group of colleagues interested in trying out the FACTs. As you (and your students) share success stories, other colleagues will want to join you in using FACTs.
- Realize that it takes time to change assessment and instructional practices.
- Don't treat formative assessment as a fad or another new initiative to come down the pike. Recognize where teachers are already using

Figure 3.3   Questions for Science Professional Learning Communities

---

Examining Instruction and Assessment in a Professional Learning Community

Questions About Learning Curricular Ideas and Concepts

1. What preconceptions seem to be most prevalent among our students?
2. Are there common misconceptions noted in the research on learning that our students exhibit?
3. Which concepts seem to be most problematic for our students?
4. What terminology do our students use to describe their ideas? Can they use scientific terms with understanding?
5. Are our students sufficiently engaged with the content?

Questions About Students

1. Which students seem to be progressing well toward the scientific ideas?
2. Are there particular students who are having more difficulty than others? Who are they?
3. Which students have a scientific understanding that could be used to support learning for other students?
4. How can we use formative assessment to differentiate for particular students?

Questions About Teaching

1. Are our students responding positively to instruction?
2. Is the pace of our instruction appropriate?
3. What does formative assessment indicate with respect to how well our curriculum matches our teaching and learning goals?
4. What do we need to do to improve our lessons so there is greater opportunity to learn?
5. Do some FACTs embed more easily in our teaching than others? Which FACTs produced the greatest results?
6. What changes or modifications do we need to make to the FACTs to improve their effectiveness?
7. What new FACTs can we add to the ones we have read about or used?

---

formative assessment and extend everyone's repertoire of strategies by trying out some new FACTs and reflecting on how they worked.

- Encourage an environment in which teachers can watch other teachers in action. Visit each others' classrooms. Seeing how formative assessment plays out with others' students helps teachers understand how they can use FACTs in their classroom.
- Use "critical friends" as sounding boards for giving feedback on formative assessment practices.
- Build time into team, schoolwide, department, or professional learning community meetings for examining and discussing formative assessment.

USING DATA FROM THE FACTS

Even with careful selection, planning, and implementation, assessment is not formative unless the information is used to inform teaching or guide learning. FACTs provide a variety of raw student-learning data that can be analyzed in various ways for different purposes.

The techniques described in this book are not formative unless teachers use the data to take action in some way. After teachers have collected formative assessment data, the important task of constructing meaning from the data and using it to inform teaching and learning is the essence of formative assessment. Data are not just the sets of test scores that often reside in a central office. There is a treasure trove of data being mined every day in the classroom that comes from listening to students interact, observing their actions, and analyzing their responses to questions posed. The challenge is not only in systematically collecting these data but understanding what to do with them. The use of formative assessment data can be described as helping teachers to "challenge their assumptions, investigate their own questions, uncover inequities, discover previously unrecognized strengths in their students, question their practice, improve instruction, and see the world anew" (Love, 2002, p. xxiv).

> "It is important to emphasize the critical criterion—formative assessment—is a process, one in which information about learning is *evoked* and then *used* to modify the teaching and learning activities in which teachers and students are engaged" (Black et al., 2003, p. 74).

> "Just as students analyze and use the information gathered during a science investigation, so too do you analyze the data and use the findings to inform instruction, promote student learning, and enhance your own professional growth" (Carlson et al., 2003, p. 59).

The following suggestions can help you use the assessment data you collect in a formative way:

- If the FACT involves feedback to students, provide that feedback as soon after the assessment as possible.
- Decide whether feedback will be written or shared through discussion. Allow adequate time to discuss FACT feedback with students.
- Let students know how you plan to use the data from the FACTs to improve your teaching and provide better opportunities for them to learn.
- Select an appropriate question that can be answered by analysis of the type of data generated by the FACT.
- Decide whether your analysis will be a qualitative "temperature taking" or whether you will quantitatively analyze the data by crunching numbers of responses and percentages of students.

- Present analyzed response data to students—engage them in examining the class data and coming up with suggestions for improving teaching and learning.
- Avoid being overwhelmed with too much data. Often you do not have the time to analyze all of the student response data. Choose "samples" of student responses to examine and share with the class or select FACTs that lend themselves to a quick scan and analysis.
- Be prepared for negative feedback. Do not feel professionally hurt if you find students' responses reveal that your instruction was not as effective as you may have thought. View it as an opportunity to improve student learning and build on your existing practice.
- Focus on facts from the data, not the inferences. Don't try to read too much between the lines and be aware that further probing is often necessary.
- Don't just gloss over results. Spend time reflecting on the data and considering what actions you need to take to improve teaching and learning. Then, take action!
- Share data with others and take collective actions to improve teaching and learning.
- Take time to further explore the research on learning and suggested interventions that can help students learn concepts they struggle with as indicated by the data. Generic instructional strategies may not be as helpful as science-content-specific pedagogical strategies. Use the student data to inform areas of research you may want to learn more about.
- Consider being a researcher in your own classroom. Use the FACTs to collect and triangulate data that can be used to investigate problems related to teaching and learning.

Ultimately, how you select, plan for, implement, and use data from FACTs depends on your purpose for using them. As you try out the FACTs, you may discover other purposes for their use in informing teaching and learning, including ways to adapt them for use in other disciplines such as mathematics, social studies, health, language arts, performing arts, and foreign language.

Examine the list of FACTs and their purposes for promoting learning and informing teaching as described in the matrix in Figure 3.4. Find a few that pique your interest and resonate with your instructional style and purpose and read the descriptions in Chapter 4. Choose one to try out. The most important take-home message of this book is to commit to trying at least one FACT and celebrating its success. It is through that first small step that large strides will soon follow!

Figure 3.4 75 FACTs and Their Use in Teaching and Learning

FACT Formative Assessment Classroom Technique	Elicit and Identify Preconceptions	Engage and Motivate Students	Activate Thinking and Promote Metacognition	Provide Stimuli for Scientific Discussion	Initiate Scientific Inquiry and Idea Exploration	Formal Concept Development and Transfer	Improve Questioning and Responses	Provide Feedback	Peer and Self-Assessment	Reflection
1. A&D Statements	•	•	•	•	•					
2. Agreement Circles	•	•	•	•	•	•				•
3. Annotated Student Drawings	•	•	•	•		•				
4. Card Sorts	•	•	•	•		•				
5. CCC—Collaborative Clued Corrections			•	•		•			•	
6. Chain Notes	•		•	•		•				
7. Commit and Toss	•	•	•	•		•				•
8. Concept Card Mapping	•		•	•	•	•				•
9. Concept Cartoons	•	•	•	•						
10. Data Match			•					•		
11. Directed Paraphrasing		•	•							
12. Explanation Analysis			•			•	•	•	•	
13. Fact First Questioning				•		•	•			
14. Familiar Phenomenon Probes	•		•	•	•	•				
15. First Word–Last Word	•	•	•			•	•			•
16. Fishbowl Think Aloud	•	•	•	•		•	•	•		•
17. Fist to Five			•			•		•	•	
18. Focused Listing	•		•	•						•
19. Four Corners	•	•	•	•		•				
20. Frayer Model	•	•	•			•				
21. Friendly Talk Probes	•	•	•	•	•					
22. Give Me Five			•	•		•		•		
23. Guided Reciprocal Peer Questioning		•	•	•					•	
24. Human Scatterplots	•	•	•	•						
25. Informal Student Interviews	•	•	•	•		•		•		•

FACT Formative Assessment Classroom Technique	Elicit and Identify Preconceptions	Engage and Motivate Students	Activate Thinking and Promote Metacognition	Provide Stimuli for Scientific Discussion	Initiate Scientific Inquiry and Idea Exploration	Formal Concept Development and Transfer	Improve Questioning and Responses	Provide Feedback	Peer and Self Assessment	Reflection
26. Interest Scale		•						•		
27. I Think–We Think	•	•	•							•
28. I Used to Think... But Now I Know			•	•	•	•				•
29. Juicy Questions							•			
30. Justified List	•	•	•	•	•	•				
31. Justified True or False Statements	•	•	•	•	•	•				•
32. K-W-L Variations	•	•	•	•	•	•			•	•
33. Learning Goals Inventory (LGI)	•	•	•		•				•	•
34. Look Back			•							•
35. Missed Conception			•	•						
36. Muddiest Point			•					•	•	•
37. No-Hands Questioning	•	•	•			•	•		•	
38. Odd One Out	•	•	•		•	•				
39. Paint the Picture	•	•	•	•		•		•		
40. Partner Speaks	•	•	•			•	•			•
41. Pass the Question	•	•	•	•		•	•	•		•
42. A Picture Tells a Thousand Words		•	•	•		•		•		
43. P-E-O Probes (Predict, Explain, Observe)	•	•	•	•	•	•				
44. POMS—Point of Most Significance						•		•		•
45. Popsicle Stick Questioning	•	•	•	•			•			•
46. Prefacing Explanations			•	•			•			
47. PVF—Paired Verbal Fluency		•	•	•			•			
48. Question Generating				•			•			•
49. Recognizing Exceptions	•		•		•	•				
50. Refutations	•		•	•	•	•				

(Continued)

Figure 3.4 (Continued)

FACT Formative Assessment Classroom Technique	Elicit and Identify Preconceptions	Engage and Motivate Students	Activate Thinking and Promote Metacognition	Provide Stimuli for Scientific Discussion	Initiate Scientific Inquiry and Idea Exploration	Formal Concept Development and Transfer	Improve Questioning and Responses	Provide Feedback	Peer and Self-Assessment	Reflection
51. Representation Analysis			•	•		•			•	
52. RERUN			•					•		•
53. Scientists' Ideas Comparison			•	•		•		•	•	•
54. Sequencing	•		•	•	•	•				•
55. Sticky Bars	•	•	•	•	•			•		•
56. STIP—Scientific Terminology Inventory Probe	•		•							
57. Student Evaluation of Learning Gains			•						•	•
58. Synectics	•	•	•	•		•		•	•	•
59. Ten-Two			•							
60. Thinking Log			•						•	•
61. Think-Pair-Share	•	•	•	•	•	•	•	•	•	•
62. Thought Experiments	•	•	•	•	•	•			•	•
63. Three-Minute Pause		•	•							
64. Three-Two-One			•						•	•
65. Traffic Light Cards		•	•			•		•	•	
66. Traffic Light Cups			•					•	•	
67. Traffic Light Dots		•	•					•	•	
68. Two-Minute Paper			•					•	•	•
69. Two or Three Before Me		•					•			
70. Two Stars and a Wish		•						•	•	
71. Two-Thirds Testing							•	•	•	
72. Volleyball—Not Ping Pong!		•	•				•			
73. Wait Time Variations	•	•	•				•		•	
74. What Are You Doing and Why?		•	•						•	
75. Whiteboarding	•	•			•	•		•	•	

44

4

Get the FACTs!

75 Science Formative Assessment
Classroom Techniques (FACTs)

The 75 FACTs selected for this chapter were gathered from a variety of sources. Many of the techniques described in this section were practiced and honed by the author during her 25 years as a middle and high school science teacher and teacher educator. Others were adapted from professional development strategies used with adult learners, gleaned from the literature on formative assessment, or contributed by classroom teachers. Each FACT selected for inclusion in this chapter was reviewed against a set of considerations:

1. *Content Validity:* Is the FACT valid for eliciting information about students' understanding of science content? For example, is the FACT useful in uncovering specific ideas students have about a science concept or ability to use a skill?

2. *Engagement:* Is the FACT engaging to students? Would students want to respond to the assessment technique?

3. *Flexibility:* Can the FACT be used in a range of classroom configurations, including individuals, small groups, and whole class? Can it be adapted to fit a range of classroom environments and diversity of student populations?

4. *Inquiry Based:* Does the FACT promote the spirit of scientific inquiry and lead into an investigation of students' ideas?

5. *Ease of Use:* Is the FACT easy to administer and respond to, and does it use minimal class time? Are the materials readily available? Can the data be quickly collected and analyzed?

6. *Reciprocal Benefits:* Is the FACT as beneficial to students' use in promoting learning as it is for teachers' use in informing instruction?

7. *Impact:* Will the FACT make a difference in the classroom learning environment and student achievement? Will instruction and opportunities to learn improve when the technique is used?

As you peruse this collection of 75 FACTs, make note of the ones that seem most appropriate for your unique classroom situation, experience, and instructional goals. Carefully read the information and example provided for each FACT. After using a FACT, add your own notes at the end of the description to describe how it worked in your setting, including any modifications or suggestions that would improve its use in your classroom.

Each FACT follows a format that includes the following:

Description: This short paragraph provides a snapshot of the FACT—a brief overview of what it is and how it is used.

How This FACT Promotes Student Learning: This section highlights the impact of the FACT on the student. It describes ways in which the FACT can enhance student learning, including stimulating metacognition, promoting student dialogue and discussion, encouraging scientific argumentation, giving and receiving feedback, providing "think time," increasing opportunities for students to respond to questions, and self-assessment and reflection. As you use a FACT, note the ways in which your students respond to it and connect it to what they are learning.

How This FACT Informs Instruction: This section highlights the impact of using the FACT on teaching practice. It describes ways in which the FACT can be used to promote discourse and inform instruction—such as elicitation techniques, gathering information on students' ideas used to modify lessons, improvements in instructional techniques such as questioning, differentiation for individuals or groups of students, student feedback on effectiveness of lessons, ways to continuously monitor learning over time, and providing feedback to students. As you use a FACT, note the extent to which it makes an impact on your teaching philosophy, beliefs about student learning, and teaching strategies.

Design and Administration: This description provides information on selecting content and the preparation needed to set up for the use of a FACT, including materials, time, modeling first-time use, and group work configurations. It also describes how to implement the FACT, including what both the teacher and the student are doing during its use.

General Implementation Attributes: This section describes three general attributes for implementing a FACT in the classroom that range from low to high. Ease of Use rates the general mechanical aspect of using a FACT, such as availability and preparation of materials, amount of practice students need before using it, and extent of teacher facilitation needed to use it effectively with students. Time Demand rates how quickly and efficiently a FACT can be used in terms of the benefits gained from its use. A low rating does not necessarily mean the FACT is not useful but rather that considerable time needs to be invested in using it effectively. Cognitive Demand describes the level of complexity of a FACT in terms of how much is required from the students to think and respond to the FACT.

Modifications: This section provides suggestions for modifying a FACT for different audiences. For example, it may describe ways to adjust the cognitive load for students depending on their age and developmental level. It also describes ways to modify the way the FACT is used, such as changing the ways students are grouped for discussion or adapting a paper-and-pencil-type technique to fit an oral discussion format.

Caveats: With every good technique, there are always cautions to consider when using a strategy to improve teaching and learning. This section describes immediate as well as long-term cautions and pitfalls to be aware of when using a particular FACT.

Use With Other Disciplines: While the FACTs in this chapter are described according to how they are used in science, many of them are readily applicable to other content areas either as is or with modification. Some, where noted, are specific to the discipline of science. As teachers work within interdisciplinary teams in their schools or in a self-contained classroom, it is helpful to use common techniques across disciplines, creating a classroom or school culture that values and uses a common language and strategies for formative assessment. When applicable, connections to the disciplines of mathematics, health, social studies, language arts, foreign languages, and the performing arts are noted. However, these connections are not set in stone. You may see ways to use a FACT with other disciplines not noted by the author.

Examples: Embedded in each of the 75 FACTS descriptions is an illustrative example of how it can be used with students. Examples are general or grade-level specific. They include actual student work, authentic student responses, a sample worksheet, or a scenario or description that illustrates its use. The examples are intended to give the user a glimpse into what a FACT actually looks like in practice.

My Notes: This is a blank area for you to record notes after you try out a FACT. Some things to record might include the date, which class you used it with, successes or challenges in using it, suggestions for modifying or improving its use, insights you gained about your students' learning, or reflections on how it affected your teaching. In addition, it is suggested that you build a file or three-ring binder of the materials you create to use with each FACT (e.g., specific worksheets for the students to reply on or sample questions or reflection prompts) as well as student artifacts that can be shared with others in your professional learning community to collectively gain insights into the use of formative assessment to enhance teaching and learning.

Now it's time to get the FACTs! The FACTs are organized alphabetically and numbered on the matrix in Figure 3.4. The matrix can help you select FACTs that match a specific purpose or stage in your instructional cycle. Some FACTs will appeal to you while others may not. There are plenty of examples to choose from. In order to use a FACT effectively, it must resonate with your teaching philosophy and instructional style. As you come across FACTs you might try out in your classroom, consider placing sticky notes on the pages so you can go back and revisit them. Start small by selecting one or two FACTs to try out initially. Make notes on how well the technique worked for you. Continue adding more techniques that fit your instructional style and teaching goals as you readily assimilate new techniques into your practice. As you become adept at using the FACTs, your repertoire of instructional strategies will increase, accompanied by improved student learning.

#1: A&D STATEMENTS

Description

Students use *A&D Statements* to analyze a set of "fact or fiction" statements. In the first part of *A&D Statements*, students may choose to agree or disagree with a statement or identify whether they need more information. In addition, they are asked to describe their thinking about why they agree, disagree, or are unsure. In the second part of the FACT, students describe what they can do to investigate the statement by testing their ideas, researching what is already known, or using other means of inquiry. Figure 4.1 shows an example of *A&D Statements* for a third-grade unit on magnetism.

Figure 4.1 *A&D Statements* for Grade 3 Magnets

Statement	How Can You Find Out?
1. **All magnets have 2 poles.** ___ agree ___ disagree ___ it depends on ___ not sure My thoughts:	
2. **All metals are attracted to magnets.** ___ agree ___ disagree ___ it depends on ___ not sure My thoughts:	
3. **Larger magnets are stronger than smaller magnets.** ___ agree ___ disagree ___ it depends on ___ not sure My thoughts:	
4. **Magnetism can pass through metals.** ___ agree ___ disagree ___ it depends on ___ not sure My thoughts:	

How This FACT Promotes Student Learning

A&D Statements provide an opportunity for students to practice metacognition—thinking about their own understanding. In addition, this FACT "primes the pump" for student inquiry by having students describe how they could design an investigation or identify information sources that would help them determine the validity of the statement. When used in small groups, *A&D Statements* provide stimuli to encourage scientific discussion and argumentation. Through the process of defending or challenging scientific arguments aimed at the statements, students may solidify their own thinking, consider the alternative views of others, and modify their own thinking as new information replaces or becomes assimilated into their existing knowledge and beliefs.

How This FACT Informs Instruction

A&D Statements are best used at the beginning of a learning cycle to elicit students' ideas about a topic. The information helps teachers identify areas where students may need targeted instructional experiences that will challenge their preconceptions and increase confidence in their own ideas. The results can be used to differentiate instruction for selected groups of students who have similar ideas about the topic. Students' descriptions of how they can find out whether the statements are correct provide data the teacher can use regarding their ability to design experiments or identify appropriate scientific sources of information.

Design and Administration

Select *A&D Statements* that focus on specific concepts and skills students will encounter in the curriculum. Develop statements that can lead into inquiry with hands-on materials, books, videos, or other information sources. Students should first be given the opportunity to respond to the FACT individually. Then, have students discuss their ideas in small groups, coming to consensus on whether they agree with the statement while noting any disagreements among group members. After they have had time to consider each others' ideas and design a way to further test or research information, allow time for small groups to investigate the statements as exploratory activities. These activities provide a common experience for whole-class discussion aimed at resolving discrepancies between students' initial ideas and discoveries made during their explorations. The teacher should listen carefully as the class shares its findings, building off the students' ideas to provide guidance and clarification that will help students accommodate new scientific understandings.

General Implementation Attributes

Ease of Use: Medium   Time Demand: Medium
Cognitive Demand: Medium

Modifications

This FACT can be modified for younger students by focusing on one statement at a time, rather than a set of statements.

Caveats

This FACT should not be used solely as a "true or false" assessment. It is important to provide the follow-up experiences for students to investigate the statements, particularly those in which there is a conflict between students' preconceptions and the scientific ideas.

Use With Other Disciplines

This FACT can also be used in mathematics, social studies, language arts, health, foreign languages, and performing arts.

My Notes

_____

_____

_____

#2: AGREEMENT CIRCLES

Description

Agreement Circles provide a kinesthetic way to activate thinking and engage students in scientific argumentation. Students stand in a circle as the teacher reads a statement. The students who agree with the statement step to the center of the circle. They face their peers still standing in the circle and then match themselves up in small groups of students who agree and disagree. The small groups engage in discussion to defend their thinking. After discussion, the students are given an opportunity to reposition themselves with those who now agree standing in the center of the circle, those who now disagree standing on the circumference of the circle. The idea is to get everyone either inside the circle or on the circumference. This is repeated with several rounds of statements relating to the same topic, each time with students starting by standing along the circumference of a large circle.

How This FACT Promotes Student Learning

Agreement Circles activate students' thinking about scientific ideas related to a topic they are studying. As the statements are made, students access their existing knowledge. They must justify their thinking to their peers about why they agree or disagree with the statement. As they engage in a scientific argument with their "opposing partners" still standing on the circle, students may modify their ideas as new information convinces them that their original ideas may need adjustment and either step into or onto the circle.

How This FACT Informs Instruction

This FACT can be used prior to instruction or during the concept development stage when formally introduced concepts may need reinforcement. The teacher can get a quick visual sense of students' understanding according to which part of the circle they are in. As the teacher circulates and listens to students' arguments, information about students' thinking is revealed that can be used to design further learning experiences or revisit prior experiences aimed at developing conceptual understanding. Giving students an opportunity to change their position after discussion indicates the extent to which the small group discussions may have changed some students' initial thinking.

Design and Administration

Develop a set of three to five conceptually challenging statements related to the topic of instruction. Statements should be a combination of true and false. False statements can be developed based on examining the research on students' commonly held ideas. See the Appendix for a description of tools from Science Curriculum Topic Study (Keeley, 2005) that can be used to identify common misconceptions. For example, a set of eighth-grade statements used to elicit students' ideas about energy might be as follows:

1. Energy is a material that is stored in an object.

2. When energy changes from one form to another, heat is usually given off.

3. Energy can never be created or destroyed.

4. Something has to move in order to have energy.

5. Energy is a type of fuel.

Begin by having students form a large circle. Read the first statement, then give students five to ten seconds of think time. Ask students to move to the center of the circle if they agree with the statement and stay on the outside if they disagree. Match students up 1:2, 1:3, 1:4, 1:5, or whatever the proportion of agree/disagree indicates and give them a few minutes to defend their ideas in small groups. Call time, read the question again, and have students reposition themselves according to whether their ideas have changed or stayed the same. Students who agree with the statement move to the inside of the circle. Students who disagree stay on the outside of the circle. Note any changes and then have students go back to the circle for another round. When finished with all rounds, the next step depends on the stage of instruction. If the FACT was used to activate and elicit student thinking, then the next step is to plan and provide lessons that will help students to explore their ideas further and formulate understandings. If the FACT was used during the concept development stage provide an opportunity for a whole-class discussion to resolve conceptual conflicts, formalize development of the key ideas, and solidify understanding.

General Implementation Attributes

Ease of Use: High   Time Demand: Medium
Cognitive Demand: Medium/High

Modifications

Limit the number of statements for younger students. If all students end up in either the middle or outside of the circle, have them pair up to explain why they agree or disagree. Often there are differences in the justification of their ideas, even if both students agree or disagree with the statement.

Caveats

Students need to be confident in their thinking when using this strategy. Encourage students to refrain from changing their answer because they see a majority of students move to the inside or outside of the circle.

Use With Other Disciplines

This FACT can also be used in mathematics, social studies, language arts, health, foreign languages, and performing arts.

My Notes

_____

_____

_____

#3: ANNOTATED STUDENT DRAWINGS

Description

"If a picture is worth a thousand words, perhaps drawing and visualizing can help science students enhance their learning potential" (National Science Teachers Association [NSTA], 2006, p. 20). *Annotated Student Drawings* are student-made, labeled illustrations that visually represent and describe students' thinking about a scientific concept.

How This FACT Promotes Student Learning

Annotated Student Drawings encourage students to access their prior knowledge and visually represent their thinking. The act of drawing to explain a concept or phenomenon encourages sense making and awareness of one's own ideas. Students are challenged to think about how to visually represent and explain an idea with minimal use of words. Students who are strong visual learners and communicators may find this technique especially helpful. These students are often at a disadvantage when asked to perform on written assessments that involve text only. Because of the graphic nature of this FACT, it can be helpful in pulling out visual thinkers' ideas and providing a medium for them to publicly share their thinking.

How This FACT Informs Instruction

Annotated Student Drawings can be used at the beginning of a learning cycle to engage students in a topic with which they have some familiarity. As an elicitation, *Annotated Student Drawings* are used by the teacher to identify conceptual difficulties that may stem from prior knowledge or experiences. They can also be used to examine how students use scientific terminology. Thinking visually and trying to draw what is in one's head can surface areas of understanding or misunderstanding that are often not captured by words. Graphic images, terminology used, and descriptions that explain the drawing may reveal gaps and misconceptions that can be addressed in subsequent lessons. For example, fifth graders may be asked to draw and label the water cycle. Students' drawings may reveal arrows labeled "evaporation" going from a body of water straight up to a cloud and to the sun. This example alerts the teacher to the need to probe further to find out a student's notion of what happens to water after it evaporates. Arrows that indicate that evaporated water goes immediately up to the clouds and sun may reveal that the student does not understand that the evaporated water first stays in the air around us in a form we cannot see (water vapor). Furthermore, the drawing might show a large, underground river labeled "groundwater." This part of the drawing indicates the need to challenge the student's idea about the commonly held misconception that groundwater exists in large, underground lakes or rivers, rather than in spaces between the particles of soil or rock. Further probing, based on ideas revealed through the drawing, may indicate the need to design targeted learning experiences that will address the student's misconceptions.

This FACT can also be used after students have had an opportunity to formally develop scientific ideas during the concept-development phase. Teachers can examine the drawings and descriptions for indications of the need to clarify scientific terminology, provide feedback to individual students on selected aspects of their drawings, or provide additional learning opportunities to further solidify understanding. Selected drawings can be used to provide additional support for concept development by giving the class an opportunity to examine each others' drawings, ask further questions, and provide peer feedback on the accuracy and appropriateness of their representations and use of terminology.

Annotated Student Drawings can also be used to encourage reflection. Drawings made prior to instruction can be recorded in students' science notebooks or collected and returned to students at the end of a unit of instruction. The initial drawings are revisited to reflect on what students learned and to describe learning experiences that helped them gain new understandings. As a self-assessment activity, students can be given an opportunity to revise their drawings, labeled terminology, and descriptions based on what they now understand, describing how and why their new drawing differs from their first one. This information can be used by the teacher to evaluate the effectiveness of the instructional unit for closing gaps and addressing student misconceptions.

Design and Administration

Choose an idea that is central to the curricular topic and that can be represented through children's drawing. Provide a clear prompt for the drawing that will elicit the information you are seeking. For example, in the water cycle task, students were asked to *draw a picture that would help someone understand what happens to water as it goes through the water cycle.* Directions for students included the following: *Draw, label, and briefly describe each part of the water cycle. Include the changes in form and location of the water.*

Show students an example from a familiar topic the first time you use this strategy, pointing out how annotations are used to briefly explain or label important ideas and words depicted in the drawing. Emphasize to the students that you are more interested in their ideas than the right answer or the artistic quality of their drawings. Use a catchy acronym, such as "MTV"—**M**ake your **T**hinking **V**isible—to engage students in drawing a representation of their thinking. While circulating among students and examining their drawings, ask probing questions to promote deeper thinking. After students have completed their drawings, provide an opportunity for them to talk about their drawings and receive feedback on their ideas from their peers as well as the teacher.

General Implementation Attributes

Ease of Use: Medium   Time Demand: Medium
Cognitive Demand: Medium

Modifications

Consider having younger students verbally describe and name parts of their drawings while the teacher annotates it for them. This FACT can also be administered as a small-group assessment, using a large sheet of paper or whiteboards. Students work collaboratively, discussing their ideas as they reach consensus on the visual components and annotations that should be included in the drawing.

Caveats

It is best to avoid assigning *Annotated Student Drawings* as an out-of-class assignment. Using the FACT in the classroom ensures that students will represent their own thinking without accessing information from other sources. This is important since the purpose of this strategy is to find out what is in students' own minds. While scientific drawings are an important part of communicating in science, students with strong verbal abilities and less developed drawing skills may find this FACT frustrating. A suggested caution is to avoid or be careful when praising students who exhibit artistic talent as it may signify to other students that their drawings are "not as good" and detract from the purpose of making their ideas visible.

Use With Other Disciplines

This FACT can also be used in mathematics, social studies, and health.

My Notes

_____

_____

_____

#4: CARD SORTS

Description

Card Sorts is a sorting activity in which students group a set of cards with pictures or words on them according to a certain characteristic or category. Students sort the cards based on their preexisting ideas about the concepts, objects, or processes on the cards. As students sort the cards, they discuss their reasons for placing each card into a designated group.

How This FACT Promotes Student Learning

Card Sorts provide an opportunity for students to access their prior knowledge. In addition, they promote metacognition by surfacing uncertainties in their thinking. As students work in pairs or small groups to sort the cards, they justify their own ideas, practice skills of scientific argumentation, consider the ideas of others, and modify their thinking as new information persuades them to modify their original ideas. The exercise in categorizing also helps students to understand that sometimes in science, things in the natural world do not always fit neatly into groups.

How This FACT Informs Instruction

Card Sorts provide a way for the teacher to elicit students' preconceptions, assess students' ability to transfer knowledge when provided with new examples or contexts, and look for areas of uncertainty or disagreement among students that may signify the need for further instructional opportunities. *Card Sorts* are best used in small groups to encourage students to talk about their ideas. While students discuss their ideas, the teacher circulates around the classroom listening to students agree, disagree, or express their uncertainty. The teacher notes ideas that are most problematic to become the focus for subsequent lessons.

Some card sorts can be used to determine whether students have developed generalizations. For example, students may be asked to sort objects on cards according to whether they reflect or do not reflect light. The cards include a variety of shiny, dull, smooth, and rough objects visible to the eye. Since the objects are visible, all of them reflect light to some degree. The teacher can quickly see at a glance whether students have developed the generalization that all visible objects reflect light by circulating through the room to visually note whether students sort the cards into one or two categories. The information gained from the card sort can help teachers determine whether students were bound by the context in which they developed ideas about reflection—for example, experiences that involved only shiny objects such as mirrors.

The cards can also be used to orchestrate whole-class discussion. The discourse that ensues provides feedback to learners to help resolve conceptual difficulties, while the teacher maintains a nonjudgmental role as listener and clarifier, guiding students toward the accepted scientific idea.

Figure 4.2 is an example of a card sort used with second graders to sort organisms as "animals" and "not animals." Several of the cards are based on commonly held ideas, including the idea that animals must have fur and legs (Driver, Squires, Rushworth, & Wood-Robinson, 1994). Examining the placement of the cards and students' reasoning provides feedback to the teacher on whether students have developed a scientific conception of "animal" or whether students hold a restricted meaning.

Design and Administration

Prepare sets of cards that align with the content goal of the lesson or cluster of lessons students will encounter. It is helpful to use tools such as Science Curriculum Topic Study (Keeley, 2005) to examine the research on student learning in order to identify common misconceptions that may be used as examples on the cards (see the Appendix). You can place text on index cards or make cards from preprinted matchbook-size squares on a sheet of paper and have students cut out the squares. Provide students with a category header under which to sort their cards. Encourage students to lay out each card in a row or column under the category header

Figure 4.2   *Card Sort:* "Is It an Animal?"

THINGS THAT ARE ANIMALS		THINGS THAT ARE NOT ANIMALS
ant	horse	fish
human	monkey	worm
giraffe	snail	lizard
spider	flower	crab
butterfly	tree	shark
whale	toad	snake
kitten	octopus	mushroom
hummingbird	caterpillar	mouse

rather than on top of each other so you can see how students sort each individual item. Have students work in small groups to discuss each of the cards and come to a common agreement on which category to place it in before sorting the next card. Listen carefully to students as they discuss and argue their ideas. Note examples where instructional opportunities may need to be designed to challenge students' ideas. If a record of student thinking is needed, provide individual students and/or small groups with a recording sheet to note where each card was placed along with a justification for its placement. See the Appendix for a source of assessment probes that can be used as card sorts.

General Implementation Attributes

Ease of Use: High   Time Demand: Medium
Cognitive Demand: Medium

Modifications

For younger students or less fluent readers, use pictures of familiar objects or combine pictures with words. Limit to no more than two sorting categories for younger students—those that fit the concept and those that do not. For older students, consider using multiple categories where appropriate. Consider adding a third category of "it depends on" or "not sure."

Caveats

This FACT can turn into a vocabulary exercise if the words are unfamiliar to students. Some students, particularly English-language learners, may need help reading the cards or require visual cues. Emphasize that students need to talk about each card before they assign it to a category. Discourage students from quickly sorting all the cards first and then discussing them.

Use With Other Disciplines

This FACT can also be used in mathematics, social studies, language arts, health, foreign languages, and performing arts.

My Notes

_____

_____

_____

#5: CCC—COLLABORATIVE CLUED CORRECTIONS

Description

CCC provides an alternative way to mark student papers with comments that encourage revision. Students complete and submit an assignment made up of selected responses or short answers. The teacher purposefully selects a sample of student papers that includes incorrect or partially correct responses. The teacher reviews the samples and provides feedback regarding the number and types of errors or areas for improvement. However, the specific questions or area for correction in each question are not explicitly identified by the teacher. They are only "clued." The sample set of "clued" papers is distributed to small groups of students, who work together to collaboratively seek out the problem areas and revise them.

How This FACT Promotes Student Learning

The purpose of this FACT is to provide feedback to students on homework or class assignments, which typically get corrected, passed back, and quickly forgotten. The CCC technique is supported by Black and Wiliam's (1998) research on how learning improves when students are given feedback on their work that encourages revision rather than marking wrong answers and giving a grade, which can have negative consequences in terms of sending an unspoken message that students lack ability. Working together as a group provides all students with an opportunity to activate and discuss their own ideas and modify them based on peer feedback. The task of identifying the areas that need improvement, based on the teacher's clues, provides greater content engagement in learning than passing back marked assignments. Feedback from the clues focuses students on the content of the learning goals rather than how well one student does in comparison to others. Marked and graded assignments, particularly when students have multiple errors and no opportunities to make revisions, are often ignored, thus contributing little to furthering content understanding.

How This FACT Informs Instruction

CCC is an example of a technique in which passing back class work or homework assignments can be used as learning opportunities while helping teachers manage feedback on student work in an efficient way. Not every student paper needs to be corrected and commented on by the teacher. By selecting representative samples of work that contain common errors that small groups of students then collaborate on to revise, the teacher is free to circulate among groups to provide additional feedback that will support student learning.

Design and Administration

CCCs are best used with short-answer assignments that can springboard into engaging learning opportunities for students to activate and explain their thinking. Select papers for the CCC that include common errors made by students in the class. Provide comments on the paper but do not explicitly point out where the error or area for improvement lies. The following is an example of clues a teacher might write on a high school homework assignment:

> I found two factual mistakes in your descriptions. One explanation lacked sufficient evidence to support it. Check your math—there are two mathematical errors dealing with conversions. There is one scientific term you used in a way that might be interpreted incorrectly. One of your explanations could be improved by using

a drawing to explain your solution to the problem. With your partners, identify and discuss the areas that need improvement and work together to revise them.

Feedback/revision groups should be formed based on the learning needs and social interaction of the individuals in the group. Each small group can include the student whose paper was marked with clues. Students work together in their small groups to identify the areas of correction or improvement, discuss their ideas related to the questions on the assignment, and collaboratively revise the work once all members of the group accept the corrections. The work is resubmitted and then becomes representative of the group, rather than the individual. This encourages others to participate even though the student work is not their own. After submitting the group's work, the teacher returns the remaining unmarked papers for students to revise on their own or with a partner. Students become more interested in reviewing their own unmarked papers and looking for areas to change or improve on, after having an opportunity to first analyze another student's work.

It is important to provide time to teach this strategy and allow students an opportunity to practice it. One way of doing this is to choose one or two samples of anonymous student work to copy, write clues, and use with the whole class in examining the clues, looking for the areas that need revision, and discussing and making revisions to improve the quality and content accuracy of the work.

General Implementation Attributes

Ease of Use: Medium   Time Demand: Medium
Cognitive Demand: Medium/High

Modifications

Use short answer, matching, fill in the blank, or multiple choice with students who have a difficult time deciphering handwriting or reading a lot of student handwritten text. Note the number of answers that need revision. Even though questions and responses are not as robust in a forced-choice assignment as they are in an open-response format, the discussions that ensue during the *CCC* provide an opportunity for rich content-focused dialogue.

Caveats

Be careful that students do not construe this as an opportunity to put less effort into their own work if they know that only a few papers will be selected for revision. This FACT works best in classroom environments where students embrace the idea that their own work is an important means for helping *all* students improve the quality of their work. Make sure that all students have an opportunity to review their own work after the CCC, regardless of whether their papers were the ones selected to be clued.

Use With Other Disciplines

This FACT can also be used in mathematics, social studies, language arts, health, foreign languages, and performing arts.

My Notes

_____

_____

_____

#6: CHAIN NOTES

Description

Chain Notes begin with a question printed at the top of a paper. The paper is then circulated from student to student. Each student responds with one to two sentences related to the question and passes it on to the next student. Upon receiving the previous "chain of responses," a student adds a new thought or builds on a prior statement.

How This FACT Promotes Student Learning

Chain Notes provide an opportunity for students to examine others' ideas and compare them to their own thinking. In the process of examining others' ideas, students build upon them or add new ideas of their own. The FACT encourages students to move beyond recall since they must first synthesize and evaluate what others have recorded before adding their own ideas. *Chain Notes* provide an opportunity for students to draw upon various levels of knowledge, including facts, definitions, specific ideas, big ideas, analogies, illustrative examples, and evidence from their own or class experiences to contribute to building the chain.

How This FACT Informs Instruction

Chain Notes elicit different ideas students have about scientific concepts they encounter during or after a lesson or sequence of lessons. *Chain Notes* are best used as a check for understanding after students have had sufficient opportunities to explore and learn about the concept addressed by the question in the note. Analysis of the notes reveals the extent to which students draw upon formal definitions and ideas presented and discussed in class as well as the hands-on experiences they have had. The notes reveal students' level of sophistication and accuracy in thinking about the concept, the terminology they use, and common misconceptions. Figure 4.3 shows a transcribed example of a seventh-grade *Chain Note* that targets concepts related to matter. Examining the chain of responses can indicate to the teacher whether the lessons students engaged in allowed them to make sufficient connections to the concept and whether they should be modified and/or revisited. Varied information about students' ideas related to the concept in question can be gathered using this FACT. For example, several students seem to have the idea that matter has mass (or weight) and takes up space, yet ideas differ when it comes to gases.

Figure 4.3   Seventh-Grade *Chain Note*

What Is Matter?

- Matter is all around us and makes up everything.
- Matter takes up space and has mass.
- Matter has volume and mass.
- You can see or feel matter.
- Some kinds of matter can't be seen, like gases.
- Matter is in solid, liquid, and gas forms.
- Matter can be solid, liquid, or gas and also elements and compounds.
- Matter has atoms in it. Almost everything has atoms in it.
- All things made out of atoms are matter.
- Atoms are small, but they are matter even without being seen.
- You can't see some kinds of matter. It's there if you can feel or smell it. Air is there; you can't see it, but you can smell it.
- Gases are matter because they can take up space that fills up. When you blow up a balloon, it doesn't weigh too much.
- Matter has weight if enough matter is there to weigh something.
- Sound doesn't weigh anything, but it's there because I can hear sound. It's not matter—it's something like energy that isn't matter but still moves around, and you can feel it sometimes.
- Heat is like that. You can feel heat, but heat isn't matter because you can't hold it, so it is something different—maybe matter that is a kind of energy.
- Some things are made of matter, and some things are made of energy. They are two different scientific things.
- They are different and kind of the same; matter and energy can both be felt.
- Some energies fill up space like light and get used up.
- Light isn't matter because it's like a gas—you can't hold it or weigh it.
- Some matter can't be weighed or held. It depends on its form, whether it is a solid or liquid or gas.

Design and Administration

Select a broad, open-ended question focused on a particular concept relevant to the curriculum. Write the question at the top of a long sheet of paper. In addition, post the question somewhere in the room so that everyone can see it. Pass the note around the class from student to student, having each student add a one- or two-word sentence that relates to the question and builds upon, extends, or disagrees with others' comments. Make sure students know they should read all the prior responses before adding their own "note." Encourage students to build upon the last note made so that it connects with the idea they are adding. Have students turn the sheet over when they run out of space on the first page. The *Chain Notes* can be passed around as students are engaged in other tasks. It should take no more than one to two minutes per student to respond and pass on. Notes should be brief—only one or two sentences in length. When completed, the *Chain Notes* can be read aloud or projected from an overhead, allowing for students to give feedback on the statements made by their peers. Students discuss whether they agree or disagree with the statements on the paper and defend their reasoning.

General Implementation Attributes

Ease of Use: High   Time Demand: Medium
Cognitive Demand: Medium

Modifications

Have students accordion-fold their paper each time they respond so only the last note or last two notes appear when they pass it on. The next student writes a note and then accordion-folds it again so that only his or her response appears when passing it on to the next student, and so on. This way, teachers can analyze how students consider and build upon the ideas of their peers without being distracted by all the previous comments.

Caveats

This FACT should be explicitly taught and modeled the first time it is used. Make sure students are not influenced by other students' ideas or merely parroting back what others have written.

Use With Other Disciplines

This FACT can also be used in mathematics, social studies, language arts, and health.

My Notes

_____

_____

_____

#7: COMMIT AND TOSS

Description

Commit and Toss is an anonymous technique used to get a quick read on the different ideas students have in the class. It provides a safe, fun, and engaging way for all students to make their ideas known to the teacher and the class without individual students being identified as having "wild" or incorrect ideas. Students are given a question. After completing the question, students crumple their paper up into a ball and, upon a signal from the teacher, toss the paper balls around the room until the teacher tells them to stop and pick up or hold on to one paper. Students take the paper they end up with and share the ideas and thinking that are described on their "caught" paper, not their own ideas.

How This FACT Promotes Student Learning

Commit and Toss incorporates an essential component of conceptual-change teaching and learning—committing to an outcome based on students' own ideas. Before students crumple and toss their papers, they must think about the question posed, commit to a response, and describe their thinking. This FACT helps students recognize that it is common for students in a class to have different ideas. There is a sense of relief when a student realizes that he or she is not alone in his or her answer. It helps students see that "wrong" answers can be just as valuable for building learning opportunities and constructing new ideas as "right" answers. It provides a nonthreatening opportunity to make everyone's ideas public regardless of whether they are right or wrong. It allows students to tap into others' thinking, comparing their own ideas with others' in the class. Since the technique is anonymous, individual students are more likely to reveal their own ideas rather than providing a "safe" answer they think the teacher wants to hear.

How This FACT Informs Instruction

Commit and Toss allows the teacher to get a quick read on ideas and explanations that are prevalent in the class. It is a very engaging way to get a class snapshot of student thinking. The information is used to design and provide targeted learning opportunities for conceptual change, including an opportunity for students to test their ideas or gather more information that will support or modify their thinking.

Design and Administration

Choose a content goal. Design or select a forced-choice assessment item that requires students to commit to an outcome and provide a justification for the answer they selected, such as the example in Figure 4.4.

Remind students not to write their names on their paper. Give students time to think about and record their response, encouraging them to explain their ideas as best they can so another student would understand their thinking. When everyone is ready, give the cue to crumple their paper into a ball, stand up, and toss it back and forth to other students. Students keep tossing and catching until the teacher says to stop. Make sure all students have a paper. Remind students that the paper they have in their hand will be the one they talk about, not the answer and explanation they wrote on their own paper.

After students catch a paper, give them time to read the response and try to "get into the other student's head" by making sense of what the student was thinking. Ask for a show of hands or use the *Four Corners* strategy to visually show the number of students who selected a particular response. Have students get into small groups according to the selected response on their paper and discuss the similarities or differences in the explanations provided for each choice and report out to the class the different explanations students provided for each answer choice. The teacher can list the ideas mentioned, avoiding passing any judgments, while

Figure 4.4   Example of a Forced-Choice Question Used With *Commit and Toss*

Sophie's Weight

Sophie stood with both feet on the bathroom scale. She recorded her weight. She lifted her left foot and stood on the scale with only one foot on it. Which best describes what happened to the reading on the scale?

 A. The weight shown on the scale increased.

 B. The weight shown on the scale decreased.

 C. The weight shown on the scale stayed the same.

Explain your thinking. Describe the reason for the answer you selected.

noting the different ideas students have that will inform the instructional opportunities that will follow.

Once all the ideas have been made public and discussed, engage students in a class discussion to decide which ideas they believe are most plausible and to provide justification for their thinking. This is the time when they can share their own ideas. Following an opportunity to examine the class's thinking, ask for a show of hands indicating how many students modified or completely changed their ideas. Also ask how many students are sticking to their original idea. With consensus from the class, select a few of the common ideas and have students decide in small groups or as a class how to go about investigating the question in order to determine the correct scientific explanation. Provide opportunities for students to test or use other resources to research their ideas. Revisit these ideas again during the formal concept-development stage to help students build a bridge between their ideas and the scientific explanation. Ask students to consider what else it would take to convince them of the scientific explanation if they are still experiencing a dissonance between their ideas and the scientific ones. See the Appendix for sources of assessment probes that can be used with this strategy.

General Implementation Attributes

Ease of Use: High   Time Demand: Low
Cognitive Demand: Medium

Modifications

This FACT can be modified to fit a less rambunctious situation by adapting it to a "commit, fold, and pass" where students fold their paper in half and pass it around the room until the teacher gives the signal to stop passing.

Caveats

This is a fun, engaging technique—for this reason, be careful not to overuse it or it will lose its effectiveness. Remind students to honor anonymity, even if they recognize someone's handwriting. It is also important to establish the norm that disparaging or other types of negative comments should never be made about the student paper they end up with.

Use With Other Disciplines

This FACT can also be used in mathematics, social studies, language arts, health, foreign languages, and performing arts.

My Notes

_____

_____

_____

#8: CONCEPT CARD MAPPING

Description

Concept Card Mapping is a variation on the familiar strategy of concept mapping (Novak, 1998). Instead of constructing their own concept maps from scratch, students are given cards with the concepts written on them. They move the cards around and arrange them as a connected web of knowledge. They create linkages between the concept cards that describe the relationship between concepts. Moving the cards provides an opportunity for students to explore and think about different linkages.

How This FACT Promotes Student Learning

Concept Card Mapping provides an opportunity for students to activate their prior knowledge, think about the relationships between familiar concepts, and make a visual representation of the connections in their own knowledge network. When students create maps collaboratively in small groups, the maps promote discussion. Individuals become more aware of their own ideas and may modify them accordingly as a result of the discussion generated in their group. Because there is no one "right answer," this FACT provides an open entry point for all learners. In the process of exploring their own and others' ideas, they use that information to connect ideas and terminology together in a coherent way, deepening their understanding of the structure of a topic. Students who tend not to speak up in class have been found to contribute freely in the nonthreatening activity of mapmaking (White & Gunstone, 1992).

How This FACT Informs Instruction

Teachers can use *Concept Card Mapping* as an elicitation prior to instruction or at key points in a sequence of lessons to gather information about how students make linkages among a connected set of concepts and terminology. Using a common set of predetermined words or phrases allows the teacher to see how different students, or groups of students, make conceptual sense of the same ideas in different ways. The student-generated sentences are examined carefully by the teacher to reveal any conceptual misunderstandings or incorrect ideas. The linkages made by students reveal the level of sophistication of their ideas, accuracy of content knowledge, and depth and breadth of their thinking. The information is used to inform the development of lessons that will provide students with an opportunity to explore and solidify important connections.

Different maps can be selected by the teacher to provide teacher-to-student and student-to-student feedback during the formal concept development phase of whole-class instruction. Discussion focuses on whether students agree or disagree with the connections made on the map and ways they may have made different linkages. The maps can also be used by the teacher to initiate questions that probe deeper for student understanding. *Concept Card Mapping* can be used again at the end of an instructional unit to help students reflect on the extent to which their knowledge increased or ideas changed since their original map was created.

Design and Administration

For the purpose of this technique, a concept is a defined as a simple one- to two-word or three-word mental construct or short phrase that represents or categorizes a scientific idea, such as ecosystem, boiling point, or erosion (Carey, 2000; Erickson, 1998). Choose concepts central to the topic of instruction and place them in squares that students cut out from a sheet of paper. See the Appendix for a description of Science Curriculum Topic Study, a process that uncovers the essential concepts in a standards-based topic (Keeley, 2005). If students have never created a concept map, start by introducing concept mapping with a familiar topic. Engage the class in practicing concept mapping through an interactive demonstration. Model and emphasize the importance of creating clear, connecting sentences. For example, in mapping the topic "States of Matter," a link between the "ice card" and the "water card" might be connected by the phrase "is the solid state of."

Concept cards can be used as an individual activity or with pairs or small groups of students. When using this FACT with pairs or small groups, encourage students to think first about their own connections and then discuss them with others. Students decide which connections best represent the pair's or group's thinking. Once students are satisfied with their maps, they can glue down their cards, write in their linkages to form sentences, and share their maps with others for feedback. Figure 4.5 shows an example of cards used for a concept mapping activity on "States of Matter."

General Implementation Attributes

Ease of Use: Low   Time Demand: Medium
Cognitive Demand: High

Figure 4.5   Concept Cards for "States of Matter"

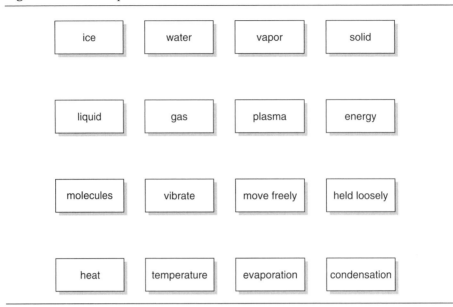

Modifications

Combine pictures with words for younger students. Include a few blank cards for students to write in their own concepts to include on their map. If students struggle with determining the connecting words or phrases, consider providing examples of different connectors that can be used with the topic chosen.

Caveats

The cognitive demand of this FACT depends on the concrete or abstract nature of the concept words selected and the number of cards to map. Choose the appropriate level of demand that matches the grade level of the students and complexity of the topic they are learning about.

Use With Other Disciplines

This FACT can also be used in mathematics, social studies, language arts, and health.

My Notes

#9: CONCEPT CARTOONS

Description

Concept Cartoons were originally developed in the United Kingdom as cartoon drawings that visually depict children or adults sharing their ideas about common, everyday phenomena (Naylor & Keogh, 2000). Students decide which character in the cartoon they agree with most and why. Cartoon characters' comments about the situation presented in the cartoon include an idea that may be more scientifically acceptable than the others as well as alternative ideas based on common misconceptions. Sometimes there is no single right answer as it may depend on factors that surface during student discussion about the cartoon. Figure 4.6 shows an example of a *Concept Cartoon* related to the topic of transfer of energy. See the Appendix for information on the *Concept Cartoons* Web site and research reports that support the use of *Concept Cartoons*.

Figure 4.6   The Snowman's Coat *Concept Cartoon*

How This FACT Promotes Student Learning

Concept Cartoons are designed to engage and motivate students, uncover students' thinking about their own ideas, and encourage scientific argumentation. This FACT is particularly effective with struggling readers or English-language learners because the ideas are set in a visual context and contain limited text. Showing cartoon characters with differing points of view reinforces the value placed in science on examining alternative ideas. Students examine these ideas and work to resolve differences in order to come up with an acceptable explanation. *Concept Cartoons* help students develop confidence and trust in making their viewpoints public. As the developers of the cartoons note, "After all, if they get one wrong, then they can always blame the cartoon character for putting forward that idea!" (Naylor & Keogh, 2000, p. 7). It is the process of surfacing and discussing their own ideas that makes this a powerful technique for promoting student learning.

How This FACT Informs Instruction

Concept Cartoons are most often used at the beginning of a learning cycle to surface students' ideas and engage them in wanting to learn more about the science related to the cartoon situation. The ideas that surface when students respond to the cartoon provide valuable information to the teacher to use in designing instructional experiences that will confront students with their ideas and beliefs about the situation presented in the cartoon.

Concept Cartoons can also be used throughout instruction to initiate starting points for inquiry, solidify concepts learned, and transfer and apply the scientific concepts students learned to a new, real-life situation. The cartoons are a particularly useful medium for engaging students in scientific argumentation, providing an opportunity for teachers to listen to students' discuss their ideas and use the information to modify lessons or plan for further instruction and assessment. Many of the cartoons lend themselves to follow-up with an inquiry investigation in which students test their ideas. For example, after students have discussed their ideas from the cartoon shown in Figure 4.6, they could work in small groups to design and carry out an investigation simulating the Snowman's Coat scenario to find out whether a frozen object melts faster when covered with material such as the type used to make winter coats.

Design and Administration

Concept Cartoons are designed to probe students' thinking about everyday situations they encounter that involve the use of scientific ideas. Teachers can use concept cartoons that are already published and available, create their own from scratch, or adapt written assessment probes to a cartoon format. Consider using students who like to draw to create the characters and the setting for your cartoon and then add your distracters to the thought bubbles. Figure 4.7 shows an example of a teacher-developed concept cartoon using the process described in Science Curriculum Topic Study for developing formative assessment probes (see Appendix). If you create your own *Concept Cartoons*, limit the amount of text. Check to be sure there are no contextual clues that might cue the "right answer" such as "happier" facial expressions or one character having a more technical and detailed explanation. Before showing the cartoon, introduce the topic to students. You can provide the cartoon as a printed handout, as a projected image, or sketch it out for students on a chart or whiteboard.

Concept Cartoons work well as a small group or whole-class discussion stimulus as long as individual students first have an opportunity to activate their own thinking.

Give students time to individually think about their own ideas and then have small groups of students discuss their ideas and try to come to some consensus. At this point, the teacher is circulating and listening to ideas being discussed but not passing judgment on students' ideas. Have each group share with the whole class the ideas they came up with

Figure 4.7   Example of a Teacher-Developed *Concept Cartoon*

perhaps followed by voting on the one that seems most acceptable to the class. When possible, follow up the discussion by providing students with the opportunity to test out their ideas and share the outcomes of their inquiries. Use the results to draw students into a whole-group discussion to share their findings, consider what they have learned, and explain how their ideas have changed or been modified in some way. Probe further to find out what evidence led students to modify or change their thinking.

General Implementation Attributes

Ease of Use: High   Time Demand: Medium
Cognitive Demand: Medium

Modifications

Consider whiting out the bubbles that contain the characters' ideas and adding your own examples of commonly held ideas you may have observed with your own students. An alternative way to generate distracters is to ask students to work in small groups to fill in the bubbles with ideas they think the characters may have and exchange them with other groups for discussion. Students can also create their own cartoons to describe specific phenomena related to a curricular topic.

Caveats

Not all cartoons have one "right answer." Consider asking students for the "best" answer given the situation presented. It is the process of discussing ideas that is most important, not determining which character is correct. Refrain from giving away the answer soon after presenting the cartoon. Allow them time to experience uncertainty and cognitive dissonance, resolving the conflict through discussion and inquiry. Allowing time for ideas to simmer and stew increases cognitive engagement as the teacher builds the bridge from students' ideas to formal scientific explanations.

Use With Other Disciplines

This FACT can also be used in mathematics, social studies, and health.

My Notes

_____

_____

_____

#10: DATA MATCH

Description

Data Match provides students with a data set from a familiar investigation and several statements about the data. Students use evidence from the data to determine which statements are accurate. Research shows that some students tend to "look for or accept evidence that is consistent with their prior beliefs and either distort or fail to generate evidence that is inconsistent with those beliefs" (American Association for the Advancement of Science [AAAS], 1993, p. 332). *Data Match* helps teachers determine whether students rely on evidence derived from data collected from an investigation or whether they make inferences and form interpretations based on their own beliefs.

How This FACT Promotes Student Learning

Making claims and drawing conclusions based on evidence from reliable data is an essential feature of scientific inquiry (National Research Council [NRC], 1996). *Data Match* provides students with an opportunity to consider what constitutes evidence, practice interpreting data, and consider how confident they are in interpreting results of an inquiry. It reinforces the notion that inquiry does not end with the collection of data—that one must make sense of the data, using it as evidence for their claims.

How This FACT Informs Instruction

Data Match helps teachers determine how well students understand the role and significance of data they obtain through investigation. As students work in groups to analyze and discuss the statements based on the data collected during an investigation, teachers listen carefully, noting instances where students ignore the data to fit the outcomes to their own beliefs or examples where they struggle to link the data with the claim made in the statement. The information is used to guide students in distinguishing between evidence that comes from data and inferences that are based on assumptions and personal beliefs.

Design and Administration

Quantitative or qualitative data can be used with this FACT, depending on the developmental level of the students. Using data students have collected themselves makes the task more meaningful. Students should record their own ideas before engaging in small group and/or whole-class discussion about the data statements. Figure 4.8 is an example of a *Data Match* developed from elementary student-collected data on the effect of different surfaces on the melting time of an ice cube.

Figure 4.8   Ice Cube Melt *Data Match*

Where We Put the Ice Cube	How Many Minutes It Took to Melt
On the blacktop in the sun	3
On the blacktop in the shade	7
On the grass	10
On the metal slide	2
On the dirt underneath the slide	5
On the top of the picnic table bench	6
On a rock	5
On a rubber tire in the sun	2
On the shaded part of the tire	5

Which of these statements match your results?

1. The ice cube on the grass took longest to melt.
2. The metal slide was hotter than the dirt underneath the slide.
3. The rock must have been in the shade.
4. The ice cube melted faster on the blacktop in the sun than on the shaded blacktop.
5. The picnic table bench was in the sun.
6. Ice placed on dark things melts faster than ice placed on light things.
7. The ice melted faster on the slide because it was shiny.
8. Ice melts faster on some surfaces than on others.
9. Ice cubes in the sun melt faster than ice cubes in the shade.
10. The time it takes an ice cube to melt on a surface depends on the surrounding conditions.

General Implementation Attributes

Ease of Use: Low   Time Demand: Medium
Cognitive Demand: Medium

Modifications

Have students generate a list of statements that can be used in a class discussion to differentiate between accurate claims and inferences.

Caveats

If data from actual student investigations are not available, use caution when developing an example of a data set to use with this FACT. Contrived data may contain inaccuracies that contribute to misconceptions. Whenever possible, use data from actual investigations or credible sources.

Use With Other Disciplines

This FACT is specific to inquiry-based science.

My Notes

_____

_____

_____

#11: DIRECTED PARAPHRASING

Description

Directed Paraphrasing involves students in translating a lesson or part of a lesson using language and examples appropriate for a specific audience (Angelo & Cross, 1993). For example, following a lesson on fossils that targeted ideas about kinds of objects that are considered to be fossils and how they became fossilized, students summarize the key points learned during the lesson as if they were talking to a younger brother or sister looking at fossils in a science museum; or, at a higher level, they may paraphrase their understandings as if they were talking to a paleontologist.

How This FACT Promotes Student Learning

Directed Paraphrasing provides an interesting, creative, and challenging way for students to summarize what they learned in their own words, use appropriate scientific terminology, and consider how to best communicate their understanding to a specific audience. Explaining what one has learned to others, in examples and words familiar to the specific audience, provides a metacognitive opportunity for the learner to examine his or her own understanding and think about how to translate it so that others can understand. When one has to explain something to others, one's own learning increases. Listening to other students share their paraphrases and providing peer feedback further enhances student learning.

How This FACT Informs Instruction

Teachers can use this FACT to have students summarize a lesson or segment of a lesson. The lesson could be from a lecture, group discussion, activity, video, or text reading. Listening to students paraphrase what they learned provides an opportunity for the teacher to gauge whether key points in the lesson were identified and understood by students, indicating the need for revision or additional opportunities to learn the scientific ideas. Listening to the ways in which students talk about their ideas also provides the teacher with useful information about students' scientific communication skills.

Design and Administration

First, decide on an appropriate time to break during the lesson so students can summarize what they learned without interrupting the conceptual flow of the lesson. Encourage students to individually record their ideas that summarize the lesson or part of the lesson selected before developing a paraphrase for their audience. Assign an audience or have students select one and challenge them to create their summary for the specific audience. Examples of audiences used for *Directed Paraphrasing* include younger students, parents, students in the same class who were absent when the lesson was taught, adults with different careers, famous persons, scientists whose work is related to the topic, or teachers in the school who teach different subject areas. Give time for students to think about how to put the summary into words and examples that would be appropriate for the intended audience. Another way to use *Directed Paraphrasing* is to assign different audiences to small groups. Have each group come up with a *Directed Paraphrase* they could share with the teacher and whole class for feedback.

General Implementation Attributes

Ease of Use: Medium   Time Demand: Medium
Cognitive Demand: High

Modifications

Consider having the class generate the key points to summarize the lesson and then assign the *Directed Paraphrase* as an individual or small group assessment.

Caveats

It may be necessary to model an example for the class the first time this FACT is used. Directing the paraphrase toward a particular audience increases the cognitive demand of summarizing information. Make sure your students are familiar with the intended audience before asking them to translate what they learned for that audience.

Use With Other Disciplines

This FACT can also be used in social studies, language arts, health, and performing arts.

My Notes

_____

_____

_____

#12: EXPLANATION ANALYSIS

Description

Explanation Analysis encourages self and peer assessment of students' ability to both construct and analyze a well-crafted scientific explanation. Teachers and students constructively critique scientific explanations for accuracy and inclusion of the key components that distinguish scientific explanations from other types of explanations: the claim, appropriate and sufficient evidence, and reasoning that links the evidence to the claim using a scientific principle (Krajcik et al., 2006). While the original work of Krajcik et al. (2006) focused on explanations using data from investigations, this FACT is also used with explanations from assessment probes and other types of assessment questions.

How This FACT Promotes Student Learning

Writing scientific explanations is an important skill that helps students make sense of data and scientific phenomena. This FACT provides an opportunity for students to hone the skill of constructing scientific explanations as well as analyzing the explanations of others. Students often think of explanations as the endpoint of a task. Teacher-led feedback on students' explanations helps students see that their written explanations are not set in stone and can be revisited, rethought, and revised (Krajcik et al., 2006). *Explanation Analysis* provides a formative opportunity for students to work in small groups to assess their own and their peers' explanations against a common set of accepted criteria. This process of analyzing explanations and providing feedback develops deeper conceptual understanding of what a scientific explanation is as well as improves students' ability to write scientific explanations.

How This FACT Informs Instruction

Scientific explanations differ from explanations in other content areas. For example, explaining what happened during a story in a language arts class is more descriptive than it is explanatory when compared with scientific explanations. In science, explanations involve reasoning that links evidence to a claim or scientific statement as opposed to descriptions that tend to be observational in nature. Students are frequently asked to provide explanations in science during activities, lessons, and assessments, yet this skill is rarely explicitly taught or self-assessed by students. An analysis of students' explanations may reveal a need to explicitly teach students how to construct explanations in order to differentiate description from explanation. Teachers can use this FACT to give feedback on explanations related to specific class activities, or experiments. The FACT is particularly useful when used with assessment probes that ask students to commit to an idea and support it with a scientific explanation. The criteria shown in Figure 4.9 can be embedded into instruction to help students construct well-developed, scientific explanations.

The cycle of feedback and revision, using the assessment criteria, helps teachers see how students improve over time in their ability to construct scientific explanations. The assessment data are used to help teachers make decisions about when to provide additional scaffolding or when to reduce the amount of scaffolding students need to construct explanations. Furthermore, when students are able to construct good explanations in science, they serve as a window into examining how well students understand science concepts and principles and how their preconceptions might be used to inform instruction. Explanations that lack grounding in scientific content and principles may indicate the need to adjust instruction accordingly.

Design and Administration

Guide students through the *Explanation Analysis* process the first time it is used by having students generate an explanation as part of an existing activity, experiment, or assessment probe. Provide students with the assessment criteria listed in Figure 4.9 or generate your own to analyze the explanations. First have students self-assess their own explanation using the criteria and then revise it and submit it for feedback from the teacher. Once students become familiar with the FACT, they can work in groups to help each other analyze and revise their explanations, providing and receiving feedback in the process. Teachers can select a sampling of student explanations to use as part of a whole-class discussion focused on critiquing explanations and providing constructive feedback.

Figure 4.9   Assessment Criteria Checklist for Analyzing Scientific Explanations

Explanation Criteria	N/A	Not at all	Partially	Yes
The Claim or Statement				
1. Is a claim or statement in response to the question made?				
2. Is the claim or statement stated as a complete sentence, without beginning with yes, no, or the answer choice?				
3. Is the claim or statement related to the question?				
4. Is the claim or statement scientifically correct?				
Evidence (from experiences outside of school, prior knowledge, or science activities and investigations)				
5. Is the type of evidence appropriate for supporting the claim or statement?				
6. Is there sufficient evidence?				
7. Is the evidence scientifically accurate?				
Reasoning (linking the evidence to the claim or statement using a scientific principle)				
8. Does the reasoning or "rule" used in the explanation stand out to the reader (i.e., is it obvious)?				
9. Does the reasoning make a link between the evidence and the claim or statement?				
10. Is a scientific principle or knowledge of scientific ideas used to describe why the evidence supports the claim or statement?				
Overall Explanation				
11. If your explanation is based on an investigation or activity from your science class, would someone who is not in your class be able to read your explanation and understand how the investigation or activity supports it?				
12. If your explanation is based on your real-life experiences or prior knowledge, would someone be able to read your explanation and understand how the experience or prior knowledge supports it?				

SOURCE: Adapted from Krajcik et al. (2006).

General Implementation Attributes

Ease of Use: Medium   Time Demand: Medium
Cognitive Demand: Medium/High

Modifications

In the early grades, the focus of science is more observational than explanatory. Scientific principles are introduced when students are developmentally ready to link them to their observations. Hence, younger students may not be ready to identify scientific principles that link evidence to a claim. Instead, encourage them to focus on the evidence that supports their claim and the "rule" they used to decide what counts as evidence.

Caveats

Students should be explicitly taught how to construct explanations in science. They need opportunities to practice using the three components of a scientific explanation before asking them to analyze their own or others' explanations. Model this FACT for students who are using it for the first time. Make sure students understand the language used in this FACT. If students are not familiar with the concept of a claim, scientific reasoning, or the concept of linking evidence to the claim, consider using a metaphor such as "building a bridge between the claim and the evidence" (Krajcik et al., 2006, p. 104). When using this FACT to help students write or analyze explanations in response to an elicitation or preassessment, such as an assessment probe, eliminate criteria #4 and #7. Students have not yet had an opportunity to develop the conceptual understanding needed to determine whether the explanation is scientifically correct. For this purpose, the focus should be on constructing an explanation that allows the reader an opportunity to understand what the student is thinking and what type of experiences or prior knowledge informed their ideas.

Use With Other Disciplines

This FACT is specific to inquiry-based science.

My Notes

_____

_____

_____

#13: FACT FIRST QUESTIONING

Description

Quality questions provide insight into students' ideas and growing knowledge base. *Fact First Questioning* is a higher-order questioning technique used to draw out student knowledge beyond recall level. It takes a factual "what" question and turns it into a deeper "how" or "why" question because you are stating the fact first and asking students to elaborate.

How This FACT Promotes Student Learning

Students, including "high achievers," can memorize, recall, and recant information with very little conceptual understanding. By stating the fact first and asking students to explain or elaborate on it, you enable students to tap into deeper thinking processes that lead to a more enduring understanding of science concepts. Stating the fact first and then allowing for wait time provides an opportunity for students to activate their thinking about the concept before being asked the higher-level question.

How This FACT Informs Instruction

This FACT helps teachers expand their repertoire of questioning strategies for the purpose of finding out what their students know and understand. A simple change in the way factual questions are asked and responded to can open up the door to providing valuable information to teachers about student understanding of the conceptual ideas related to an important scientific fact. The information helps teachers determine whether students recall important knowledge at a superficial level or have developed deeper conceptual understanding. The information can be used to examine whether terminology and facts are overemphasized at the expense of scientific understanding and adjust instruction accordingly to focus on concepts instead of terminology and facts.

Design and Administration

Any factual question can be thoughtfully turned into a *Fact First Question.* Use the general template: State the fact followed by "Why is X an example of Y?" (Black et al., 2003). For example, instead of asking, "Which essential life process releases energy from food?" turn it around to ask, "Cellular respiration is an example of an essential life process. Why is cellular respiration an essential life process?" Instead of the factual recall answer—cellular respiration—from the first question, the *Fact First Question* produces a much deeper response that involves describing cellular respiration as a process that happens within cells to break down carbohydrates in order to release the energy required for cells to function. Figure 4.10 lists a variety of other *Fact First Questions* used at different grade levels.

General Implementation Attributes

Ease of Use: High   Time Demand: Low
Cognitive Demand: Medium

Modifications

Consider modifying traditional textbook recall questions into *Fact First Questions.* Have older students come up with their own *Fact First Questions* and responses.

Caveats

Use *Fact First Questions* after students have had an opportunity to experience and learn the content. Some "why" questions are not appropriate for younger students in cases when observations are developed before explanations. For example, K–2 students should know the fact that the moon can sometimes be seen in the daytime. This can be observed by students and assimilated into their knowledge about the Earth, moon, and

Figure 4.10   Examples of *Fact First Questions*

- Glucose is a form of food for plants. Why is glucose considered a food for plants?
- A cell is called the basic unit of life. Why is the cell called the basic unit of life?
- Density is a characteristic property of matter. Why is density considered a characteristic property?
- The small intestine is an organ of the digestive system. Why is it considered part of the digestive system?
- The patterns of stars in the night sky stay the same. Why do the patterns of stars in the night sky stay the same?
- Sandstone is a sedimentary rock. Why is sandstone considered a sedimentary rock?
- Bacteria in the soil are decomposers. Why are bacteria in the soil considered to be decomposers?
- Quartz is a mineral. Why is quartz an example of a mineral?
- Electricity requires a closed circuit in order to flow. Why is it necessary to have a closed circuit in order for electricity to flow?

sun system. However, it is beyond the developmental level of primary-age students to respond to a *Fact First Question* such as the following: The moon can sometimes be seen in the daytime. Why can the moon sometimes be seen during the day?

Use With Other Disciplines

This FACT can also be used in mathematics, social studies, language arts, health, foreign languages, and performing arts.

My Notes

_____

_____

_____

#14: FAMILIAR PHENOMENON PROBES

Description

Familiar Phenomenon Probes are two-tiered questions consisting of a selected response section and a justification for the selected response. They are designed to elicit students' ideas about a familiar phenomenon. The distracters (wrong choices) used for the selected response section include commonly held ideas noted in the research on children's misconceptions in science. Students are asked to provide an explanation to support the answer they selected. Figure 4.11 is an example of a *Familiar Phenomenon Probe* used to elicit ideas about the bubbles in a pot of boiling water (Keeley, Eberle, & Tugel, 2007).

How This FACT Promotes Student Learning

Familiar Phenomenon Probes are used to draw out students' ideas related to phenomena they have encountered in their everyday experiences. They engage students in thinking about the scientific ideas related to the phenomenon and committing to a response that matches their thinking. After sharing their own thinking and considering the ideas of others, students will sometimes modify their ideas when new information and supporting arguments override their existing conceptions. The nature of the probes also creates a "desire to know" on the part of the student, leading to further investigation, questions, or researching sources of information.

Figure 4.11   Example of a *Familiar Phenomenon Probe*

What's in the Bubbles?

Hannah is boiling water in a glass tea kettle. She notices large bubbles forming on the bottom of the kettle that rise to the top and wonders what is in the bubbles. She asks her family what they think, and this is what they say:

Dad: They are bubbles of heat.

Calvin: The bubbles are filled with air.

Grandma: The bubbles are an invisible form of water.

Mom: The bubbles are empty—there is nothing inside them.

Lucy: The bubbles contain oxygen and hydrogen that separated from the water.

Which person do you most agree with and why? Explain your thinking.

SOURCE: Keeley, Eberle, and Tugel. (2007). Reprinted by permission.

How This FACT Informs Instruction

Familiar Phenomenon Probes provide a quick way for teachers to gather data on students' preconceptions, including commonly held ideas noted in the cognitive research literature. Teachers take these ideas into account when designing instruction and monitoring student learning. The probe initiates discussion about scientific ideas and may lead to inquiry-based investigations. This FACT can also be used as an application of students' ideas in a context different from the one they experienced in their learning activities. The results of the probe are useful in determining how well students can transfer their learning to a new context. If results indicate that transfer did not take place, it may signify the need to provide additional learning opportunities or the need to be more explicit in developing the big ideas and broader generalizations related to the topic.

Design and Administration

Design or choose assessment probes that use examples of familiar phenomena to elicit ideas related to a specific learning goal. See the Appendix for sources of *Familiar Phenomenon Probes*. The probe can be administered as a written task or used orally to stimulate small- or large-group discussion. This FACT is best used at the start of a sequence of instruction, although it can be used after conceptual development to determine whether transfer has taken place. Encourage students to write as much as they can in their explanation so you can use their ideas to help them learn. Consider sharing the results with students so they can see the variety of ideas held by their classmates. In addition, it is helpful to provide an opportunity for students to discuss their ideas in small groups or as a whole class, but let them know that you are not going to reveal the answer right away. Assure them that they will revisit the probe again after they have had an opportunity to further explore and investigate their ideas. After students have experienced lessons related to the probe, revisit their initial ideas, discuss them as a group, and reflect on whether they have modified or changed them. This FACT can be combined with other strategies such as *Commit and Toss, Four Corners, Sticky Bars, Human Scatterplots,* and *Traffic Light Cards.*

General Implementation Attributes

Ease of Use: High   Time Demand: Medium
Cognitive Demand: Medium

Modifications

Where appropriate, bring in props to demonstrate the phenomenon. For example, when using the example shown in Figure 4.11, *safely* demonstrate by boiling water in a large, clear beaker or glass kettle so students can see the bubbles forming and rising to the surface. These types of probes can also be turned into open-response questions by omitting the distracters. For example, the prompt in Figure 4.11 can be changed to "What do you think is in the bubbles?"

Caveats

Before developing or using a *Familiar Phenomenon Probe,* make sure all students are familiar with the phenomenon. Avoid using unfamiliar objects or contexts.

Use With Other Disciplines

This FACT is specific to science because of its emphasis on science phenomena.

My Notes

_____

_____

_____

#15: FIRST WORD–LAST WORD

Description

This FACT is a variation of acrostics. Students construct statements about a concept or topic before and after instruction that begins with a designated letter of the alphabet. The acrostic format provides a structure for them to build their idea statements off different starting letters that make up the topic word (Lipton & Wellman, 1998).

How This FACT Promotes Student Learning

The *First Word* acrostic is used to activate student thinking about the concept or topic students will be studying prior to beginning a unit. Writing conceptual statements that reflect one's understanding is a metacognitive task that requires students to think about what they already know. The *Last Word* provides a metacognitive opportunity for students to examine where they were in their thinking at the beginning of a unit of instruction and reflect on how their present understanding extends or modifies their initial understandings.

How This FACT Informs Instruction

This FACT provides an opportunity at the beginning of instruction to uncover likely barriers to learning, such as tenaciously held misconceptions. After instruction, it helps teachers examine how students' ideas may have changed, solidified, or become more sophisticated throughout the course of their learning. Figure 4.12 is an example of a seventh grader's *First Word*, before a series of lessons on photosynthesis. The teacher can scan the *First Word* to determine what the student already knows, how sophisticated his or her knowledge or terminology is, and any misunderstandings he or she may bring from prior experiences. In this example, the student has a significant misconception about plants getting their food directly from the soil. The teacher may notice similar ideas in other students' papers. The teacher uses this information to plan a lesson that will challenge the students' concept of "plant food."

The *Last Word* provides a postinstruction opportunity for teachers to assess how students have progressed in conceptual understanding, scientific accuracy, and sophistication of ideas compared to their initial statements about the concept. It also reveals misconceptions that continue to persist. The example of the *Last Word* in Figure 4.13 indicates that the student changed her idea that plants get their food from the soil. Other ideas were revised that reflect an accurate and more sophisticated understanding. The information from *Last Word* also signifies whether additional learning experiences or modifications to lessons are needed.

Figure 4.12 Seventh Grader's *First Word* on the Topic of Photosynthesis

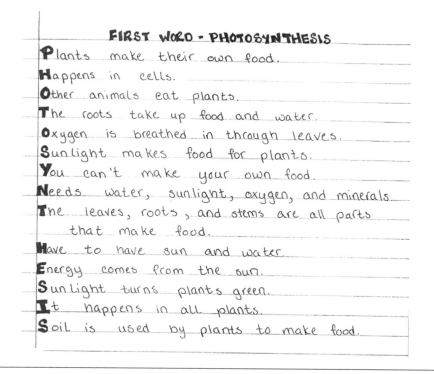

FIRST WORD - PHOTOSYNTHESIS

Plants make their own food.
Happens in cells.
Other animals eat plants.
The roots take up food and water.
Oxygen is breathed in through leaves.
Sunlight makes food for plants.
You can't make your own food.
Needs water, sunlight, oxygen, and minerals.
The leaves, roots, and stems are all parts
    that make food.
Have to have sun and water.
Energy comes from the sun.
Sunlight turns plants green.
It happens in all plants.
Soil is used by plants to make food.

Design and Administration

Choose one word or a short phrase that represents a major concept or focus of the curricular topic you are teaching. The *First Word* is given to students before beginning a sequence of instruction. Have students write the word vertically down the page. Start with the first letter in the acrostic to begin a statement related to the topic. Remind students that there is no such thing as a blank slate in their heads. Everyone can write something that springs to mind. Encourage students to write full sentences, not single words or short phrases. If students struggle with writing ideas as sentences rather than words or short phrases, create an example of a *First Word* acrostic using a concept they previously studied, to show students what the FACT should look like. Collect the *First Words* for analysis and save them for a final reflection. After completing a series of lessons on the concept or topic, the students repeat the process on a new sheet of paper called the *Last Word*. Pass back the saved *First Words* and have students examine them to compare their ideas at the beginning of instruction to their current thinking. They write a *Last Word* by repeating what they stated before, if their idea has not changed; revising prior statements to include more detail, complexity, and appropriate terminology; or correcting

Figure 4.13   Seventh Grader's *Last Word* on the Topic of Photosynthesis

LAST WORD - PHOTOSYNTHESIS

Producers such as plants use energy from the sun to make their food.

Happens in cells that have structures called chloroplasts.

Organisms that eat plants are using stored energy from the plant.

The roots take water up to the leaves where it reacts with sunlight and carbon dioxide.

Oxygen is given off during photosynthesis and is used by plants and animals for respiration

Sunlight provides the energy so plants can make food.

You need to have cells with chlorplasts and chlorophyll to make food.

Need water, carbon dioxide, and sunlight to make food.

The leaf is the food making part.

Have to have sunlight, water, and carbon dioxide.

Energy comes from sunlight.

Sunlight is trapped in the chlorphyll.

Is a necessary life process for all plants

Soil holds the water for plants and gives some minerals.

misunderstandings by completely rewriting the statement to be scientifically correct. Students are often quite surprised and excited to see how their ideas have changed considerably. They are able to recognize and acknowledge the extent to which new and deeper understanding developed as a result of their instructional experiences.

General Implementation Attributes

Ease of Use: Medium   Time Demand: Medium
Cognitive Demand: Medium

Modifications

Use shorter words for the acrostic with younger students. This FACT can be used in pairs for students who lack strong language skills and need the support of a peer. It can also be used as a whole-class activity, charting the class ideas as the *First Word* and revisiting it to create a *Last Word* chart that reflects the class consensus after a sequence of instruction.

Caveats

Don't assume students know what acrostics are. It may help to model the strategy with a familiar concept the first time it is used and/or begin some of the sentence stems with the class to start them off.

Use With Other Disciplines

This FACT can also be used in mathematics, social studies, language arts, health, foreign languages, and performing arts.

My Notes

_____

_____

_____

#16: FISHBOWL THINK ALOUD

Description

The *Fishbowl Think Aloud* is a technique used to listen in on the thinking of a sampling of students in the class. Four or five students are selected to be in a "fishbowl," sitting together in a cluster or the front of the room. The rest of the class and the teacher face or surround the students who are in the "fishbowl" and listen attentively to their conversation. The conversation is a response to a prompt in which the students "think aloud," discussing and defending their ideas as the teacher and other students listen in and reconcile their own thinking with that of their peers in the "fishbowl."

How This FACT Promotes Student Learning

This FACT requires the students in the "fishbowl" to think out loud, describe their thinking, and explain the reasons for their ideas. While the students in the "fishbowl" are thinking through and talking about their ideas, the other students are mentally comparing their ideas to what they are hearing in the "fishbowl." This continuous reflection on learning helps students think about their own ideas, strive to put them together in a coherent way, and compare their thinking with that of ideas of other students.

How This FACT Informs Instruction

The students selected to sit in the "fishbowl" represent a sample of the class. The sample may surface some of the ideas and ways of thinking that are indicative of the group as a whole. As the teacher listens in on the conversation, understandings and misconceptions can be noted that may need to be addressed in subsequent instruction. The FACT also provides an opportunity for the teacher to see how well students can engage in "science talk" that is supported by evidence and explanation. If students have difficulty engaging in discussions that require them to justify their ideas with various forms of evidence, it indicates the need to further develop this hallmark skill of science. The observing students are allowed to ask questions or make comments at the end of the fishbowl discussion. This provides another opportunity to see how well students understand a concept, including their ability to identify inaccuracies and challenge statements that may conflict with their own thinking.

Design and Administration

This FACT can be used during the elicitation or formal concept-development stage of the learning cycle. Choose students for the fishbowl who, as a group, are representative of the class as a whole. Seat them so they can see each other and so the class can see them. These are the only students who can talk. Remind the other students that they are to listen during the fishbowl and note any questions or comments they want to make at the end.

Provide the students in the fishbowl with an interesting open-ended prompt for discussion to begin the thinking process. For example, *Is air necessary for gravity to act on an object?* One student will begin the process of thinking out loud, sharing his or her answer and the reasoning behind it. Other students join in, agreeing or disagreeing, building on each others' ideas. If students have not experienced techniques such as *Volleyball—Not Ping-Pong!* the teacher may have to help facilitate the conversation the first time the strategy is used. It is important to encourage all students in the fishbowl to participate and focus on each other, not the students who are watching and listening to them. After the fishbowl conversation ends, the students who have been listening and processing what they heard have an opportunity to share whether they agree or disagree with any of the ideas discussed in the fishbowl.

General Implementation Attributes

Ease of Use: Low   Time Demand: Medium
Cognitive Demand: Medium/High

Modifications

Students outside the circle can come up with the questions for the fishbowl, in addition to the prompt provided by the teacher. Students can also ask a question of the fishbowl group after they finish their fishbowl conversation. Each questioner then takes the seat of the student in the fishbowl who answered and becomes part of the fishbowl responses while the fishbowl student joins the rest of the class. This can be repeated several times, encouraging students to question each other and widening the opportunity for other students to participate.

Caveats

It is important to set norms before this FACT is used so that students in the fishbowl feel comfortable with the public display of their thinking.

Use With Other Disciplines

This FACT can also be used in mathematics, social studies, language arts, and health.

My Notes

_____

_____

_____

#17: FIST TO FIVE

Description

Fist to Five asks students to indicate the extent of their understanding of a concept or procedure by holding up a closed fist (no understanding), one finger (very little understanding), and a range up to five fingers (I understand it completely and can easily explain it to someone else). For example, after giving instructions for a lab activity, teachers might ask for a *fist to five* to do a quick check on whether students understand the directions before proceeding with the lab.

How This FACT Promotes Student Learning

Fist to Five provides a simple feedback opportunity for all students in a class to indicate when they do not understand a concept or skill and need additional support for their learning. It is especially effective with individual students who are reluctant to let the teacher know that they are experiencing difficulty during a lesson. It encourages metacognition by raising self-awareness of how well a student feels he or she understands a concept, skill, or procedure.

How This FACT Informs Instruction

Fist to Five is a feedback and monitoring technique used to check understanding or skills at any point in a lesson. It is particularly useful when new material is presented, a new procedure is introduced, or directions for a task are given. It allows the teacher to direct the challenge and pace of lessons toward the needs of the students rather than follow a prescribed instructional plan. The quick read of the class provides teachers with the feedback they need to modify the lesson or pair students up to help each other.

Design and Administration

At any time during a lesson, ask students to hold up their hands for a check of understanding. The closed fist indicates "I have no idea," one finger means "I barely understand," two fingers mean "I understand parts of it but I need a lot of help," three fingers indicate "I understand most of it but I'm not sure I can explain it well enough to others," four fingers mean "I understand it pretty well and can do an adequate job explaining it," and five fingers indicate "I understand it completely and can easily explain it to someone else." Some teachers post a "Fist to Five" chart in the room so students remember how many fingers to hold up. Make sure all students hold up their hands. It can be used to group students for peer assistance by putting the students who hold up two to three fingers together with the students who hold up four to five fingers. The teacher can then take the closed-fist and one-finger responses aside for differentiated assistance.

General Implementation Attributes

Ease of Use: High   Time Demand: Low
Cognitive Demand: Low

Modifications

This FACT can be modified as a three-finger strategy: one finger: I don't get it, two fingers: I partially get it, and three fingers: I get it.

Likewise, you can use thumbs up: I get it, thumbs sideways: I'm not sure I understand, and thumbs down: I don't get it.

Caveats

When matching students who claim to understand with students who need help, make sure that the students who held up four to five fingers really do understand well enough to explain it to others before putting them into peer-assistance groups.

Use With Other Disciplines

This FACT can also be used in mathematics, social studies, language arts, health, foreign languages, and performing arts.

My Notes

_____

_____

_____

#18: FOCUSED LISTING

Description

Focused Listing asks students to recall ideas and experiences related to a science topic they encountered in a prior instructional unit or grade. Students list as many concepts, facts, and ideas as they can recall from prior instruction (Angelo & Cross, 1993).

How This FACT Promotes Student Learning

This is a knowledge-comprehension level activity designed to activate thinking and improve ability to recall information and experiences from previous instruction. It helps students differentiate between what they think they learned in school and prior conceptions they may have developed outside of formal learning experiences. It also helps students avoid the common complaint of "we already did that in X grade" by recognizing that teaching and learning require revisiting previous concepts and experiences in order to build upon them for deeper understanding.

96 Science Formative Assessment

How This FACT Informs Instruction

Focused Listing helps the teacher gauge students' readiness and familiarity with facts, ideas, knowledge, or skills from a previous unit of instruction. The lists students generate provide information to the teacher about the web of recalled information and classroom experiences students associate with a curricular topic. The information is used to make decisions on how to best build from students' prior experiences and knowledge. Figure 4.14 shows a sixth-grade example of a *Focused List* that recalls students' knowledge and experiences related to reflection of light. Students previously learned about the reflection of light in third grade.

Design and Administration

Select a topic that is an important part of your curricular unit. Make sure it is not too broad or too narrow. Have students write the word or phrase at the top of a sheet of paper and list as many terms, facts, ideas, concepts, definitions, or experiences as they can that they remember from previous lessons in other grades or units of study. Students can also work in small groups to develop collective *Focused Lists*. Examine the lists or have small groups post their charts. Look for similarities, noting which things students readily recall and whether the ones that are critical to learning are missing.

Figure 4.14   Sixth-Grade Focused List on Light Reflection

REFLECTION OF LIGHT

light bounces off things

light goes in different directions

light goes in straight lines

mirrors

full moon reflects light

water reflects light

bike reflectors

light waves

sunburn from reflection off water

shiny things

General Implementation Attributes

Ease of Use: High   Time Demand: Low
Cognitive Demand: Medium

Modifications

This FACT can also be conducted as a whole-class brainstormed list.

Caveats

Generating items on the list does not always equate with understanding. Be aware that students can recall information and experiences without conceptual understanding or the ability to make connections between the words and statements on their list.

Use With Other Disciplines

This FACT can also be used in mathematics, social studies, language arts, health, foreign languages, and performing arts.

My Notes

_____

_____

_____

#19: FOUR CORNERS

Description

Four Corners is used with selected response questions to identify groups of students with similar responses to the question asked. Students move to a corner of the room designated to match their response or similar way of thinking.

How This FACT Promotes Student Learning

Four Corners provides an opportunity for students to make their ideas public. By meeting "in the corner" with students who have similar ideas, students can further discuss and clarify their own thinking with others before returning to their seats and engaging in scientific argumentation with the class or small groups of students with different ideas. In the process of explaining their thinking, students sometimes notice gaps or inconsistencies in their own reasoning and question whether they have enough information to be certain their ideas are plausible.

How This FACT Informs Instruction

Teachers can visually see which idea individual students have as well as which idea is most prevalent in the class. By circulating among corners as students are discussing and clarifying their ideas, the teacher gains insight into students' *foothold* ideas—those ideas students assume to be true at that point in time (Hammer & Van Zee, 2006). The information is used to inform instructional strategies that can help students gradually move toward and accept the scientific ideas.

Design and Administration

Choose a selected response assessment that includes an explanation and label the four corners of a room with the letter or name that matches the response. Examples of FACTs in this chapter that can be used with *Four Corners* include *Concept Cartoons, Familiar Phenomenon Probes, Friendly Talk Probes,* and *P-E-O Probes.* Ask students to individually think through their response, commit to an answer, and write their explanation. When students are finished with the task, have them go to the corner of the room that matches their selected response. Give students up to five minutes to share and discuss their thinking with others who selected the same response. Teachers can follow up the discussion at the *Four Corners* with a class debate about the ideas by having students return to their seats for mixed small groups and whole-class discussion. Another alternative is to have students remain in each of the corners and work together as a group to support their arguments in front of their peers. As students listen to and consider the arguments of other groups, they may move to a different corner when they give up their idea in favor of a new one. The challenge is to try to get all students over to one corner, ideally the one that represents the scientific view.

General Implementation Attributes

Ease of Use: High   Time Demand: Low
Cognitive Demand: High

Modifications

Use different areas of the room or designated tables for more than four responses, or use only three corners for selected response items that include fewer than four selected responses.

Caveats

This FACT works best in a classroom environment where students feel comfortable expressing and defending their own ideas without being influenced by others' responses.

Use With Other Disciplines

This FACT can also be used in mathematics, social studies, language arts, health, foreign languages, and performing arts.

My Notes

_____

_____

_____

#20: FRAYER MODEL

Description

The *Frayer Model* graphically organizes prior knowledge about a concept into an operational definition, characteristics, examples, and nonexamples (Buehl, 2001). An example of a *Frayer Model* template is shown in Figure 4.15.

How This FACT Promotes Student Learning

The *Frayer Model* helps activate students' prior knowledge about a scientific concept. It provides students with the opportunity to clarify what they think the concept is and communicate their understanding by providing an operational definition, describe characteristics, and list examples and nonexamples from their own background knowledge or experiences with the concept. This FACT can also be used to help solidify conceptual understanding after students have had an opportunity to learn about the concept.

How This FACT Informs Instruction

The *Frayer Model* is used to determine students' prior knowledge about a concept or technical terminology before planning a lesson. Barriers that can hinder learning may be uncovered with this FACT. The *Frayer Model* can also be used after students have explored a concept and are ready to

Figure 4.15 *Frayer Model* Template

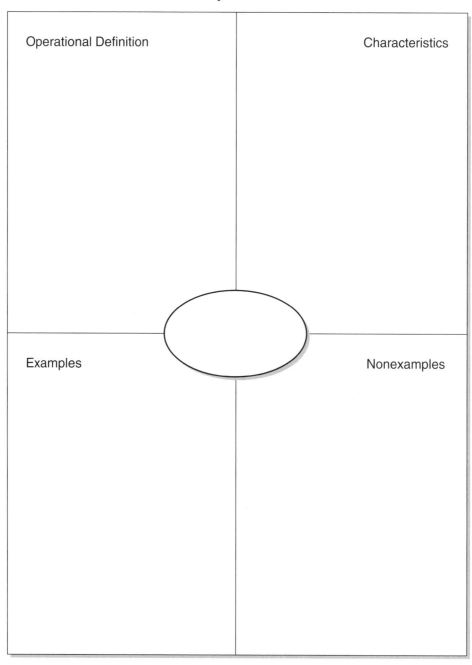

Frayer Model

SOURCE: Created by Frayer, D., Frederick, W. C., & Klausmeier, H. J. (1969).

develop formal conceptual understanding. Students' completed *Frayer Models* provide a starting point with an operational definition and understandings gained through instructional experiences that can be further refined through class discussion and formal clarification of the concept.

Design and Administration

The *Frayer Model* is best used with concepts that might be confusing because of their relational qualities. For example, the middle school concept of characteristic properties may be confusing to students because of their difficulty in distinguishing between intensive and extensive properties of matter. Begin by using a familiar concept to explain the *Frayer Model* diagram and demonstrate how to fill it in. Provide students with the concept you want them to think about and give them time to complete the diagram. Once the diagram is complete, let the students share their ideas with other students, modifying their diagrams as they accept new information. Students can also work in groups to create their Frayer diagrams, using them in a whole-class discussion about the concept and refining them as new information is added to their existing model. Frayer models can also be used after students have had an opportunity to develop conceptual understanding using the *Scientists' Ideas Comparison.* Students can apply the formal understandings gained from the scientists' ideas to the *Frayer Model.*

General Implementation Attributes

Ease of Use: High   Time Demand: Low
Cognitive Demand: Medium

Modifications

The center bubble is typically used to insert the concept word. It can also be used for a student drawing or other visual representation of the concept.

Caveats

Frayer Models have been used in language arts to support vocabulary development and word recognition prior to a reading assignment. In science, their primary purpose should extend beyond vocabulary development and focus on enhancing conceptual understanding.

Use With Other Disciplines

This FACT can also be used in mathematics, social studies, language arts, health, foreign languages, and performing arts.

My Notes

_____

_____

_____

#21: FRIENDLY TALK PROBES

Description

Friendly Talk Probes are two-tiered questions that consist of a selected response section followed by a justification. The probe is set in a real-life scenario in which friends, family members, or familiar adults talk about a science-related concept or phenomenon. Students are asked to pick the person they most agree with and explain why. There is usually one best answer that most closely matches the scientific idea. Distracters are based on commonly held ideas from the research on students' misconceptions. The conversation between the characters draws students into the ideas almost as if they are participating in the conversation (Keeley et al., 2007).

How This FACT Promotes Student Learning

This FACT can be used to engage students in surfacing and examining their preconceptions as well as solidifying concepts and applying understandings in a new context. It promotes engagement with ideas in an accessible way by having friends, family, or familiar student and adult roles legitimize the act of putting alternative ideas forward for scrutiny. When a student can relate an incorrect or naive idea he or she has to one of the characters in the probe, he or she is less apt to feel uncomfortable about revealing a "wrong answer."

How This FACT Informs Instruction

Friendly Talk Probes can be used at multiple points prior to or throughout instruction to find out what students are thinking in relation to an important curricular goal. It can be used to engage students in thinking about the concepts they will encounter during their instructional experiences and provide them with an opportunity to share their ideas and explain their thinking. This FACT can also be used as an application of students' learning following the conceptual development phase of instruction. Choose a probe that targets the concept taught and presents ideas in a context different from the students' instructional materials and learning experiences. The responses are useful in determining how well students can transfer their ideas to a new context. Results may signify the need to provide additional activities or be more explicit about developing the big idea and broader generalizations related to the targeted concept.

Design and Administration

The challenge in designing these types of probes is to not oversimplify a complex idea. Design or choose probes that use examples of familiar events, processes, or objects that can be realistically discussed by the characters represented. The Appendix describes the *Uncovering Student Ideas in Science* series, a source of *Friendly Talk Assessment Probes.* The probe can be administered as a paper-and-pencil task or used orally to stimulate small- or large-group discussion. It can be combined with other FACTs in this chapter, such as *Commit and Toss, Four Corners, Sticky Bars,* and *Human Scatterplots,* to determine the range of ideas held in a class. An example of a *Friendly Talk Probe* is shown in Figure 4.16.

General Implementation Attributes

Ease of Use: High   Time Demand: Low
Cognitive Demand: Medium/High

Modifications

To help auditory learners, select students to act out the probe by representing the characters and reading their viewpoints. For visual learners,

Figure 4.16   *Friendly Talk Probe*

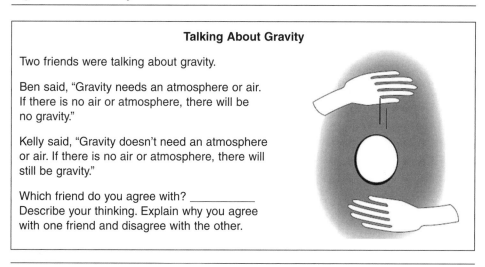

Talking About Gravity

Two friends were talking about gravity.

Ben said, "Gravity needs an atmosphere or air. If there is no air or atmosphere, there will be no gravity."

Kelly said, "Gravity doesn't need an atmosphere or air. If there is no air or atmosphere, there will still be gravity."

Which friend do you agree with? _____
Describe your thinking. Explain why you agree with one friend and disagree with the other.

SOURCE: Keeley, Eberle, and Farrin (2005). Reprinted by permission.

these probes can be readily turned into *Concept Cartoons* by giving the text to students who demonstrate a talent for drawing or cartooning.

Caveats

Sometimes students will not agree with anyone because they feel there is not enough information or they have an idea that is very different from the characters in the probe. Acknowledge this if it occurs and provide an option for these students to add their own statement.

Use With Other Disciplines

This FACT can also be used in mathematics, social studies, and health.

My Notes

_____

_____

_____

#22: GIVE ME FIVE

Description

Give Me Five is a technique used to promote and publicly share personal reflections that collectively provide feedback from the group. Students are given a prompt and take a minute or two for a "quiet think." Five students then volunteer to publicly share their reflection.

How This FACT Promotes Student Learning

Give Me Five provides students with an opportunity to individually and publicly reflect on their learning during or after a lesson. This FACT encourages students to be thoughtful reflectors and demonstrates teachers' respect and value for students sharing personal insights into their learning.

How This FACT Informs Instruction

Selecting five students to publicly share their reflection provides a sample collage for the teacher to gain feedback on how students perceived the impact of a lesson on their learning. *Give Me Five* is a simple, quick technique for inviting and valuing public reflection and welcoming feedback from students that will be used to design responsive instruction.

Design and Administration

Provide a reflection prompt that is inviting and open to a variety of responses by all students. Be sure to give time for individuals to quietly reflect, perhaps through a quick write, before asking for five volunteers to share their reflection. Practice the use of wait time if, at first, students are hesitant to share their thoughts publicly. This FACT can be used at any critical juncture in a lesson or at the end of a lesson or class period as closure. Hold up your fist, showing a finger each time a student shares a reflection until you have completed five fingers. Some examples of reflection prompts are as follows:

- What was the most significant learning you had during today's lesson?
- How "in the zone" do you feel right now as far as understanding the cell as a system is concerned?
- How did today's lesson help you better understand the rock cycle?
- What was the high point of this week's activities on chemical change?
- How well do you think today's science discussion worked in improving our understanding of balanced and unbalanced forces?

General Implementation Attributes

Ease of Use: High   Time Demand: Medium
Cognitive Demand: Medium

Modifications

Five is an arbitrary number. Depending on time and number of students, you might consider additional reflections, such as a *Give Me Five Plus Three* (hold up one hand and three fingers). You can also ask for a show of hands for how many students had a similar reflective thought each time a student shares his or her thoughts.

Caveats

Don't overuse this technique or it may become a trivial exercise, particularly if the same reflective prompts are used. Be sure to vary the prompts. Make sure the same students are not the ones whose reflections are most frequently selected to be shared.

Use With Other Disciplines

This FACT can be used in mathematics, social studies, health, language arts, foreign languages, and performing arts.

My Notes

_____

_____

_____

#23: GUIDED RECIPROCAL PEER QUESTIONING

Description

Guided Reciprocal Peer Questioning is a FACT in which students question each other about the content they are learning using higher-order, open-ended question stems. The questions are used to promote thinking and generate focused discussions in small groups.

How This FACT Promotes Student Learning

When students ask questions of each other, they activate their own thinking, elicit ideas from others, and promote shared learning within their group. Asking higher-order questions in a mutually supportive peer environment allows students to articulate their thoughts and exchange ideas in ways that differ from their interactions with the teacher. The scaffolded approach to asking questions that they are interested in seeking answers to help them become better questioners. *Guided Reciprocal Peer Questioning* supports metacognition as students must think about what they already know or need to know in order to frame their questions.

How This FACT Informs Instruction

Questioning is an essential strategy for monitoring student understanding. Typically, questions are asked by the teacher, and responses are used to inform instruction. In this FACT, the students ask the questions, which provide an additional layer of formative assessment information by allowing the teacher to circulate among groups and note the kinds of questions students ask each other and how they respond. Raising a question is an indication of a student's need to understand a concept better. Teachers can carefully listen to the questions asked to identify areas to target in their instruction as well as glean information on students' understanding by listening to their responses to the questions. As teachers circulate among the groups, they can provide feedback on students' responses, probe further, or redirect to focus on a particular insight, particularly when students in a group are having difficulty with a response or the potential for a misconception arises.

Design and Administration

This FACT is typically used after students have had an opportunity to learn about the concepts in question, drawing on their conceptual understanding developed through instruction. The teacher provides students with a prompt directly related to the lessons or sequence of lessons the questions will target and gives them a few minutes to formulate questions using a list of question stems such as the one shown in Figure 4.17. For example, the teacher might say,

> *For the past few days we have been learning about rocks and the different processes that formed them. Think about what you have learned. Write down two or three questions you would like to ask your classmates that will help you improve your understanding of rocks and rock formation. Use the question stems on the list to make up your questions.*

Students then form small groups of three to four and take turns asking their questions and discussing their answers. Each small group notes any questions they have difficulty with. The teacher can choose to help individual groups work through the questions they are having difficulty with, note them for discussion with the whole class, or use them to select additional learning opportunities to solidify students' understanding.

General Implementation Attributes

Ease of Use: Medium   Time Demand: Medium
Cognitive Demand: Medium/High

Modifications

This FACT can also be used after an inquiry-based investigation or homework assignment. Consider having students use *Traffic Light Dots* to mark how well they feel the group was able to answer the questions. Have students turn in their *Traffic Light Dotted* questions as an indication to the teacher of questions that students felt they could answer, partially answer, or could not answer to inform further support for learning. Questions can also be used later for summative assessment.

Caveats

The task of developing good questions is a complex process for teachers, let alone students. When students are first introduced to this FACT, it is important to give them feedback on the questions they develop to ensure they can be answered by students based on the learning experiences provided in class.

Figure 4.17   Question Stems for *Guided Reciprocal Peer Questioning*

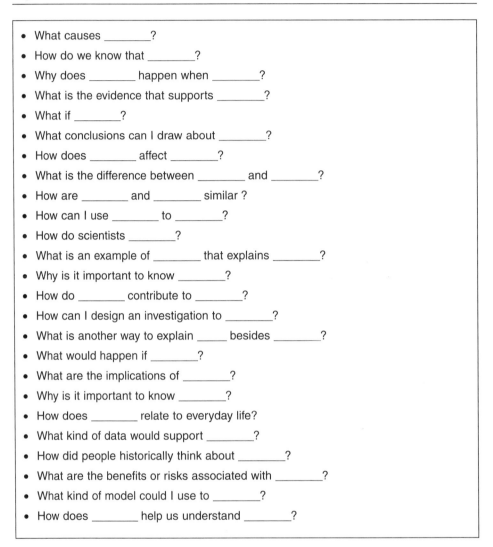

- What causes _____?
- How do we know that _____?
- Why does _____ happen when _____?
- What is the evidence that supports _____?
- What if _____?
- What conclusions can I draw about _____?
- How does _____ affect _____?
- What is the difference between _____ and _____?
- How are _____ and _____ similar ?
- How can I use _____ to _____?
- How do scientists _____?
- What is an example of _____ that explains _____?
- Why is it important to know _____?
- How do _____ contribute to _____?
- How can I design an investigation to _____?
- What is another way to explain _____ besides _____?
- What would happen if _____?
- What are the implications of _____?
- Why is it important to know _____?
- How does _____ relate to everyday life?
- What kind of data would support _____?
- How did people historically think about _____?
- What are the benefits or risks associated with _____?
- What kind of model could I use to _____?
- How does _____ help us understand _____?

Use With Other Disciplines

This FACT can also be used in mathematics, social studies, language arts, health, foreign languages, and performing arts.

My Notes

_____

_____

_____

#24: HUMAN SCATTERPLOTS

Description

The *Human Scatterplot* is a quick, visual way for teachers and students to get an immediate classroom snapshot of students' thinking and the level of confidence students have in their ideas. The technique gets the class up and moving as students position themselves on a "floor graph." As students position themselves around the room according to their response to the question and their confidence level, it creates a visual scatterplot of class results.

How This FACT Promotes Student Learning

This FACT can be used to engage students in examining their own ideas as well as ideas from the whole class. Seeing that students in the class vary in their answers and confidence levels can be both a surprise and a relief to students who learn that they are not alone in their thinking or in how much confidence they have in their ideas. It sends a message that the class must work together to develop their understanding so that everyone can eventually come to an agreement on the answer to the question and raise their confidence in their own ideas.

How This FACT Informs Instruction

This FACT can be used at the beginning of a lesson or sequence of instruction to elicit students' initial ideas and motivate them to want to further explore and discover scientific ideas. It can be used during the exploration and discovery stage of instruction to determine how well students are making sense of different phenomena. Looking about the room to see where clusters of students and individuals place themselves gives immediate feedback to the teacher on the different ideas students have and their levels of confidence. *Human Scatterplots* can be used to initiate scientific argument among students who hold different ideas, by pairing them up with students standing in different areas of the scatterplot. Students who are low on the confidence scale can be asked what it would take to raise the level of confidence in their thinking, sparking discussion and/or providing opportunities to test ideas. They can also be matched with students who have a similar idea and higher level of confidence to draw out ideas that may increase their confidence level.

Design and Administration

Choose selected response questions with at least three and no more than four choices for this FACT. Label the wall (*Y*-axis) on one side of the room with the choices (e.g., A, B, C). Label the adjacent wall (*X*-axis) with a range of low confidence to high confidence. Have students position themselves according to where they feel they fall on "the graph." Figure 4.18 shows an example of a prompt and the distribution of students positioned on the scatterplot.

Figure 4.18   *Human Scatterplot* for the Mirror Problem

Emma is standing 3 meters away from a regular mirror placed flat on the wall. She can see her body from the waist up in the mirror. She steps forward so she is 1 meter away from the mirror. How will this affect how much of her body she can see in the mirror?

A. She will see less of her body.

B. She will see more of her body.

C. She will see the same amount.

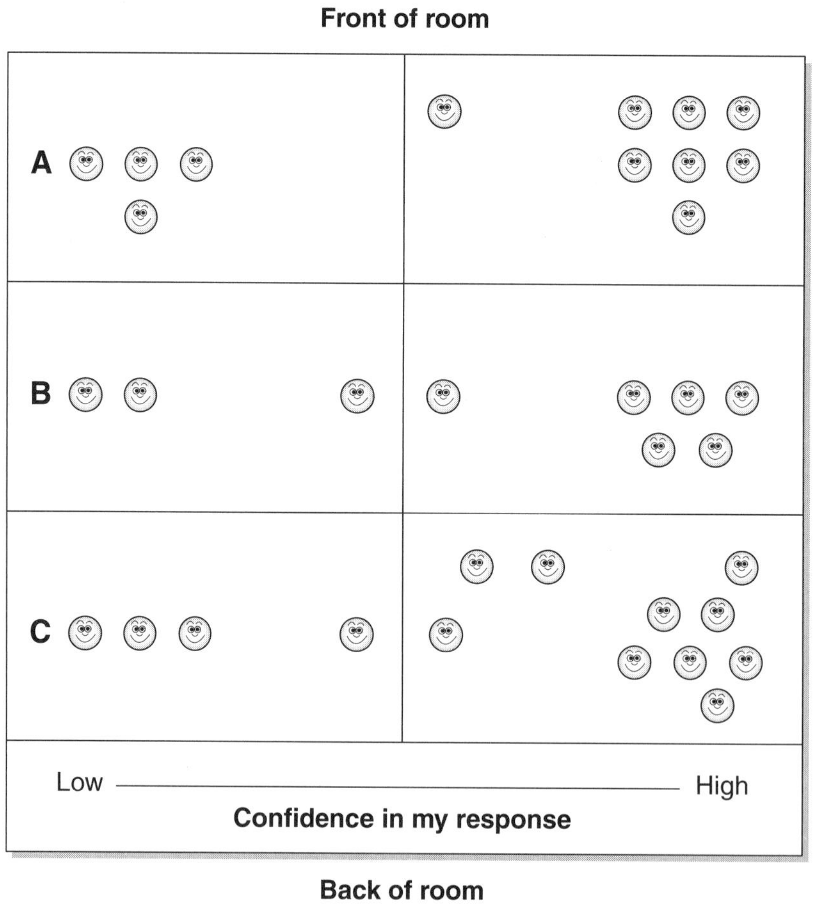

Front of room

Low ————————————————————— High
Confidence in my response

Back of room

General Implementation Attributes

Ease of Use: Medium   Time Demand: Low
Cognitive Demand: Medium

Modifications

A paper version can be used instead of a human graph. Pass the graph, with axis labeled, around the class and have students put their initials on it according to where their answer falls and their level of confidence. With this method, teachers also have a written record. The scatterplot can then be passed back later after students have had an opportunity to explore the question. Students then reinitial their position, drawing a line to connect their initial and later position, showing the extent to which their confidence level changed or if they changed their response to the question.

Caveats

Students who have difficulty with spatial thinking may need help positioning themselves on the floor graph.

Use With Other Disciplines

This FACT can also be used in mathematics, social studies, language arts, health, foreign languages, and performing arts.

My Notes

_____

_____

_____

#25: INFORMAL STUDENT INTERVIEWS

Description

The *Informal Student Interview* is a variation of the formal, structured student interview. This FACT involves conversational interviews with students in informal settings, such as lunch, recess, hallway talks, bus duty, riding on the bus to a field trip, and other contexts where students are not in a formal classroom setting. The *Informal Student Interview* uses a series of probing questions to sample a set of representative students for their ideas about concepts in science.

How This FACT Promotes Learning

Informal Student Interviews provide an engaging way for students to share their thinking. Because they happen outside of a formal classroom setting, students who may be reluctant to speak out in the "judgmental" environment of a classroom may be more apt to freely share their thinking. The interviews promote metacognition by making students more aware of their own ideas and the reasons for their thinking.

How This FACT Informs Instruction

Informal interviews with a handful of carefully selected students with a range of ability, diversity, and experiences enable the teacher to understand the different ideas the class is likely to have and how student ideas may have developed prior to instruction. The information helps the teacher determine an effective starting point for instruction by indicating how well students understand a concept as well as identify misconceptions, areas of confusion or difficulty, and gaps in understanding that may be common among students. The data are useful in understanding the different types of ideas students are likely to bring to a planned instructional unit, modifications that should be considered, and the types of prior experiences or reasoning that informed their preconceptions.

Design and Administration

Select a topic that is going to be taught in a future unit of instruction. Interview questions, even when used informally, should be thought about and planned in advance. Since informal interviews do not involve the structured setting of a formal student interview, open the door to spontaneous conversation with a group of students by starting off with an inviting, opening statement such as the following:

I was wondering if you could help me think through some ideas about science. I have been talking with several people who seem to have different ideas, and I'm curious as to what you think.

Pose questions so that they are clear and open-ended, and do not cue students as to the answer they think you are looking for. For example, a question might be the following:

Have you ever watched the liquid go up or down in a thermometer? I'm trying to figure out what would happen if I held a thermometer upside down while I put something hot on the bulb. What do you think would happen to the liquid inside the thermometer when I hold it upside down and put something hot on it?

Allow students to share their different ideas but also probe for their explanations. For example, Sam says, "Well, I think the red stuff won't go anywhere because it's used to going up when it gets bigger." Jenna says, "It will go down in the same place it would go if it were held the right way." Other students jump in and share their ideas.

At this point you might say,

I'm hearing several different ideas—some of you are saying the liquid in the thermometer won't go up or down; it will stay the same. Some of you think it will be pushed downward. And some of you think it will only move a tiny bit. Can you tell me more about why you think that?

This provides the entry point for students to further explain their thinking. Other questions asked might include "Have you ever tried anything like this? How do you think a thermometer works?" Continue asking questions that will help you understand how students think about the concept or phenomenon. Make sure you do not interject any bias or leading statements into the questions. When you are finished, thank the students for sharing with you. After the conversation, make notes describing the important things you heard. Figure 4.19 lists examples of interview stems you can use.

General Implementation Attributes

Ease of Use: High   Time Demand: Medium
Cognitive Demand: Medium/High

Modifications

This strategy can be modified as a formal, structured interview, focusing on one student at a time. See the Appendix for video examples of student interviews. The scope and type of questions should match the developmental levels of the students.

Caveats

Keep in mind that interviews elicit the most useful information when the students have a good rapport with the teacher. It is essential to help the students feel relaxed. They should consider the verbal exchange as a fun

Figure 4.19   Example Stems for Informal Interview Prompts

- What can you tell me about . . . ?
- Have you ever tried to . . . ? What happened?
- Have you ever seen a . . . ? What can you tell me about it?
- What does it take to . . . ?
- What does it mean when someone says . . . ?
- The other day I saw . . . . What could that be?
- What do you think causes . . . ?
- How can I explain this to my friend?
- Is there some way you can demonstrate this?
- Can you tell me more about that?
- Can you help me understand . . . ?
- Some people think. . . . What are your ideas about this?
- What do you think would happen if . . . ?
- Did you learn this in school? If not, where did your ideas come from?
- What do you think is different about . . . ?
- What do you think is the same about . . . ?
- How could you convince others about . . . ?
- Why do you think there are so many different ideas about this?

chance to talk with the teacher outside of a formal classroom learning experience. Remember this should be a friendly conversation about science—not an interrogation! Do not correct, revise, or provide instruction when the students are sharing their ideas with you. This is not intended to be a teachable moment but rather an opportunity for students to openly share their thinking with you in a nonjudgmental way. Resist the temptation to pass judgment on their ideas with statements such as "Oh, that's a great idea," "Well, that's not quite what I am looking for," or "Are you sure about that?"

Use With Other Disciplines

This FACT can also be used in mathematics, social studies, and health.

My Notes

_____

_____

_____

#26: INTEREST SCALE

Description

The *Interest Scale* is a way to gauge student interest in the topic being taught. The technique uses a chart with a marked scale in which students place Post-it notes on a scale of low to high to indicate their level of interest in the topic being studied.

How This FACT Promotes Learning

Student interest is a strong, contributing factor to student learning. Providing an opportunity to express their interest level shows students that you value knowing their level of engagement in the learning process.

How This Fact Informs Instruction

This simple strategy can be used to identify the level of interest before instruction, or during certain points in a unit when student interest in a topic may be waning. The teacher uses the feedback to modify lessons as appropriate in order to make the content more relevant and engaging to students. The strategy helps spot particular students or groups of students who may be disengaged and need differentiated strategies for motivating and interesting them in learning about the topic.

Design and Administration

Start with having students identify their interest level before you begin instruction in the topic. Give them a few minutes to discuss what they think the topic is about. Make a chart with a range from high (10) to low (1) or a scale of your choosing, such as the thermometer chart in Figure 4.20. Give students Post-it notes and ask them to place them by the range value that matches their current level of interest. Encourage students to be thoughtful and honest. Encourage students to think about why the topic interests or does not interest them. Revisit during different points in the instructional sequence to allow students to reposition their Post-it notes according to whether their interest level has changed. If the level of interest in the class significantly drops, engage students in a discussion to find out why. Conversely, it is also helpful to have a discussion if the interest level rises to find out what led to increased interest.

General Implementation Attributes

Ease of Use: High   Time Demand: Low
Cognitive Demand: Low

Figure 4.20   *Interest Scale*

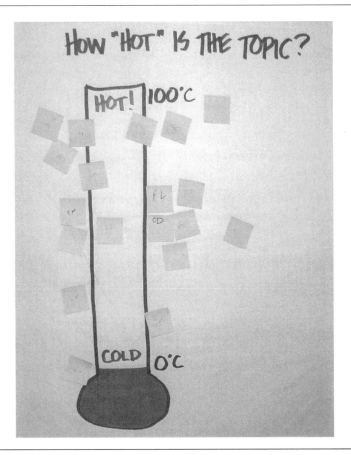

Modifications

Students can be given the option of anonymously sharing their interest level. Have students write the number that expresses their level of interest on a slip of paper that is dropped in a box. These slips of paper are later analyzed by the teacher.

Caveats

Students need to understand that expressing a lack of interest does not mean that the content of instruction will be changed. This FACT is intended to provide feedback to the teacher to help make the topic more interesting and relevant to students. Teachers should not take results personally, particularly since different topics have different levels of appeal to students' interest. That does not make them any less important than topics that are very engaging. It is important to establish an environment of trust and respect in order to use this strategy effectively.

Use With Other Disciplines

This FACT can also be used in mathematics, social studies, language arts, health, foreign languages, and performing arts.

My Notes

_____

_____

_____

#27: I THINK–WE THINK

Description

In *I Think–We Think*, students use a two-column sheet of paper to record their own individual ideas (*I Think*), prior to group discussion, and ideas their group or class has that surface through group discussion (*We Think*) (Goldberg, Bendall, Heller, & Poel, 2006).

How This FACT Promotes Student Learning

The *I Think–We Think* strategy provides an opportunity for students to think about and record their own ideas prior to engaging in small- or large-group discussions. First, students must explicitly formulate and record their own ideas. When students compare their own ideas (*I Think*) to the group's ideas (*We Think*), they clarify their initial thinking, may modify their own thinking to accommodate new ideas offered through group interaction or recognize how their ideas informed the group's thinking. In the concept-development stage of instruction, students can self-assess how closely their individual and group ideas match the scientific ones developed through sense-making discussions and formal concept development. *I Think–We Think* can also be used as an individual or whole-class reflection on how students' ideas have changed, contributed to, or been modified throughout the course of instruction.

How This FACT Informs Instruction

This FACT provides teachers with an opportunity to become aware of students' initial ideas and monitor how they contribute to the group's learning or change as they interact with other students during activities and small group and class discussions. The information is used to guide students toward development of conceptual understanding of the ideas targeted in the lesson or sequence of lessons.

Design and Administration

Provide students with a two-column sheet to record their ideas. Begin by having students record their initial, individual ideas. You may choose to collect responses and analyze them to inform instructional decisions as well as determine groupings for small group work. After students have described their own thinking, provide an opportunity for small groups to engage in discussion and argumentation, recording the ideas that emerge from the group discussion, both consensus ideas and ideas that differ among group members. Listen nonjudgmentally as students discuss their ideas and encourage as many ideas as possible. In the whole-class discussion, point out the similarities and differences in student thinking and keep a record of ideas to refer to throughout instruction, particularly as they change or are modified.

General Implementation Attributes

Ease of Use: Medium   Time Demand: Medium
Cognitive Demand: Medium

Modifications

This FACT can be modified as a preassessment of individual and group ideas prior to engaging in instructional activities. It can be reassigned during the concept development stage to examine whether students have changed their ideas as they worked through exploratory activities. *I Think–We Think* can be used with small group discussions. For whole-class discussion, make a *The Class Thinks* chart that is a compilation of the small group ideas. Figure 4.21 is an example of a *The Class Thinks* wall chart in which the teacher listed the consensus ideas from small groups about melting and how to distinguish it from other processes such as dissolving. The ideas on this chart are used in whole-group discussion to come to a class consensus about distinguishing the process of melting from other processes.

Caveats

I Think–We Think is a record of an individual's and group's original thinking. Make sure students do not change their original record over the course of discussion.

Use With Other Disciplines

This FACT can also be used in mathematics, social studies, and health.

Figure 4.21   Class Ideas From *I Think–We Think*

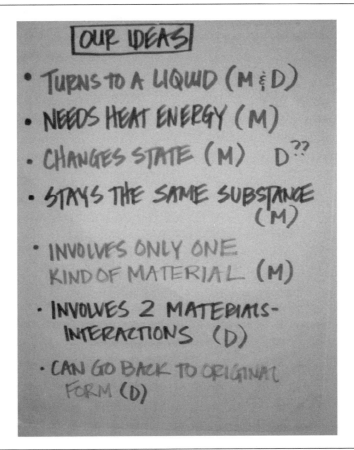

My Notes

_____

_____

_____

#28: I USED TO THINK . . . BUT NOW I KNOW

Description

I Used to Think . . . But Now I Know asks students to compare verbally or in writing their ideas at the beginning of a lesson or instructional sequence to the ideas they have after completing the lesson(s). It differs from *K-W-L Variations* because both parts of the reflection occur after instruction.

How This FACT Promotes Learning

This FACT is a self-assessment and reflection exercise that helps students recognize if and how their thinking has changed at the end of a sequence of instruction. It prompts students to recall their ideas at the beginning of the instructional sequence and consider how they changed. Metacognition involves not just the ability to self-regulate learning, recognize the demands of a learning task, and know of one's own learning strengths and weaknesses (Bransford et al., 1999). It also involves knowledge about what one has learned. *I Used to Think . . . But Now I Know* provides an opportunity for students to self-assess and reflect on their current knowledge and how it may have changed or evolved from their previously held ideas.

How This FACT Informs Instruction

A comparison of students' before-and-after thinking can be used to examine the extent to which a sequence of instruction was effective in bridging where students' ideas were at the beginning of instruction to how close they come to the scientific idea. If a significant number of students have not traversed the bridge between their initial conceptions and the scientific idea, the teacher may use the information to design additional lessons that target students' difficulties or modify activities.

Design and Administration

Provide students with a copy of a recording sheet, or have them make one similar to the one shown in Figure 4.22. Provide time for a quiet write. Explain to students that they should describe how their ideas changed or how they became more detailed compared to what they knew at the beginning of instruction. Use *Think-Pair-Share, Partner Speaks,* or other pair strategies to have students share reflections with a partner.

Figure 4.22   Example Recording Sheet

I USED TO THINK . . .	BUT NOW I KNOW . . .

General Implementation Attributes

Ease of Use: High   Time Demand: Medium
Cognitive Demand: Medium/High

Modifications

An additional column can be added to include . . . *And This Is How I Learned It* to help students reflect on what part of their learning experiences helped them change or further develop their ideas. This addition provides additional feedback to the teacher on what was effective for learning from the students' viewpoint. The FACT can also be used as a whole-class shared reflection after a lesson or a series of lessons by going around the class and having each student orally share one thing to fill in the blanks: I used to think___, but now I know___.

Caveats

Some students may have difficulty recalling their initial ideas. If a class record exists from other FACTs, it may be helpful to share with the class some of the earlier ideas that were noted.

Use With Other Disciplines

This FACT can also be used in mathematics, social studies, language arts, health, foreign languages, and performing arts.

My Notes

_____

_____

_____

#29: JUICY QUESTIONS

Description

Like squeezing an orange to get the juice out, *Juicy Questions* require students to think deeply and extract knowledge that will help them answer a rich, novel question. A *Juicy Question* often requires students to work on a series of smaller questions and ideas before they take a stab at answering it. For example, a *Juicy Question* for a high school chemistry class might be the following: *What could happen if someone developed and accidentally released a substance into the Great Lakes that behaved like a catalyst?*

What would the implications be if this catalyst-like substance changed the density of ice so that it was greater than water? The question requires students to think about a series of smaller questions, such as the following: What are the characteristics of a catalyst? How would ice behave if it were denser than water? What are the environmental implications of ice sinking rather than floating? The question leads to all sorts of interesting and intriguing cause-effect ideas.

How This FACT Promotes Learning

This FACT requires students to activate their knowledge and "squeeze out" a variety of ideas that come from the *Juicy Question*. Students must think deeply to come up with smaller questions and ideas that will help them answer the bigger question.

How This FACT Informs Instruction

By providing a robust, engaging question to bring students' prior and existing knowledge to the fore in discussing the novel situation posed by the question, the teacher can gauge what students know, partially know, and do not know related to the concepts targeted by the *Juicy Question*. The teacher is able to listen carefully and guide students in upgrading and moving their complete or partial knowledge forward toward a fuller understanding and application of the concepts involved.

Design and Administration

A *Juicy Question* is one that cannot be answered immediately and requires several smaller questions and ideas in order to answer it. *Juicy Questions* often involve integrating ideas from topics taught in separate units. For example, in the ice and catalyst example, students must integrate ideas about density, properties of ice, catalysts, water in the earth system, and public water supplies. Begin by having students identify the knowledge they need to answer the question. Identify in advance what the smaller questions might be that will help students respond to the *Juicy Question*. Use these smaller questions to guide the class discussion, taking note of where students may be having difficulty with some concepts.

General Implementation Attributes

Ease of Use: Medium   Time Demand: Medium
Cognitive Demand: High

Modifications

Consider asking students to write a story or essay in response to the *Juicy Question* after they have had an opportunity to share the knowledge they need to respond to the question.

Caveats

Avoid developing questions that use little-known facts or knowledge students have not had instructional opportunities to develop.

Use With Other Disciplines

This FACT can also be used in language arts, social studies, and health.

My Notes

_____

_____

_____

#30: JUSTIFIED LIST

Description

A *Justified List* begins with a statement about an object, process, or concept. Examples that fit or do not fit the statement are listed. Students check off the items on the list that fit the statement and provide a justification explaining their rule or reasons for their selections.

How This FACT Promotes Student Learning

Justified Lists activate students' thinking about a concept. They require students to think beyond the context in which they may have learned about the concept. For example, prior activities, such as building and observing vibrations from musical instruments, may have helped students learn that sound is made when an object vibrates. A *Justified List* probe, such as the one shown in Figure 4.23, prompts them to think how this idea may apply to other objects that differ from musical instruments. The FACT also leads into an opportunity for students to investigate the items on the list and modify their ideas based on new evidence. *Justified Lists* can be used to solidify ideas during formal concept development. The items on the list can be used to encourage argumentation during small-group discussion or class discourse, further promoting student thinking and resolving discrepancies between students' own ideas and those of their peers. *Justified Lists* can also be used again for reflection at the end of a unit of instruction. Students examine their original list, reflecting on how they might respond differently based on new knowledge they have.

How This FACT Informs Instruction

Justified Lists can be used to elicit students' prior ideas, particularly about a topic in which students may have become context bound in their learning. This FACT helps determine whether students have developed a narrow or overgeneralized idea of a particular concept in science. If results show students have a narrow view of the concept, it indicates to the teacher that instruction needs to explicitly address the big ideas and generalizations, in addition to the examples used in the students' instructional materials. The items on the list can springboard into opportunities to

Figure 4.23   *Justified List* Probe

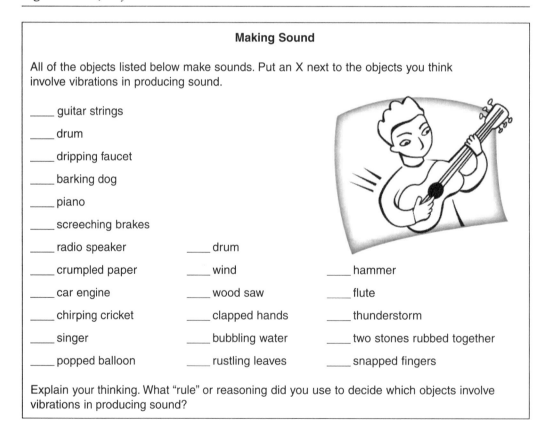

Making Sound

All of the objects listed below make sounds. Put an X next to the objects you think involve vibrations in producing sound.

_____ guitar strings

_____ drum

_____ dripping faucet

_____ barking dog

_____ piano

_____ screeching brakes

_____ radio speaker   _____ drum

_____ crumpled paper   _____ wind   _____ hammer

_____ car engine   _____ wood saw   _____ flute

_____ chirping cricket   _____ clapped hands   _____ thunderstorm

_____ singer   _____ bubbling water   _____ two stones rubbed together

_____ popped balloon   _____ rustling leaves   _____ snapped fingers

Explain your thinking. What "rule" or reasoning did you use to decide which objects involve vibrations in producing sound?

SOURCE: Keeley, Eberle, and Farrin. (2005). Reprinted by permission.

develop inquiry-based investigations or engage students in small-group or whole-class discourse, orchestrating argumentation supporting why or why not particular items belong on the list.

Listen carefully to the justification students use, as it may point out the need for targeted instructional interventions that will confront students with their existing ideas about the relationship between the items on the list and the targeted concept. This FACT can also be used as an application to determine the extent to which students are able to transfer the ideas they developed during the formal concept development stage to new contexts or examples. It may indicate the need to revise or include additional activities to support transfer of learning to new situations.

Design and Administration

Design *Justified Lists* that probe a "big idea" in science and preferably have a body of cognitive research behind them that informs the selection of distracters to put in the list. Science curriculum topic study (see the Appendix) includes a process for developing these types of probes. You can use ready-made *Justified List* probes in the *Uncovering Student Ideas* series. This FACT can be given individually as a written assessment, or it can be given to pairs or small groups to discuss their ideas and come to an agreement as to what should be checked off on the list. Encourage students to check off the examples that fit the statement according to ideas they have, not what they think the answer is that the teacher is looking for. Encourage them to provide a detailed explanation that supports the reasoning they used to decide if an item on the list fits the statement. Small groups can share their lists with the whole class for discussion and feedback. If used as an individual written task, consider collecting the task, analyzing the data to inform the instructional opportunities you will need to design, and passing it back at the end of a unit for student reflection. The lists can also be tallied and posted as a class chart for students to examine the range of ideas held by the class, signifying the need to develop a class consensus.

General Implementation Attributes

Ease of Use: High   Time Demand: Medium
Cognitive Demand: Medium/High

Modifications

Some students may not recognize a word on the list or may be unfamiliar with an object. Have students cross off any examples on the list they do not recognize, including unfamiliar words, and focus only on the familiar items. It may be helpful to provide picture icons for younger students or students who are English-language learners. The items on the list can also be put on cards and used as a *Card Sort* FACT.

Caveats

Make sure students are familiar with the words and items on the list. Otherwise, this FACT may end up being a vocabulary exercise or run the risk of being developmentally or contextually inappropriate.

Use With Other Disciplines

This FACT can also be used in mathematics, social studies, language arts, health, foreign languages, and performing arts.

My Notes

_____

_____

_____

#31: JUSTIFIED TRUE OR FALSE STATEMENTS

Description

Justified True or False Statements provide a set of claims or statements that are examined by students. The students draw upon evidence from data, prior knowledge, or other sources to analyze their validity. Students describe the reasoning they used to decide whether each claim or statement is true or false.

How This FACT Promotes Student Learning

Justified True or False Statements provide individuals or small groups of students an opportunity to activate their thinking about a particular science topic. Furthermore, this FACT supports one of the hallmarks of inquiry-based science instruction: "How do we know what we know?" Students need to consider the evidence that supports their ideas about a claim or statement in science and use critical reasoning skills to make a case for or against its validity.

How This FACT Informs Instruction

This FACT is used to examine students' existing ideas, including what they consider as information or evidence that supports their ideas. It can be used individually or in pairs, small groups, and whole-class discussions at the beginning of a lesson, at different points during a sequence of lessons, or at the end of an instructional unit as a reflection activity. Listen carefully as students discuss their own ideas and argue with the views of their classmates. Note strengths or weaknesses in their use of critical reasoning skills that may need to be further strengthened through targeted instruction. Identify areas of agreement or disagreement that could be addressed in subsequent lessons and discussions. Careful listening may also reveal areas of uncertainty that indicate the need to ensure adequate time for additional activities and sense making.

Design and Administration

Use no more than three statements for younger children. Up to six statements work well for older students. Provide individuals or each group of students with a handout of the set of statements, such as the example shown in Figure 4.24. This FACT can also be administered orally, posting the list of statements on a chart or overhead for students to see and discuss with their small group or whole class. Students discuss and justify each statement, one at a time, trying to come to an agreement on whether it is true or false, noting any areas on which they cannot reach consensus.

General Implementation Attributes

Ease of Use: Medium   Time Demand: Medium
Cognitive Demand: Medium/High

Modifications

For struggling readers, post the statements on a chart and read them aloud with the class.

Caveats

Avoid simple recall statements of factual information. Statements should provoke student thinking, drawing out commonly held ideas that students might have that are related to the topic.

Use With Other Disciplines

This FACT can also be used in mathematics, social studies, language arts, health, foreign languages, and performing arts.

Figure 4.24   Justified T/F for a Sixth-Grade Landforms Unit

Statement	T	F	Why I (We) Think So
1. Mountains are made mostly of rock.			
2. As mountains get older, they keep growing taller.			
3. Volcanoes are found only in areas of the world with warm climates.			
4. Beach sand comes from rocks under the ocean.			
5. Some mountains were once volcanoes.			

My Notes

_____

_____

_____

#32: K-W-L VARIATIONS

Description

K-W-L is a general elicitation technique in which students describe what they **K**now about a topic, **W**ant to know about a topic, and **L**earned about the topic. There are different variations of K-W-L, depending on the students' age and the teacher's purpose.

How This FACT Promotes Student Learning

K-W-L provides an opportunity for students to become engaged with a topic, particularly when asked what they would like to learn. It is a metacognitive exercise that requires students to think about what they already know. K-W-L provides a mechanism for self-assessment and reflection at the end, when students are asked to think about what they learned. The three phases of the K-W-L help students see the connections between what they already know, what they would like to find out, and what they learned as a result.

How This FACT Informs Instruction

K-W-Ls provide information to the teacher about students' prior knowledge at the beginning of a unit of instruction as well as at the end. Teachers can use the "what I know" information to determine readiness to learn, examine students' familiarity with the topic, and identify preconceptions so that instruction can focus on building new knowledge and experiences from students' starting points. Students' ideas can be used by the teacher for discussion starters. The "what I want to know" provides an opportunity to design instructional experiences that include students' own ideas about what they would like to learn during the unit of instruction. Finally, the "what I learned" column provides an opportunity to examine the scope and depth of student learning and make adjustments as needed to improve instructional activities and further develop student understanding.

Design and Administration

Provide students with a K-W-L handout, such as the template in Figure 4.25. Remind students to fill in only the first two columns. Collect and save their K-Ws and return the student papers at the end of the unit when they are ready to revisit their initial ideas and reflect on the "L." Students' K-Ws can be collected, synthesized, and posted as a class chart to refer to throughout the instructional unit.

General Implementation Attributes

Ease of Use: High   Time Demand: Medium
Cognitive Demand: Medium

Modifications

Other versions include **K-W-F:** This is what I **K**now, This is what I **W**onder about, This is how I will **F**ind out; **K-T-F:** This is what I **K**now for sure, This is what I **T**hink I know, This is how I **F**ound out; **O-W-L:** This is what I **O**bserved, This is what I **W**onder about, This is what I **L**earned; and **P-O-E:** This is what I **P**redict, This is what I **O**bserved, This is how I can **E**xplain it. A fourth column can be added to the standard K-W-L, making it a K-W-L-H. The **H** stands for This is **H**ow I learned it.

Figure 4.25 K-W-L

K- This is what I already KNOW	W- This is what I WANT to find out	L- This is what I LEARNED

Caveats

Be careful not to overuse this strategy as students quickly tire of it if it is used in the same way with every instructional unit. Be aware that the open-ended nature of this FACT is not as effective in pinpointing specific misconceptions, learning gaps, or conceptual difficulties as some of the other specific probing techniques.

Use With Other Disciplines

This FACT can also be used in mathematics, social studies, language arts, health, foreign languages, and performing arts.

My Notes

_____

_____

_____

#33: LEARNING GOALS INVENTORY (LGI)

Description

An *LGI* is a set of questions that relate to an identified learning goal in a unit of instruction. Students are asked to "inventory" the extent to which they feel they have prior knowledge about the learning goal. They also describe the prior experiences they had to learn about it.

How This FACT Promotes Student Learning

The *LGI* activates student thinking about a topic of instruction that targets explicitly identified learning goals. It requires them to think about what they already know in relation to the learning goal statement as well as when and how they may have learned about it. It also helps make the target learning goals explicit to students. A key principle of learning is that students must know what the learning target is. Explicitly sharing learning goals with students raises their awareness of what their learning will be focused on.

How This FACT Informs Instruction

The *LGI* provides information to teachers on students' perceptions of their existing knowledge in relation to identified learning goals, including state or national standards. It also provides information on when and how students may have had opportunities to learn the ideas related to the goal. This information is particularly helpful when students are coming from other schools or classes within a school where there is not a consistent curriculum. It provides an opportunity for teachers to see which goals may be "new" to students and which may provide an opportunity to revisit and build upon previous learning experiences.

Design and Administration

Identify the goals from the instructional unit and/or the state and/or national standards targeted in the unit of instruction. Create a question inventory on one goal such as the one shown in Figure 4.26 for a high school biology unit on cells that targets a learning goal from *Maine's Learning Results* (Maine Department of Education, 2007). Give time for students to fill it out. Post the goals on a chart throughout the instructional unit so students will know what the learning targets are. The *LGI* can be given back to students at the end of the instructional unit as a self-assessment and reflection on their learning, noting the difference between their ratings before and after the instructional unit.

Figure 4.26   *LGI* for a High School Biology Unit on Cells

Learning Goal: Describe structure and function of cells at the intracellular and molecular level including differentiation to form systems, interaction between cells and their environment, and the impact of cellular processes and changes on individuals (MLR 9-12/E3 Cells) (Maine Department of Education, 2007)

What do you think this learning goal is about?
List any facts, concepts, or ideas you are familiar with related to this learning goal:
List any terminology you know of that relates to this goal:
List any experiences you have had (in or outside of school) that may have helped you learn about the ideas in this learning goal:

General Implementation Attributes

Ease of Use: Medium   Time Demand: Medium
Cognitive Demand: Medium

Modifications

The *LGI* can be used in an oral discussion format with younger students or completed as a whole-class inventory.

Caveats

Learning goals that come from state and national standards are interpreted in a variety of ways by teachers. Consequently, expect the same variation in interpretation from students. How one student may interpret a learning goal may be very different from how another student interprets it.

Use With Other Disciplines

This FACT can also be used in mathematics, social studies, language arts, health, foreign languages, and performing arts.

My Notes

_____

_____

_____

#34: LOOK BACK

Description

A *Look Back* is a recount of what students learned over a given instructional period of time. Students recount specific examples of things they know now that they didn't know before and describe how they learned them (B. Chagrasulis, personal communication, 2005).

How This FACT Promotes Student Learning

This FACT provides students with an opportunity to look back on and summarize their learning. Asking students "how they learned it" helps them think about their own learning and the different ways, as learners, they are able to integrate new scientific information.

How This FACT Informs Instruction

Teachers can use the information from this FACT to examine aspects of an instructional sequence students seemed to get the most out of and why. The student feedback can be used to inform the use of various strategies that may work well in the existing unit as well as in other instructional units. *Look Back* also alerts teachers to strategies and activities that seem to be most effective for individual students. The information can be used to differentiate instruction for individual learners, based on their descriptions of what helped them learn.

Design and Administration

This FACT is best used no more than three weeks or midway into a sequence of instruction. It is important to model this FACT with students the first time you use it. Use a template such as the one shown in Figure 4.27. An example of a high school prompt used with this FACT is as follows:

For the last two weeks, we have been studying genetic traits and how they are passed onto offspring. Please take 15 minutes to make a list of all the things you learned in the last two weeks that you didn't know before or know as well when we started the unit. Next to each new learning you identified, please describe how you learned it and why that way of learning was effective for you. Your descriptions will be used by me to think about ways I can make your science learning more relevant and effective.

General Implementation Attributes

Ease of Use: Medium
Cognitive Demand: Medium

Time Demand: Medium

Figure 4.27   Template for *Look Back*

What I Learned	How I Learned It

Modifications

With younger students, use shorter amounts of time to look back. For example, use the end of the week for them to look back on the week's activities.

Caveats

Be aware that failure to mention some key ideas taught during the instructional period does not mean that students did not learn them. This FACT reveals what stood out most for students in their learning, not necessarily how much they learned. Some students may have a difficult time looking back more than a few days. Provide the daily syllabus, sections used in the curriculum materials, or outline of the unit to help them retrace the instructional sequence.

Use With Other Disciplines

This FACT can also be used in mathematics, social studies, language arts, health, foreign languages, and performing arts.

My Notes

_____

_____

_____

#35: MISSED CONCEPTION

Description

A *Missed Conception* is a statement about an object or phenomenon that is based on a commonly held idea noted in the research on students' ideas in science. Students are asked to analyze a statement, describe why some people may believe it is true, describe what one could do to help someone change his or her "missed conception" in favor of the scientific idea, and reflect on their own ideas in relation to the statement.

How This FACT Promotes Student Learning

Many commonly held ideas in science may interfere with students' learning. This FACT provides an opportunity to examine a commonly held idea associated with the curricular topic students have studied. Some students may have held a similar idea at the start of an instructional unit and, over the course of carefully sequenced instruction, revised their ideas and integrated the scientific view into their new framework. Working through the prompts that accompany the *Missed Conception* provides a self-assessment opportunity to examine whether one has a similar misconception that may still persist. Even with good instruction, some misconceptions are so tenacious that there may be some students who still hold on to their own private ideas even though they may give the "correct answers" on a summative assessment or during a class activity. This exercise provides a metacognitive opportunity for students to reexamine their ideas or beliefs and develop the intellectual empathy to understand why other students, as well as the general public, have different ideas about scientific topics. The interactive nature of this FACT may provide an additional opportunity for some students to be confronted with their own thinking, better understand why their own ideas may not fully match the scientific view, and work to resolve the discrepancy by understanding more about how others think and the evidence needed to help change their own strongly held belief.

How This FACT Informs Instruction

Missed Conception provides an opportunity for teachers to identify which students may need differentiated experiences to help them work toward resolving the discrepancy between their ideas and the scientific explanation that is presented during the formal concept development phase of instruction. Teachers use the information to learn more about how students think about their own thinking and gain feedback on how various instructional experiences helped students learn. On the other hand, this FACT can also point out gaps or ineffective lessons that may need to be improved in order to help students transition from a strongly held misconception to the scientifically accepted view of the concept.

Design and Administration

This FACT is best used after students have had opportunities to formally develop an understanding of the concept involved. Develop the *Missed Conception* statements from ideas you may have heard your own students express when using other FACTs. See the Appendix for a source of materials that can help you identify commonly held misconceptions. Explain the reason for using this FACT to your students. Have them work in small groups to discuss and respond to the statement and the prompts. Circulate and listen to the discussions, noting areas that may be conceptually challenging. Ask small groups to share their ideas during a whole-class debrief. The teacher may provide additional commentary as needed.

If some students still believe the *Missed Conception,* even after instruction, there are times when a teacher needs to make the decision to move forward. As hard as this may be to move forward when not all students have achieved the desired scientific understanding, some students may not be ready to change their ideas, regardless of how much additional instruction is provided. Thus, it may be best in some situations to revisit ideas later in a new context or different grade when some students may be more developmentally or cognitively ready to build new understanding. Figure 4.28 shows an example of using *Missed Conception* after students had an opportunity to formally develop a scientific understanding of what causes the seasons.

General Implementation Attributes

Ease of Use: Medium   Time Demand: Medium
Cognitive Demand: Medium

Modifications

For topics that have several commonly held ideas associated with them, develop a cluster of statements and assign one to each group to work on and report out for feedback from the whole class. Have students interview their parents, nonscience teachers, or other adults about the idea to help them see how strongly some ideas persist into adulthood.

Caveats

Do not give this FACT at the beginning of a unit. The commonly held idea in the statement surfaces as a preconception through the use of other

Figure 4.28   Example of a *Missed Conception* on the Seasons

Missed Conception: "The reason we have seasons is that, as the Earth revolves around the sun, it is closer to the sun in the summertime; therefore, it is warmer in summer and colder in winter."

1. Why do you think some people have this idea about the reason for seasons?

2. What things could you do to help someone understand the scientific explanation for seasons? How would this help someone give up his or her original idea in favor of the scientific one?

3. Did you ever have a similar *Missed Conception* at the beginning of this unit or sometime during your life? Do you think you might still hold on to your previous ideas or parts of them? How and/or why has your thinking changed or not changed?

FACTs at the beginning of instruction and during the exploration of ideas phase. *Missed Conceptions* should not be explicitly identified as misconceptions for students until students have had sufficient instructional opportunity to work through and resolve their own ideas, which may be similar to the missed conception and provide a starting point for instruction.

Use With Other Disciplines

This FACT can also be used in mathematics and social studies.

My Notes

_____

_____

_____

#36: MUDDIEST POINT

Description

Muddiest Point is a commonly used, quick monitoring technique in which students are asked to take a few minutes to jot down what the most difficult or confusing part of a lesson was for them (Angelo & Cross, 1993).

How This FACT Promotes Student Learning

The *Muddiest Point* provides a metacognitive opportunity for students to think about their own learning and what is difficult or easy for them to understand. It is especially helpful when students encounter new information, deal with complicated procedures, or engage in discussions that result in cognitive conflict. This FACT provides a comfortable way for students who are reluctant to speak out and let others know when they are having difficulty understanding a concept or performing a skill.

How This FACT Informs Instruction

The *Muddiest Point* is a feedback and monitoring strategy used to efficiently collect information on what students find most difficult or confusing about a lesson or part of a lesson. It can be used any time during instruction, including the spur of the moment, when teachers detect that students may be experiencing difficulty understanding or performing a scientific procedure. The information is used as instructional feedback to address student difficulties. Teachers can quickly administer, collect, and sort responses to make immediate decisions about instruction for the class or for individual students. It can also be used at the end of a lesson to assess where students are in understanding the key ideas or skills of the lesson. The information helps the teacher prepare for strategies or activities that will address students' difficulties in the next lesson.

Design and Administration

At a determined point during an activity, lab, presentation, discussion, video, or assigned reading, distribute half sheets of paper or index cards. Ask students to describe the "muddiest point" of the lesson thus far. Clarify what is meant by *muddiest point.* For example, a high school chemistry teacher using this FACT at the end of a lesson to assess students' content understanding might say,

> *So far today we have been learning about the patterns that informed the design of the Periodic Table. What has been the muddiest point so far in today's lesson for you? Please take a few minutes to jot down any ideas or parts of the lesson that were confusing or difficult for you to understand so I can address them in class tomorrow.*

An elementary teacher might use this FACT to determine how well students can perform a scientific procedure:

> *You have been looking for microorganisms in a drop of pond water. What is the muddiest point for you thus far when it comes to using the microscope? I will use the information you give to me to think about ways to help you better use the microscopes in tomorrow's lesson.*

Let students know why you are asking for this information. Collect their responses and decide how the information will inform the rest of the lesson or the following lesson. Be sure to let students know how you plan to use their responses. When they understand that the information is seriously considered by you to make changes that will benefit them, they will respond thoughtfully and with detail. After reading the responses and taking action, share with students examples of the responses that informed your instructional decisions.

General Implementation Attributes

Ease of Use: High   Time Demand: Low
Cognitive Demand: Low/Medium

Modifications

This strategy can also be used with homework and in-class assignments. It can be combined with a question asking students what could be done to help clear up the "muddy points" for them.

Caveats

This FACT focuses on the negative, rather than the positive. Vary this strategy with *POMS—Point of Most Significance* to provide opportunities for students to identify the most significant part of a lesson or the parts of the lesson that were best understood.

Use With Other Disciplines

This FACT can also be used in mathematics, social studies, language arts, health, foreign languages, and performing arts.

My Notes

_____

_____

_____

#37: NO-HANDS QUESTIONING

Description

Students typically raise their hands when they wish to respond to a teacher's question. With *No-Hands Questioning*, students do not put their hands up to respond to a teacher's question. The teacher poses a question, practices wait time, and calls on students randomly. This FACT acknowledges that everyone needs to be ready to share his or her ideas. It reinforces the notion that everyone's response is important, not just the students who show they know the answer by raising their hand (Black et al., 2003).

How This FACT Promotes Student Learning

No-Hands Questioning is used to stimulate thinking and provide an opportunity for all students to be asked to share their thinking, not just students who raise their hands. Often when a question is asked, hands will shoot up immediately. As a result, the students who take longer to think about an idea stop thinking once they see that others already have the answer. This FACT can increase students' engagement and motivation to think about their ideas and frame a quality response, since everyone in the class has an equal chance of being called upon to respond.

How This FACT Informs Instruction

This FACT, combined with wait time, is a way for teachers to encourage all students to be active participants in the learning process. Many students have been habituated to raise their hands. *No-Hands Questioning* provides an opportunity for teachers to hear from a wide range of students in the class, not just those who raise their hands or opt out by not raising their hands. It is particularly useful when you need to learn what certain students in the class, who typically do not raise their hands, are thinking.

Design and Administration

Prepare a set of quality questions ahead of time (see the Appendix for source material on developing quality questions). Practice wait time both before and after posing a question. Call on a student by name after posing the full question and then extend the question further to probe for his or her ideas, giving the student additional time to think. In addition, the manner in which questions are asked by the teacher when a student is called upon indicates to the student that the teacher is interested in his or her thinking. The following example shows how questions can be framed using this FACT:

Teacher: *"What do you think would happen if all the microbes on Earth suddenly died?"*

  Teacher uses wait time.

  "Jana, what ideas do you have about this?"

Jana: *"Well, I think it would be a good thing because there would be fewer diseases and less people would die."*

  Teacher uses wait time after Jana's response.

Teacher: *"What do others think about Jana's idea?"*

  Teacher pauses for wait time.

  "Tyrone, what are your thoughts?"

Tyrone: *"I think it would be good that people wouldn't get as many diseases, but I think it would be bad for the Earth because there wouldn't be anything to break down all the things that die so they would just build up."*

  Teacher uses wait time.

Teacher: *"Would someone like to add to Tyrone's idea or share a different thought?"*

  Teacher pauses.

  "Petra, what are you thinking about right now?"

Share the reason for using this FACT with students so they understand that it is intended to help them think, provide an opportunity for any student to be heard, and share various ideas that students may have. Make sure students know that every idea is valued, not just the "right answer," so all students feel they have something to share in response to the question asked.

General Implementation Attributes

Ease of Use: High   Time Demand: Low
Cognitive Demand: Depends on the question

Modifications

You may choose to use random selection techniques such as cards with students' names on them or the *Popsicle Stick Questioning* FACT to select specific students you have a need to hear from. A modified version of *No-Hands Questioning*, combined with *Wait Time Variations*, is to have students put their hand up when they have an idea or comment to share. The teacher nods to the individual student when a hand goes up. The nod is the signal to then put his or her hand down. Once a significant number of hands have gone up, and then down, call on selected students.

Caveats

Avoid the use of recall questions, as they tend to result in more "I don't know" responses and provide little feedback on conceptual understanding.

Use With Other Disciplines

This FACT can also be used in mathematics, social studies, language arts, health, foreign languages, and performing arts.

My Notes

_____

_____

_____

#38: ODD ONE OUT

Description

Odd One Out combines seemingly similar items and challenges students to choose which item in the group does not belong. Students are asked to justify their reason for selecting the item that does not fit with the others (Naylor et al., 2004).

How This FACT Promotes Student Learning

Odd One Out provides an opportunity for students to access scientific knowledge to analyze relationships between items in a group. By thinking about the similarities and differences, students are encouraged to use their reasoning skills in a challenging and engaging way. The FACT can be used to stimulate small-group discussion after students have had an opportunity to think through their own ideas. As students discuss their ideas in a group, they may modify their thinking or come up with ways to further test or research their ideas.

How This FACT Informs Instruction

Odd One Out can be used at the beginning of instruction to find out what students already know about a topic. It can also be used during the development of conceptual understanding to examine the reasoning students use in comparing and contrasting the items on the list. Teachers can use this FACT to examine how their students make connections among concepts and ideas. The information is helpful in considering instructional experiences that can challenge students' commonly held ideas. *Odd One Out* can also be used to assess how well students can transfer their learning to a new context if there is a possibility that they could be limited by the instructional context in which they learned about the ideas. Results from *Odd One Out* may indicate the need to design additional learning opportunities so that students can experience examples different from the ones used in their instructional materials.

Design and Administration

Select items that lend themselves to a grouping where one item justifiably does not fit with the others. Be sure to choose items and a relationship that is not immediately obvious in order to promote deeper thinking. Provide the list as a handout, overhead projection, or chart. Alert students to what the topic of the *Odd One Out* is before they examine the list of items. Make it clear to students that they should explore what they think rather than guess the answer they think you, the teacher, are expecting. Have students record their own thinking before discussing their ideas with a partner or in groups. Allow students enough time to discuss the various possibilities before homing in on "the odd one out." Figure 4.29 shows an example of an *Odd One Out* designed for middle school students studying the topic of properties of matter.

General Implementation Attributes

Ease of Use: High   Time Demand: Medium
Cognitive Demand: Medium/High

Figure 4.29 *Odd One Out* for Properties of Matter

Properties of Matter: In each set, circle the **Odd One Out** and describe why it does not fit with the others.

Which Is the Odd One?	Why It Is the Odd One Out
Weight Density Length Color	

Which Is the Odd One?	Why It Is the Odd One Out
Melting Point Density Solubility Mass	

Which Is the Odd One?	Why It Is the Odd One Out
Length Volume Temperature Mass	

Which Is the Odd One?	Why It Is the Odd One Out
Burn Float Stretch Dissolve	

SOURCE: Based on Odd One Out Strategy created by Naylor, S., Keogh, B., and Goldsworthy, A. (2004). *Active assessment—Thinking, learning and assessment in science.* London, England: David Fulton Publishers.

Modifications

With younger children or less fluent readers, consider using pictures with words. Use only one or two sets for younger students. Instead of "Odd One Out," use "Which of These Things Is Not Like the Other?"

Caveats

Make sure students are familiar with the words or objects listed before they are asked to examine the relationship between them.

Use With Other Disciplines

This FACT can also be used in mathematics, social studies, language arts, health, foreign languages, and performing arts.

My Notes

_____

_____

_____

#39: PAINT THE PICTURE

Description

Paint the Picture visually depicts students' thinking about an idea in science without using any annotations. The FACT involves giving students a question and asking them to design a visual representation that reveals their thinking and answers the question. The picture needs to stand alone without labels and can be used to explain their thinking.

How This FACT Promotes Student Learning

Paint the Picture provides an opportunity for students to organize and represent their thinking in a visual format. It allows every student a creative and unique way to make their thinking visible to themselves and others. Furthermore, it provides a stimulus for further discussion about students' ideas. The act of describing and explaining their representation to others further supports and solidifies their learning. In addition, *Paint the Picture* reinforces the importance of scientists' use of representations to convey ideas in science.

How This FACT Informs Instruction

Paint the Picture is used after students have had an opportunity to learn about the ideas generated by the question. For example, a teacher might hold up a large syringe and ask, "What happens to the air molecules in this syringe if I push the plunger in when the cap is on? Draw a before-and-after picture of the molecules inside the syringe that shows what you think happens to the molecules." A student drawing might show a potential misconception about the size of molecules decreasing when pushed closer together as well as the belief that there is some type of matter between the molecules. This idea may come out explicitly from the drawing itself, when the student describes the drawing, or when the teacher probes further to learn more about the student's ideas. Teachers can group similar drawings and engage the class in a feedback discussion, comparing different drawings to help students bridge the gap between their own ideas and the scientific view.

Design and Administration

Provide students with drawing materials. Pose a question designed to probe their conceptual understanding and ask them to draw a picture, without using any words, which represents their thinking about the answer. Encourage students to draw what is in their head, representing it so someone else can understand their ideas. After students have finished their drawings, use various pairing strategies or small group configurations to allow students an opportunity to explain their drawing to their peers, giving each other feedback on the representation of their ideas. The teacher circulates and listens carefully, noting particular drawings that may be used to facilitate a class discussion or design appropriate interventions.

General Implementation Attributes

Ease of Use: Medium   Time Demand: Medium
Cognitive Demand: Medium/High

Modifications

Paint the Picture can be conducted as a pair or small group activity where students work with others to create a representation of their collective thinking. It can also be used with *Whiteboarding.*

Caveats

Avoid commenting on students' artistic abilities. The drawings should be for the purpose of making student thinking visible. Students may disengage in the strategy if they feel judgments are being made about artistic quality. Students with strong verbal and writing communication skills may have less developed visual communication skills, necessitating a probe beyond the picture.

Use With Other Disciplines

This FACT can also be used in social studies, language arts, performing arts, and health.

My Notes

_____

_____

_____

#40: PARTNER SPEAKS

Description

Partner Speaks provides students with an opportunity to talk through an idea or question with another student before sharing with a larger group. When ideas are shared with the larger group, pairs speak from the perspective of their partner's ideas. This changes the emphasis from the student's ideas to consider the ideas of his or her partner and encourages careful listening between student pairs.

How This FACT Promotes Student Learning

Having a partner to talk with allows students to think through and articulate their ideas to others for feedback before sharing with a larger group. It helps students develop careful listening and paraphrasing skills since the strategy requires them to share their partner's thinking, not their own. *Partner Speaks* provides an opportunity for shy, less confident students who may not be comfortable sharing their own ideas in a large group to let their ideas be heard through someone else. It also teaches overconfident, dominating students to honor and share the ideas of others rather than focusing solely on their own ideas.

How This FACT Informs Instruction

This FACT can be used during any point in a lesson when social engagement enhances the development and sharing of ideas. As teachers listen to the interaction, they learn more about student thinking in preparation for the next steps in a lesson or sequence of instruction. *Partner Speaks* can be used to promote deeper engagement with an idea, especially when there is a need to have students think through a new idea, difficult question, or novel context.

Design and Administration

Have students turn to their "elbow partner" and provide time for them to take turns discussing a question or idea. If there is an uneven number of students, assign some groups as triads. When using this strategy for the first time, it may be helpful to model for students what it looks and sounds like when two people are engaged in dialogue (e.g., one person speaks while the other listens and vice versa, with the purpose of deepening thinking) and the pairs share what their partner's ideas were. Encourage students to make eye contact and think about what their partner is saying as they respectfully listen without interrupting. The following is an example of how a teacher might describe this strategy to fourth-grade students:

Today we are going to investigate how objects float or sink in water. What kinds of things do you think affect whether an object floats or sinks in water? Are there things you can do to change how an object floats or sinks? Turn to your partner and take turns discussing your ideas. Be sure to listen carefully, without interrupting, as your partner shares his or her thinking. When you describe your own thinking, be sure to explain to your partner the reasons for your ideas. When you are finished taking turns, each of you will need to be prepared to share your partner's ideas with the rest of the class. You will not be talking about your own ideas but rather the ideas of your partner. Thus it is very important for you to be a good listener and not interrupt your partner's thoughts.

General Implementation Attributes

Ease of Use: High   Time Demand: Medium
Cognitive Demand: Medium/High

Modifications

Combine this strategy with various methods for mixing up students and assigning partners so that students are not always talking with the same person.

Caveats

In some classes, gender and friendship issues may hinder the use of *Partner Speaks.* It is recommended that teachers establish norms for partner discussions. Students should also be reminded not to pass judgment on their partner's ideas when they report to the class.

Use With Other Disciplines

This FACT can also be used in mathematics, social studies, language arts, health, foreign languages, and performing arts.

My Notes

_____

_____

_____

#41: PASS THE QUESTION

Description

Pass the Question provides an opportunity for students to collaborate in activating their own ideas and examining other students' thinking. Students begin by working together in pairs to respond to a question, partially finishing a response. When the time is up, they exchange their written, partially completed response with another pair to finish—modifying, adding to, or changing it as the pair deems necessary.

How This FACT Promotes Student Learning

The interactive nature of the pair discussion provides an opportunity for students to think about what they know and come to a consensus of thinking with their partner. After the partially finished written response is passed to a new pair of students, the new pair must examine the thinking of their peers and decide whether they agree with their thinking. If so, the pair continues the response by completing what was already started by the other pair. If their ideas differ, they may modify or change the response the other pair started and complete it for them. Pairs then get together to give feedback to each other on why they did or did not change the responses as well as feedback on how well they felt the other pair's thinking helped them pick up where the original pair's response left off.

How This FACT Informs Instruction

As teachers listen carefully to students exchange ideas in response to the question posed, they gather evidence on the nature and depth of students' understanding. The information may surface disagreements students have about the content, furthering the need to design additional opportunities that will address the concept in question. The student responses can also be collected and examined to see the range of students' thinking about the question, indicating the need for differentiation with certain groups of students.

Design and Administration

Develop a question that will elicit a rich explanatory response based on students' prior knowledge or experience. Questions can also be a new application of the concepts students have been learning about in their instructional unit. Arrange students in pairs. Write the question on a chart, on the board, or state orally. Give pairs two to three minutes to collaboratively begin drafting a response to the given question. Make sure students know they need to develop enough of a response so that another pair can follow their thinking but not so much that it doesn't leave room for the other pair to complete it. After two to three minutes have passed, pairs swap their partially completed answer with another pair. The pairs then continue to pick up from where the other pair left off. Encourage pupils to cross off parts they don't agree with and modify or exchange the crossed-off part with their own ideas. They may continue adding their own ideas to enhance, extend, and complete the response. When both pairs are finished, they share the completed responses with each other, defending their reasons for any changes they made and providing feedback on each others' thinking. They also examine whether their ideas converged or diverged. The teacher may ask pairs to share some examples, providing feedback from the teacher and the rest of the class on the response to the question.

General Implementation Attributes

Ease of Use: Medium   Time Demand: Medium
Cognitive Demand: High

Modifications

This FACT can also be used with individuals. An individual student starts the response and then exchanges with another student for completion and sharing. It can also be a written exchange between two different classes studying the same topic.

Caveats

Make sure time is provided to debrief the class about the question and engage students in a discussion about the ideas. Include how a scientist or someone who knows the content well would respond to the question. Without this opportunity to compare their responses to the scientific ideas, some students may be left accepting misconceptions or inaccurate statements that were made by their peers.

Use With Other Disciplines

This FACT can also be used in mathematics, social studies, language arts, health, foreign languages, and performing arts.

My Notes

_____

_____

_____

#42: A PICTURE TELLS A THOUSAND WORDS

Description

In this FACT, students are digitally photographed during an inquiry-based activity or investigation. Students are given the photograph and asked to describe what they were doing and learning during the "inquiry moment" (Carlson et al., 2003). Students write their description under the photograph.

How This FACT Promotes Student Learning

Students enjoy seeing themselves in photographs. There is a high level of engagement and an intrinsic desire to want to explain what is happening in a picture when the student is part of it. Asking students to annotate their photograph as they are engaged in an inquiry activity helps them reflect on their learning and value the skills that are part of scientific inquiry. This FACT can motivate reluctant writers to write more vivid, detailed accounts of their experience since the photograph personalizes it for them.

How This FACT Informs Instruction

Periodically taking digital photographs of the class during important inquiry moments provides the teacher and the class with a documented way to track how students' scientific ideas and skills are developing through inquiry. The images can be used to spark student discussions, explore new directions in inquiry, and probe their thinking as it relates to the moment the photograph was snapped. By asking students to annotate the photos with a description of what they were learning and the skills they were using, teachers can better understand what students are gaining from the inquiry experience and adjust it as needed. If students can't describe what they were learning, then this is a signal to the teacher that the purpose of the activity was not clear. It also helps the teacher see how students' conceptual understanding evolves throughout an investigation and what might be done differently to help students move forward in the investigation. The photographs can also be used to spark whole-class discussions that provide an opportunity to probe deeper into students' ideas and thinking processes. At the end of a unit, the photographs can be posted on a reflection wall and used as a class reflection to metacognitively retrace their thinking and learning.

Design and Administration

Digital cameras make it quick and easy to take and print a picture. This FACT can be used any time during students' inquiry investigations. It is particularly effective when students are excited about a discovery, experience something unexpected, or have an "ah-ha" moment during inquiry. Choose situations where students can relate to and remember what happened in the photograph. Allow students to call you over to take a picture that they think is important to share what happened during an inquiry-based experience. After taking photographs, download and copy them onto a page that allows enough space on the paper for students to describe their "inquiry moment." Distribute the photograph to students for reflection as soon as possible after taking the photograph. Encourage students to write a detailed description of what they were doing, thinking, and learning about when the photograph was taken. In addition, the teacher or other students in the class can add feedback notes to comment on the students' picture and annotations. Posting the annotated photos further reinforces the importance of sharing students' experiences and thinking.

The reflective, annotated writing can be assigned to individual students or as a group reflection by the students seen in the photograph. The group reflection provides an additional opportunity for students to discuss and share their thinking about what they were doing and learning during an investigation. A collection of class photographs, with annotations, can be displayed as a visual record of students' learning during inquiry for others to see, read, and reflect upon.

General Implementation Attributes

Ease of Use: Depends on availability of camera and printer
Cognitive Demand: Medium
Time Demand: Low

Modifications

Younger students may dictate their descriptions to the teacher to include as annotations on the photographs.

Caveats

It may not be possible to photograph every student during every activity. Make sure over the course of a unit that all students have an opportunity to see and describe themselves in a photograph. Try not to take more than one day to return the photographs for annotation.

Use With Other Disciplines

This FACT is specific to inquiry-based science.

My Notes

_____

_____

_____

#43: P-E-O PROBES (PREDICT, EXPLAIN, OBSERVE)

Description

P-E-O Probes present a phenomenon or situation in which students are asked to make a prediction or select a prediction from a set of forced-choice responses that matches their thinking. Students must explain the reasoning that supports their prediction. The probe is followed by an opportunity for students to test their prediction, observe the results, and modify their explanation as needed. Figure 4.30 shows an example of a *P-E-O Probe.*

How This FACT Promotes Student Learning

P-E-O Probes draw out students' ideas and explanations related to a phenomenon that can then be tested and observed by students. This FACT activates student thinking about scientific ideas and provides an opportunity to discuss their thinking with others. The probe provides an entry point into inquiry that engages students in wanting to know if their prediction is accurate. When their observation does not match their prediction, it creates a dissonance that leads to further investigation or concept resolving. *P-E-O Probes* also help students develop a critical skill in inquiry-based science—the importance of revising one's explanation when new evidence becomes available.

How This FACT Informs Instruction

P-E-O Probes provide a quick way for teachers to gather data on students' preconceptions, including commonly held ideas noted in the cognitive-research literature that may have been reinforced through previous experiences. For example, in Figure 4.30, the student shows a commonly held idea that if one's eyes have time to adjust to the darkness, they will eventually be able to see an object, even though they may not see the color. This response indicates a lack of understanding the role of light in how we see. *P-E-O Probes* are best used as an elicitation and exploration into testing students' ideas. This FACT can be used individually as a written assessment or given to pairs and small groups to discuss their ideas

Figure 4.30   *P-E-O Probe*

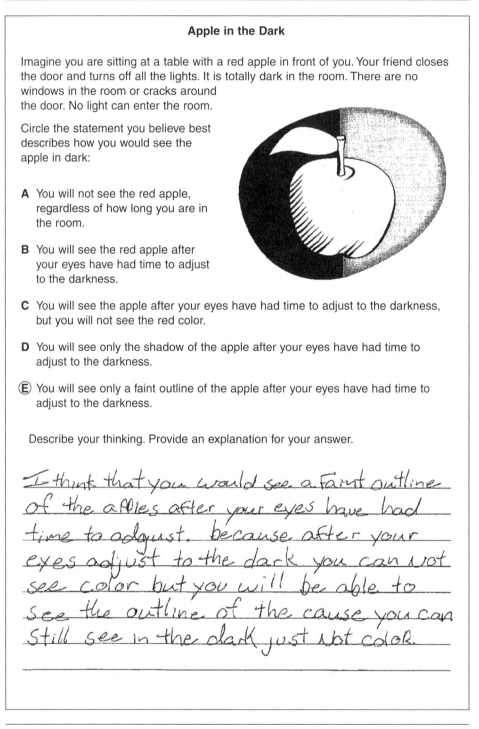

Apple in the Dark

Imagine you are sitting at a table with a red apple in front of you. Your friend closes the door and turns off all the lights. It is totally dark in the room. There are no windows in the room or cracks around the door. No light can enter the room.

Circle the statement you believe best describes how you would see the apple in dark:

A You will not see the red apple, regardless of how long you are in the room.

B You will see the red apple after your eyes have had time to adjust to the darkness.

C You will see the apple after your eyes have had time to adjust to the darkness, but you will not see the red color.

D You will see only the shadow of the apple after your eyes have had time to adjust to the darkness.

E You will see only a faint outline of the apple after your eyes have had time to adjust to the darkness.

Describe your thinking. Provide an explanation for your answer.

I think that you would see a faint outline of the apples after your eyes have had time to adjust. because after your exes adjust to the dark you can not see color but you will be able to see the outline of the cause you can still see in the dark just not color.

Source: Keeley, Eberle, and Farrin (2005).

and come to agreement on a prediction. They can then test their prediction in a dark room. Teachers examine or listen carefully to the students' justification for their prediction and monitor students' explanations after they test their prediction, especially if they find that their results do not match their original prediction. This is an opportunity to guide students toward reconciling what they believed would happen and what the actual result was. Teachers can use this opportunity to help students think through, discuss, and get feedback on their revised explanations in order to accommodate the change in their thinking that resulted from their investigation. For example, when students test their ideas with an apple in a dark room and find out that they can't see the apple, that experience provides an ideal time to introduce the role of light reflecting off an object and entering our eye to explain how we see. The discussion might reveal that students picked up a common misconception from the popular activity of observing the pupils in their eye after they have been in the dark and a light is then turned on. They might believe that the pupils "adjust to the dark" by getting bigger, rather than understanding the pupils are opening wider to try to let more light in, even if there is no light. It is also an opportunity to discuss how most people have never experienced total darkness; that there is usually some ambient light present, which explains why they see things in their dark bedroom at night.

Design and Administration

Design *P-E-O Probes* to target important learning goals in science that can be tested using simple materials. You can also use ready-made probes that have been extensively field tested. A source for these probes is described in the Appendix. Encourage students to record their own prediction and explanation before discussing their ideas in small groups. After students have had an opportunity to discuss their predictions and modify their alternative explanations as needed, have small groups engage in inquiry to test their predictions in a context similar to the one described in the probe. After they observe the result, be sure to provide time for students to revisit and revise their explanation, extending the probe to become *P-E-O-E*. Engage the whole class in a discussion to help students accommodate the result and solidify their conceptual understanding of the explanation of the phenomenon.

General Implementation Attributes

Ease of Use: Medium   Time Demand: Medium/High
Cognitive Demand: Medium/High

Modifications

After students have committed to an outcome and discussed their explanations with others, teachers can use the probe scenario as a whole-class demonstration if materials or time is limited. The results of the demonstration can be used in orchestrating discourse to help students revise their original explanation and further develop their conceptual understanding.

Caveats

To use this FACT effectively, make sure you provide adequate time for students to explain their thinking before testing their prediction and observing the result.

Use With Other Disciplines

This FACT is specific to inquiry-based science.

My Notes

_____

_____

_____

#44: POMS—POINT OF MOST SIGNIFICANCE

Description

POMS is the opposite of the *Muddiest Point*. In this quick technique, students are asked to identify the most significant learning or idea they gained from a lesson.

How This FACT Promotes Student Learning

POMS is a metacognitive strategy used to help students connect with the important goals of a lesson. Students reflect back on the lesson and identify the key points that contributed to their learning.

How This FACT Informs Instruction

POMS is used at the end of a lesson to gather information on what students feel were the most significant points made during a lesson. Teachers can quickly administer, collect, and sort responses to make judgments about how well the key ideas intended by the lesson were perceived as important learnings by the students. If the *POMS* of the students differs from the important points the lesson was intended to develop, the teacher can use this information to clarify and add more emphasis to the key points of the lesson.

Design and Administration

At the end of a lesson, ask students to describe orally or in writing the most significant point made during the lesson that contributed to their learning. For example, a fifth-grade lesson on animal adaptations might conclude with, *"Today we investigated and discussed adaptations and how some species of animals have characteristics that help them survive in a changing environment. What point made during today's activity or discussion best helped you understand what adaptations are and why they are important to a species' survival?"* Collect and analyze students' responses to decide if the lesson met its goal or needs to be modified. Be sure to let students know how you used their responses. When they understand that the information is seriously considered by you for making changes that will benefit them, they will respond thoughtfully and with detail.

General Implementation Attributes

Ease of Use: High   Time Demand: Low
Cognitive Demand: Low/Medium

Modifications

POMS can be changed to *Part of Most Significance* to be used as a reflection on the most effective part of a lesson, rather than the key points that contributed to their learning.

Caveats

Focusing only on the most significant point of the lesson may result in overlooking areas where students are experiencing conceptual difficulties. Vary this strategy with *Muddiest Point,* in order to provide opportunities for students to express what was difficult for them as well.

Use With Other Disciplines

This FACT can also be used in mathematics, social studies, language arts, health, foreign languages, and performing arts.

My Notes

_____

_____

_____

#45: POPSICLE STICK QUESTIONING

Description

Popsicle Stick Questioning is a technique used to selectively choose students for *No-Hands Questioning*. The purpose of this technique is to ensure that certain students, identified in advance by the teacher, are called on during "random" class questioning. Names are written on Popsicle sticks and placed in a cup. An inner cup, placed inside the outer cup, holds the Popsicle sticks with the names of students the teacher wants to be sure to call on. The names can be pulled out from the inner cup when needed, while giving the appearance that students are all randomly selected when called upon to respond to a question (Wiliam, 2005).

How This FACT Promotes Student Learning

This is a type of *No-Hands Questioning* strategy that encourages all students to think and be prepared to answer questions when randomly called upon. Since hands are not raised, students who do not raise their hands cannot opt out of the questions; therefore, students tend to engage more in their own thinking to prepare for the chance of being called upon for a response. All students think they have an equal chance of being called upon, and thus this selection strategy ensures that students who need to be heard from have an opportunity to think and formulate their ideas.

How This FACT Informs Instruction

There are times when it is important for the teacher to gather specific information about individual students in a class. This FACT provides a way for teachers to ensure that certain students are called upon to share their thinking without their feeling as if they had been singled out. The teacher can use the information to examine how individual students are progressing in their learning and select differentiated strategies as needed to improve their learning.

Design and Administration

Write all students' names on the Popsicle sticks and place them in an opaque cup, such as a coffee mug. Place another smaller cup inside the larger cup. The names of a few preselected students the teacher wants to be sure to call on are placed in the inner cup. The inner cup is visible only to the teacher. The other Popsicle sticks are placed outside of the inner cup. When the teacher feels a need to call on a particular student, a name is drawn from the inner cup. The following describes how a teacher might use this FACT:

Mrs. Johnston was questioning students about their ideas related to the phases of the moon. She noticed that several students were struggling through the previous day's activity. She decided she needed to call on them during the class discussion so they would make their thinking visible to the class and receive feedback to help them move toward a scientific understanding. In order to ensure that they would be selected during the "random" Popsicle stick draw, she placed their Popsicle sticks in the center, inner cup, where she could easily draw them out when necessary.

General Implementation Attributes

Ease of Use: High   Time Demand: Low
Cognitive Demand: Depends on the question asked

Modifications

Use different-colored inks for particular subgroups of students. Write some students' names down more than once to increase the probability of being selected.

Caveats

Don't allow students to see the inner cup!

Use With Other Disciplines

This FACT can also be used in mathematics, social studies, language arts, health, foreign languages, and performing arts.

My Notes

_____

_____

_____

#46: PREFACING EXPLANATIONS

Description

Prefacing is a technique in which students learn how to preface explanations in order to encourage their peers to improve communication of their ideas. This FACT is used with inquiry-based activities that require students to explain their findings to other students.

How This FACT Promotes Student Learning

Prefacing is used to support explanations during inquiry. It provides a way for students to draw ideas out from their classmates and improve the quality of their explanations. For the student who is explaining his or her ideas, prefacing encourages that student to delve deeper into his or her thinking.

How This FACT Informs Instruction

Prefacing helps facilitate communication of students' explanations. As students use this FACT during small-group discussions, the teacher circulates through the classroom, listening to and noting areas where students may be having difficulty explaining and supporting their thinking. The teacher may note areas where the outcome of the investigation was not clear to students. The teacher may also use the same prefacing statements to further help students develop their reasoning and explanation skills during inquiry.

Design and Administration

Prefacing is a skill that needs to be taught. Teachers should model prefacing with students, explicitly pointing out various ways prefacing can be used for encouraging communication of explanations. Examples of prefacing statements are included in Figure 4.31. A chart showing examples of prefacing statements may be posted in the room. This chart is used by students when they are discussing their ideas about an investigation and engaged in argumentation to evaluate the explanations of others.

General Implementation Attributes

Ease of Use: Medium/High   Time Demand: Medium
Cognitive Demand: Medium/High

Figure 4.31   Examples of *Prefacing Statements*

- I'm not sure I know what your conclusion [or claim] is.
- I'm not sure I understand your reasoning.
- It would help me to understand if you could give me an example.
- I'm wondering where your evidence came from.
- It would help if you could describe why you think that counts as evidence.
- I'm wondering if you considered other possibilities.

Modifications

Simplify the language of the prefacing statements if students are not familiar with the terminology.

Caveats

This FACT is best used with middle and high school students.

Use With Other Disciplines

This FACT is specific to inquiry-based science.

My Notes

_____

_____

_____

#47: PVF—PAIRED VERBAL FLUENCY

Description

PVF is a technique used for partner discussion or reflection. Partners take turns in timed rounds, talking "off the top of their heads" about an assigned topic or prompt. While one person talks, the other listens until time elapses and partners switch roles (Lipton & Wellman, 1998).

How This FACT Promotes Student Learning

The purpose of *PVF* is to activate student thinking. The act of talking nonstop for a specified interval stimulates students to construct meaning through language while digging deeper into their existing knowledge base. Active listening by the partner stimulates additional thinking about the topic. The structured protocol provides a vehicle for students to be metacognitive in a verbally active way. In a very short period of time, students can surface a significant amount of knowledge, beliefs, wonderings, and understandings from their instructional experiences.

How This FACT Informs Instruction

After students have engaged in *PVF*, they may have identified unresolved issues or difficulties to bring to the attention of the teacher. These issues or difficulties are then addressed by the teacher to further develop conceptual understanding through class discussion or additional learning experiences.

Design and Administration

PVF can be used prior to instruction, as a review of a lesson, or for reflection purposes at the end of a sequence of instruction. It also works well as a prelude to whole-class discussion. Some ways to use *PVF* include having students talk about a topic to be introduced by sharing what they already know about the topic; having students discuss a recent laboratory experiment, including the significance of their findings; or having students reflect at the end of a kit-based science unit by talking about their key learnings. Start by asking students to find an "eye contact partner" by standing up and making eye contact with someone who is not sitting near them. The partners move together and wait for the teacher's instructions. Ask each pair to decide who will be Partner A and who will be Partner B (usually the student who wants to go last chooses Partner B, so you may want to announce that Partner B will go first!). Give the class a discussion prompt or topic to discuss. Announce that when you give the signal, one partner will talk for exactly one minute while the other partner only listens. Announce "switch," and partners trade roles and repeat. At the next "switch," the first partner talks for 30 seconds, followed by "switch" and the other partner talks for 30 seconds. At the end of the activity, ask for a few volunteers to share what they learned from their partner or to comment on any learning issues they discussed that may need to be resolved.

General Implementation Attributes

Ease of Use: High   Time Demand: Low
Cognitive Demand: Medium/High

Modifications

Students can be paired by using a variety of strategies. The time intervals can be changed to other configurations such as 1 minute–40 seconds–20 seconds, 60 seconds–30 seconds–10 seconds (for a closing statement), or other configurations the teacher or students select.

Caveats

This strategy may be difficult for English-language learners or students who have a hard time concentrating or hearing. There is a high level of noise in the classroom when many students are talking at the same time.

Use With Other Disciplines

This FACT can also be used in mathematics, social studies, language arts, health, foreign languages, and performing arts.

My Notes

_____

_____

_____

#48: QUESTION GENERATING

Description

Question Generating is a technique that switches roles from the teacher as the generator of questions to the student as the question generator. The ability to formulate good questions about a topic can indicate the extent to which a student understands ideas that underlie the topic.

How This FACT Promotes Student Learning

Students typically think that asking questions is easy and answering them is difficult (Naylor et al., 2004, p. 120). When they are put in a position to develop thinking questions that go beyond recall, they realize they have to draw upon their own understanding of the topic. Generating good questions in science requires more than superficial knowledge of the topic. It requires the student to delve deeper into his or her existing knowledge base. As they formulate "thinking questions," students practice metacognition by recognizing their level of understanding needed not only to form the question but to respond to it as well.

How This FACT Informs Instruction

Question Generating can be used at the beginning of instruction in a topic to find out what students already know about the topic. The number of questions students come up with, the quality of the questions (recall versus thinking questions), and the sophistication of the ideas embedded in the question reveal the extent of student knowledge about the topic. As students learn to distinguish productive questions from nonproductive questions, their higher-level questions reveal interesting insights into their thinking about the content. Teachers can also have students exchange or answer their own questions, revealing further information about students' ideas related to the topic. Selected student-generated questions can be saved and used at the end of a unit of instruction for self-assessment, reflection, or summative assessment.

Design and Administration

Provide a stimulus, such as an object, picture, statement, or problem around which students can generate their questions. For example, in a fifth-grade unit on soils, the teacher might show two different-colored soil samples and ask the students to think of some good questions to ask about differences in soils. To help students develop good questions, the teacher can provide a list of question stems or post a chart of question stems to refer to in the classroom. Figure 4.32 shows examples of *Question Generating* stems.

General Implementation Attributes

Ease of Use: Medium (depends   Time Demand: Medium
   on readiness and grade level)
Cognitive Demand: High

Modifications

If individual students have difficulty generating questions, provide an opportunity for students to develop questions in small groups. Questions can also be developed as a whole-class activity.

Figure 4.32   Sample *Question Generating* Stems for Inquiry-Based Science

Question Generating Stems
Why does ____?
How does ____?
What if ____?
What could be the reason for ____?
What would happen if ____?
How does ____ respond to ____?
How does ____ compare to ____?
Does ____ when ____?
How could we find out if ____?

Caveats

Some students, particularly younger students, lack the scientific knowledge base to answer "How does" or "Why does" questions. These questions could be better phrased with stems such as "Why do you think ..." rather than "Why does ..." and shows that students' thinking about their own ideas is valued just as much as correct answers.

Use With Other Disciplines

This FACT can also be used in mathematics, social studies, language arts, health, foreign languages, and performing arts.

My Notes

_____

_____

_____

#49: RECOGNIZING EXCEPTIONS

Description

Recognizing Exceptions targets the tendency of students to form over-generalizations. Students are presented with a question that encourages them to look for exceptions. For example, *Do all seeds need only warm temperatures in order to germinate?* shows how this FACT encourages students to think beyond the general notion that seeds need warmth in order to germinate. For example, there are exceptions in which seeds, such as acorns, require a period of cold before warm temperatures and other conditions support germination.

How This FACT Promotes Learning

Recognizing Exceptions allows students to test out facts, rules, and conclusions that have been developed through activities and inquiry-based investigations. Students examine how applicable their "generalizations" are across various contexts and examples. The FACT helps students recognize limitations in describing general characteristics of natural objects, organisms, events, and processes. It also stimulates higher-order thinking by requiring students to delve deeper into a concept to explore other situations, such as the acorn germination example. Questions that elicit student thinking about generalizations stimulate thinking more than a recall question such as *What do seeds need to germinate?*

How This FACT Informs Instruction

This FACT allows teachers to examine whether students overgeneralize information that is presented to them, read, or constructed through inquiry. It allows the teacher to identify what students know, what they partially know, and what they may not know at all. The teacher can use this information to provide examples that will help students recognize exceptions to their own rules and student-generated conclusions they have developed in the science class.

Design and Administration

Choose an applicable question that reveals exceptions to a concept, rule, or student-generated conclusion developed in class. Use stems such as the ones shown in Figure 4.33.

Use the questions in conjunction with other FACTs, such as *Think-Pair-Share* or *Partner Speaks*, to initiate individual thinking, small-group discussion, and whole-class discussion. Provide students with exceptions if they do not surface and help students understand why they are "exceptions to the rule."

General Implementation Attributes

Ease of Use: High   Time Demand: Low
Cognitive Demand: Medium/High

Modifications

This FACT can be modified to focus on undergeneralizations. For example, use question stems such as the following:

- Are these the only examples that fit this rule?
- What other examples can you think of?
- What would help us decide if this is true for other things?

Figure 4.33   *Recognizing Exceptions*

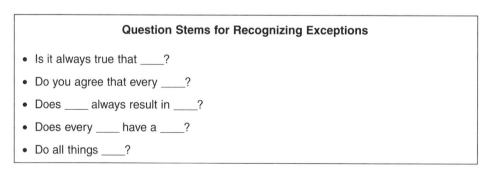

Question Stems for Recognizing Exceptions
• Is it always true that ____?
• Do you agree that every ____?
• Does ____ always result in ____?
• Does every ____ have a ____?
• Do all things ____?

Caveats

Use only with topics that have a scientific basis. Beware of topics that may encourage pseudoscientific beliefs and arguments against well-established scientific theories. For example, intelligent design and creationism are not scientific exceptions to the theory of biological evolution.

Use With Other Disciplines

This FACT can also be used in mathematics, social studies, and health.

My Notes

_____

_____

_____

#50: REFUTATIONS

Description

Refutations are used to check students' declarative and procedural knowledge. This FACT involves analyzing statements about scientific ideas, processes, or procedures that contain both accurate and incorrect information. Students make corrections to the statements so they are scientifically accurate and justify why they made the changes.

How This FACT Promotes Student Learning

Analyzing a *Refutation* provides an opportunity for students to think about and clarify their own ideas. Using this FACT in small groups provides a mechanism for students to make their ideas public and engage in scientific argumentation. It supports metacognition by having students explain their thinking to others and encourages feedback on others' ideas as students work collaboratively to revise the statements.

How This FACT Informs Instruction

Refutations can be used prior to instruction to grab the learner's attention and identify where students have strong or weak factual and conceptual knowledge related to a topic. This FACT can also be used to monitor student learning throughout instruction. Figure 4.34 shows an example of a ninth-grade *Refutation* used with the topic of the nature of particulate matter during a change in state. Commonly held ideas, including specific misconceptions, can be included in a *Refutation* to help teachers identify students who may have similar ideas. If the teacher sees that these ideas go unnoticed in the refutation, this information can be used to design learning experiences that will confront students with their ideas and move them toward the scientifically accepted view. Justifications and corrections students make to the incorrect statements provide information to the teacher on how students think about the content or procedures. Teachers may determine the need to revisit basic ideas and build upon them so that students develop understandings at a level of sophistication appropriate for their grade or developmental level.

Design and Administration

Refutations are designed to address science content knowledge or procedures and results from a classroom inquiry-based investigation. They can be written as a story, article, or textbook-like passage. *Refutations* should be a reasonable length for both the content and the grade level of the students. Students can underline or highlight the areas of text they think need correcting, revise as necessary (individually or in groups), and justify their revisions. Engage the class in a whole-group discussion in which they justify why they think a statement is incorrect and what they would do to correct it. The Appendix includes a source of materials that can be used to identify commonly held ideas to include in refutations.

General Implementation Attributes

Ease of Use: Medium   Time Demand: Medium
Cognitive Demand: Medium

Modifications

The *Refutation* may consist of text, include text and graphics, or be used as a "read aloud." When used as a read aloud, read the entire passage first

Figure 4.34   *Refutation* Example

Ice to Water

I put an ice cube in a jar and made observations as the ice melted. The ice and the molecules that make up the ice are cold and hard. As the ice melted, the water spread out in the jar. If I could see the molecules moving in the jar, I would notice they are moving faster than they were in the ice and they are much farther apart. The molecules would also be larger since they have to expand in order to spread out in the jar. The water gets a lot warmer while the ice is melting. The water molecules lose energy and move faster so they are free of each other. The water in the jar now has more mass than it did when it was in the form of an ice cube.

while students listen carefully. Then repeat and have students raise hands when they spot a mistake and discuss their reasons for correcting it.

Caveats

Do not let scientifically incorrect statements go uncorrected. Give students time to think through the corrections and discuss them, realizing that all students may not spot all the inaccuracies, particularly if they have ideas that go unchallenged. Make sure all students eventually have an opportunity to examine and discuss the corrected version of the *Refutation*.

Use With Other Disciplines

This FACT can also be used in mathematics, social studies, language arts, foreign languages, health, and performing arts.

My Notes

_____

_____

_____

#51: REPRESENTATION ANALYSIS

Description

Scientific representations include pictures, analogies, simulations, graphs, charts, physical models, or diagrams that convey a scientific idea. Since they are not exactly like the real thing, representations in science often have limitations that can sometimes convey incorrect ideas. In this FACT, students analyze a scientific representation by comparing it to the real thing and pointing out flaws, inaccuracies, limitations, or discrepancies in the representation.

How This FACT Promotes Student Learning

Representation Analysis is used to provoke student thinking about a scientific representation and how it compares to a real-life object, event, or process. Students use their own ideas to decide whether the representation is an accurate depiction of the phenomenon or object it is intended to convey. This FACT also helps students become more critically aware of the limitations of scientific representations. For example, Figure 4.35 shows a typical representation of the Earth's orbit around the sun, used to teach the concept of seasons and why they change. Students can point out several inaccuracies, such as the Earth's size in relation to the sun; Earth's highly elliptic orbit, which makes it appear as if the Earth is much closer to the sun during parts of its orbit; Earth's relative distance from the sun; or the length of the orbit in comparison to the Earth's diameter. During discussions about the representation, students may be confronted with inadequacies in their own thinking about the representation. As other students point out flaws or limitations in the representation, some students may modify their own ideas as they assimilate new knowledge.

How This FACT Informs Instruction

This FACT provides an opportunity for teachers to determine whether students may have a misconception that is supported by a representation. It also reveals whether they can apply their scientific knowledge to determine when a representation of a scientific idea is flawed or limited. *Representation Analysis* helps teachers recognize when particular representations used during lessons or contained in students' instructional materials may contribute to misconceptions. When these inadequacies in representations are further supported by students' failure to recognize the flaws or limitations, it provides evidence to the teacher that either these representations should not be used or their limiting features need to be explicitly addressed when used with students.

Design and Administration

Select representations that match the content goals of the lesson. Science textbooks and Internet sites often contain flawed representations.

Figure 4.35   Representation of the Seasons

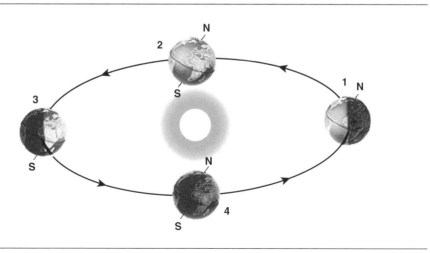

SOURCE: NASA.

Provide the representation on a handout, overhead, or played as a computer simulation. *Representation Analysis* is used after students have had an opportunity to learn the scientific ideas depicted in the representation. They use their knowledge to analyze the representation. Have students, individually or in groups, note aspects of the representation that may lead to misunderstandings or are incorrect. Students should be encouraged to justify their reasons for why they think the representation is flawed. Have students note what could be done to improve the representation. See the Appendix for a source of information on the instructional quality of representations used in science and selected examples.

General Implementation Attributes

Ease of Use: Medium   Time Demand: Low
Cognitive Demand: Medium/High

Modifications

Student drawings can also be used for *Representation Analysis.* Help students be aware that many flawed representations in textbooks and on the Internet go unnoticed by teachers and students. Encourage students to find inaccuracies in the representations they may encounter both in and outside of school and share them with the class.

Caveats

Make sure students understand that limitations are an inherent characteristic of representations. It is not always possible to represent all features accurately (e.g., simultaneously representing scale size and distance in the universe in a textbook diagram). However, when there are limitations such as scale, they should be noted in the captioning.

Use With Other Disciplines

This FACT is specific to scientific representations.

My Notes

_____

_____

_____

#52: RERUN

Description

RERUN is an acronym that stands for **R**ecall, **E**xplain, **R**esults, **U**ncertainties, and **N**ew learnings. Students are asked to write one or two sentences for each letter of the acronym, related to a laboratory experience or other type of inquiry-based investigation.

How This FACT Promotes Student Learning

RERUN is used to help students reflect on their laboratory experiences or other inquiry-based activities. It provides a structured opportunity for students to reflect on what they did, how they did it, and what they learned from it.

How This FACT Informs Instruction

This FACT provides an opportunity for the teacher to examine, from the students' perspective, learnings gained from a laboratory or other inquiry experience. *RERUN* helps the teacher determine how well the learning goals that were targeted for the investigation matched what students gained from it. Results can be used to modify labs and inquiry-based activities to make the learning goals of the lab more explicit and achievable. The teacher can also use the students' comments to provide constructive feedback to the student on his or her laboratory experience for the purpose of helping that student improve subsequent laboratory experiences.

Design and Administration

Post a *RERUN* chart in the classroom. Figure 4.36 shows an example of a *RERUN* wall chart that can be used in a middle or high school science laboratory or classroom. Provide time after an investigation for students to complete the *RERUN* while the experience is still fresh in their minds. *RERUN* can be assigned individually or completed collaboratively by lab groups. Teachers may choose to have students share their reflections with others using *PVF* or other FACTs that encourage shared reflection.

General Implementation Attributes

Ease of Use: Medium   Time Demand: Medium
Cognitive Demand: Medium/High

Figure 4.36 *RERUN* Chart

Recall: Summarize what you did in the Lab.

Explain: Explain the purpose of the Lab.

Results: Describe the results of the Lab and what they mean.

Uncertainties: Describe what you are still unsure about.

New: Write at least two new things that you learned from this Lab.

Modifications

Teachers can choose to focus on just one part of the *RERUN* chart for reflection after each lab or investigation. "**New**" can be modified to ask for a new question that resulted from the investigation.

Caveats

RERUN should be used for formative purposes. Avoid using it in place of a formal lab report and assigning a grade to it.

Use With Other Disciplines

This FACT is specific to inquiry-based science.

My Notes

#53: SCIENTISTS' IDEAS COMPARISON

Description

With *Scientists' Ideas Comparison*, students are given a summary sheet of scientists' ideas, including appropriate terminology, related to a topic they have been studying. Students compare their existing ideas to the scientists', looking for differences and similarities.

How This FACT Promotes Student Learning

Scientists' Ideas Comparison is used to help students make connections between the ideas they developed through a sequence of instruction and the formal, accepted scientific ideas. It provides a metacognitive opportunity for students to examine their thinking to see how close their ideas match the scientific ideas.

How This FACT Informs Instruction

This FACT is best used during the sense-making phase of instruction. It can also be used as a reflection and self-assessment activity. The students or teacher records the consensus ideas students have developed through a series of lessons or during an elicitation probe. Students are then asked to compare their ideas with a summary of the scientists' ideas. Figure 4.37 shows an example of a comparison between sixth graders' ideas about objects that reflect light and how a scientist would describe those ideas to a sixth grader. The teacher orchestrates class discussion of the similarities and differences, noting where there is discord or agreement. If there is a wide gap between the students' ideas and the scientists' ideas, this is a signal to the teacher that additional instructional opportunities are necessary to develop conceptual understanding. When combined with other FACTs, *Scientists' Ideas Comparison* provides an opportunity for the teacher to assess how far students have moved toward the scientific view compared to where they were when they started the unit of instruction. The extent of movement toward the scientific idea is an indicator of the effectiveness of instruction and readiness of the students to move on to the next phase in learning.

Design and Administration

Prepare a summary list or paragraph of scientists' ideas. The scientists' ideas are a formal, scientific explanation of the concept or phenomenon written at a level students can understand at their grade level. Ask students to list their ideas about the concept or phenomenon before giving them the scientists' ideas. Encourage students to list ideas that were developed during their discussions or class activities, citing where their ideas came from, or discuss their ideas in response to an assessment probe, such as the ones described in the Appendix. Alternatively, keep a record of the class ideas noted throughout the instructional sequence, including class discussions, and provide students with this list. Use a valid reference source, teacher background information from instructional materials, and explanations from the teacher notes in the assessment probes described in the Appendix, or consult with a scientist or science-content specialist to develop the scientists' ideas. Provide students with the scientists' ideas. Have students discuss in pairs or small groups how close they think their

Figure 4.37   Example of Sixth-Grade *Scientists' Ideas Comparison*

Our Ideas About Objects That Reflect Light	Scientists' Ideas About Objects That Reflect Light
• They have to be smooth. • They have to be shiny. • Light has to bounce off the object. • Not everything reflects light. • White objects reflect all colors. • Light reflects in a straight line but does not go around corners. • A new shiny penny reflects light, but a dull one does not. • Mirrors are good reflectors. • Rocks and soil do not reflect light because of their color and roughness.	• All visible objects reflect some light. • Something is seen when light emitted from or reflected off an object enters the eye. • Most materials will absorb some wavelengths of light and reflect the rest, which explains why we see different colors. • When we see white, all colors have been reflected. • Some materials reflect light better than others. • Ordinary mirrors and light, shiny, smooth objects reflect light to the observer because the light bounces off the surface at a definite angle. • When light hits rough surfaces, it is scattered and bounces back in many different directions. This scattering makes some objects appear dull.

own ideas are to the scientists' ideas. Engage students in a discussion about what they think it would take to help them move more toward the scientists' ideas. Use the feedback to design targeted learning opportunities that will move students closer to the scientific view or would improve opportunities to learn the next time the same lessons are used.

General Implementation Attributes

Ease of Use: Medium   Time Demand: Medium
Cognitive Demand: Medium/High

Modifications

Instead of a comprehensive list, use only one or two ideas with younger students. A Venn diagram, with two overlapping circles—"Our Ideas" and "Scientists' Ideas"—can be used as a graphic organizer to compare students' ideas with scientists' ideas. In the intersection of the two circles, students record ideas they had that were similar to the scientists' ideas. In the Scientists' Ideas circle, they record ideas that they did not consider that were the ideas of the scientists. In the Our Ideas circle, they record ideas they had that were not listed in the scientists' ideas. Or provide students with a three- or four-column chart. The first column lists the ideas students have that they are willing to give up, based on the scientists' ideas. The second column lists ideas they have that they are still not sure about. The third column lists ideas they had in common with the scientists. And the fourth column lists new ideas or more fully developed ones they gained from the scientists that they did not consider before.

Caveats

Make sure the terminology and descriptions of the scientific ideas are not too technical for the grade level in which you use this FACT. If a scientist helps develop the list of scientists' ideas, you may need to serve as a translator to make sure it is developmentally appropriate.

Use With Other Disciplines

This FACT is specific to science.

My Notes

_____

_____

_____

#54: SEQUENCING

Description

Sequencing is used to examine students' ideas about the sequence of events or stages that happen during a natural occurrence or investigation. This FACT involves taking a set of statements, pictures, ideas, or a combination of all three and arranging them in a logical order (Naylor et al., 2004).

How This FACT Promotes Student Learning

The act of thinking about and describing the order of stages or events activates student thinking. *Sequencing* can also be used as an elicitation to help students make predictions about what they think will happen during a scientific investigation or event. The FACT provides a focal point for students to discuss what they anticipate they will observe or learn when they begin an activity, research into a topic, or engage in an investigation. Revisiting the sequences produced at the beginning of a sequence of instruction after students have had an opportunity to investigate their ideas can help students reflect on their learning experience.

How This FACT Informs Instruction

Sequencing allows the teacher to examine how students string together a natural or laboratory-initiated sequence and whether the student views stages or events as discrete, disconnected occurrences. The information can be used to provide real or vicarious experiences that will help students improve their understanding of a sequence of scientific events or processes. When used collaboratively, this FACT encourages students to talk about each of the ideas, words, or statements on the sequence cards. Teachers can carefully listen for any misconceptions, uncertainties, and prior experiences that surface. The information is used by the teacher to plan for instruction or modify lessons to target students thinking about the sequence of events.

Design and Administration

Select a sequence that aligns with a targeted idea to be developed through a series of lessons or investigations. Place statements, words, or pictures on cards that represent the sequence of changes, stages, or events that occur during a natural process or laboratory activity. The cards allow students to arrange their ideas as they think through the sequence. Provide an opportunity for students to justify why they placed their cards in a particular sequence. When a group of students reaches consensus on their sequence, have them glue the cards down or sketch their sequence. These can then be revisited and revised after students have had an opportunity to experience or learn about the stages, processes, or events. Some examples that can be used for sequencing include life cycles of different types of organisms, a type of physical or chemical change, decomposition of an object in the environment, cell division, weathering and erosion, astronomical events such as phases of the moon or day/night cycle, life processes such as what happens to food after it is eaten, changes in states of matter, life cycle of a star, the water cycle, ecological succession of a forest, and energy transformations.

General Implementation Attributes

Ease of Use: Medium   Time Demand: Medium
Cognitive Demand: Medium/High

Modifications

Use pictures with younger children and limit the number of cards to no more than four or five. Leave out a stage or step in the sequence and insert a blank card. Have students come up with the missing stage or step and write or draw it on the card.

Caveats

Don't use sequences for events, processes, or abstract changes about which students may not have any prior knowledge or experience. Make sure students are familiar with the pictures or words on the cards. The number of steps or stages in the sequence should depend on the topic and the developmental level of the students.

Use With Other Disciplines

This FACT can also be used in social studies, language arts, health, and performing arts.

My Notes

_____

_____

_____

#55: STICKY BARS

Description

Sticky Bars help students recognize that there is often a range of ideas students in the class have about a scientific topic. Students are presented with a short answer or multiple-choice question. The answer is anonymously recorded on a Post-it note and passed in to the teacher. The teacher or a student arranges the notes on the wall or whiteboard, as a bar graph, representing the different student responses.

How This FACT Promotes Student Learning

Sticky Bars makes students' ideas public. It shows that the ideas students hold in the class vary. It helps students understand and accept that ideas may differ and that science learning involves the process of working together to develop a common understanding.

How This FACT Informs Instruction

Sticky Bars can be used as an elicitation to publicly share students' ideas before instruction. The data can be revisited at any time during instruction to identify the extent to which students have changed their original ideas as a result of their learning experiences and interactions in group science talk. *Sticky Bars* provide a quick way to identify the range of ideas held by the class, including the percentage of students who may hold misconceptions. The teacher can use this information to plan targeted learning experiences.

Design and Administration

Develop a short-answer or multiple-choice question that elicits students' thinking beyond factual recall. *Familiar Phenomenon Probes, Friendly Talk Probes,* and *P-E-O Probes* developed by the teacher or obtained through source material described in the Appendix can be used for this FACT. Remind students to record their own answer, regardless of whether they think it might be right or wrong. Keep the Post-it notes anonymous. Collect and quickly sort them into like responses (use a student assistant if needed). Create a bar graph by placing each similar response atop the other. Figure 4.38 shows what a *Sticky Bar* wall graph looks like. Provide time for students to discuss the data and what they think the class needs to do in order to come to a common understanding.

General Implementation Attributes

Ease of Use: High   Time Demand: Low
Cognitive Demand: Depends on the question used

Modifications

For teachers with more than one class, consider using a different color for each class and making a combined histogram of responses from all classes. Compare differences or similarities across classes. A high-tech version of *Sticky Bars* involves the use of personal response systems (prs) commonly referred to as "clickers."

Caveats

Avoid questions that produce data that are difficult or time-consuming to categorize, such as answers that involve long descriptions or sentences. *Sticky Bars* work best with data from multiple-choice or one-word responses that can easily be categorized.

Use With Other Disciplines

This FACT can also be used in mathematics, social studies, language arts, health, foreign languages, and performing arts.

Figure 4.38   *Sticky Bars*

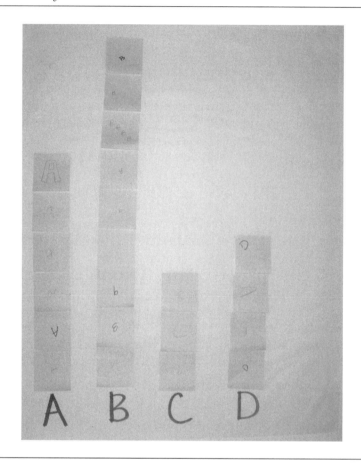

My Notes

_____

_____

_____

#56: STIP—SCIENTIFIC TERMINOLOGY INVENTORY PROBE

Description

*STIP*s are short, simple questionnaires that ascertain students' familiarity with a scientific term. Students select a response based on their level of familiarity. If students claim to be familiar with the term, they are asked to provide a description to reveal the extent to which they connect conceptual understanding to terminology.

How This FACT Promotes Student Learning

This FACT provides a metacognitive opportunity for students to determine how familiar they are with the scientific terminology used in an instructional unit. Students may recall a scientific term but have minimal conceptual understanding as to what it means. Conversely, some students may realize they not only recall a term from prior experiences but understand it well enough to explain it to another student.

How This FACT Informs Instruction

*STIP*s are used at the beginning of a sequence of lessons to determine how familiar students are with the scientific terminology they will encounter in the topic they will study. The results are used to consider ways to effectively introduce terminology into an instructional unit so that students can hang conceptual meaning onto a scientific term.

Design and Administration

Select no more than 12 words from the key scientific terminology that students will learn and use during the topic of instruction or encounter in their instructional materials. Figure 4.39 shows an example of a *STIP* for a ninth-grade earth science unit on plate tectonics. Leave plenty of space for students who know the term to be able to describe it, using formal or operational definitions, descriptions, or examples. Collect and save student responses if you are planning to administer the *STIP* again as a postassessment, providing an opportunity for students to reflect on their pre- and postfamiliarity with scientific terminology and conceptual understanding of the words used during the unit of instruction.

General Implementation Attributes

Ease of Use: Medium   Time Demand: Medium
Cognitive Demand: Low/Medium

Modifications

For the third selected response (I have some idea what it means), consider leaving a blank space to have students describe their preconceived ideas about the term. With younger students, consider using only a few key scientific terms, providing an opportunity for them to explain their understanding of the word orally or in drawings.

Figure 4.39   *STIP* for a Ninth-Grade Earth Science Unit

Plate Tectonics	Continental Drift	Pangaea
☐ I have never heard of this. ☐ I have heard of this but I'm not sure what it means. ☐ I have some idea what it means. ☐ I clearly know what it means and can describe it:	☐ I have never heard of this. ☐ I have heard of this but I'm not sure what it means. ☐ I have some idea what it means. ☐ I clearly know what it means and can describe it:	☐ I have never heard of this. ☐ I have heard of this but I'm not sure what it means. ☐ I have some idea what it means. ☐ I clearly know what it means and can describe it:
Lithosphere	**Mantle**	**Faults**
☐ I have never heard of this. ☐ I have heard of this but I'm not sure what it means. ☐ I have some idea what it means. ☐ I clearly know what it means and can describe it:	☐ I have never heard of this. ☐ I have heard of this but I'm not sure what it means. ☐ I have some idea what it means. ☐ I clearly know what it means and can describe it:	☐ I have never heard of this. ☐ I have heard of this but I'm not sure what it means. ☐ I have some idea what it means. ☐ I clearly know what it means and can describe it:
Oceanic Ridge	**Rift Valley**	**Density**
☐ I have never heard of this. ☐ I have heard of this but I'm not sure what it means. ☐ I have some idea what it means. ☐ I clearly know what it means and can describe it:	☐ I have never heard of this. ☐ I have heard of this but I'm not sure what it means. ☐ I have some idea what it means. ☐ I clearly know what it means and can describe it:	☐ I have never heard of this. ☐ I have heard of this but I'm not sure what it means. ☐ I have some idea what it means. ☐ I clearly know what it means and can describe it:

Caveats

Be aware that students can memorize definitions without conceptual understanding. *STIPs* are used to gauge familiarity with terminology, not assess for deep conceptual understanding.

Use With Other Disciplines

This FACT can also be used with other types of terminology encountered in mathematics, social studies, language arts, health, foreign languages, and performing arts.

My Notes

_____

_____

_____

#57: STUDENT EVALUATION OF LEARNING GAINS

Description

The *Student Evaluation of Learning Gains* is a teacher-designed instrument used to gather feedback on students' perceptions of how well a unit of instruction helped them learn. It consists of statements, on a three-to-five point scale, about the "degree of gain" in areas such as skills, content knowledge, attitudes, and dispositions toward science.

How This FACT Promotes Student Learning

Use of a student evaluation instrument provides an opportunity for students to reflect upon their own learning processes and to become aware of what they think enables or impedes their learning. It provides an opportunity for students to self-assess the extent to which they feel they gained new knowledge, skills, attitudes, or dispositions. It increases engagement in learning and student motivation when students see that their teacher takes the feedback seriously to improve their teaching for the benefit of their students.

How This FACT Informs Instruction

A formal student evaluation instrument of a unit of instruction can spotlight teaching strategies and components of an instructional unit that are seen by students as best supporting student learning and those that need improvement. The FACT provides an opportunity for teachers to analyze their instruction through the eyes of their students. The feedback allows teachers to effectively adjust their teaching strategies and activities to better meet student learning needs.

Design and Administration

Translate your instructional unit into evaluation statements that reflect the content, instructional strategies, and activities that occurred during the sequence of instruction. Use the example in Figure 4.40 as a guide. For middle and high school students, see the Appendix for a link to a Web site that will help you create a survey students can complete online or use Web-based survey software that your school may have available and post the survey online for students. For each item, keep in mind that you are trying to get feedback on students' personal learning gains for each component of the instructional unit that you deem important. Check the questions to ensure that they are clear, unambiguous, and do not ask about more than one thing. Explain to students how to fill out the form and when it is due. You might consider giving it as a homework assignment in order to provide enough time for students to thoughtfully complete it online or as a paper-and-pencil survey. Emphasize the importance and usefulness of the feedback the students provide for you and the seriousness with which their responses and comments are taken. After responses are analyzed, consider sharing with students what you learned from their comments and how they will be used with them as well as with future classes.

General Implementation Attributes

Ease of Use: Medium   Time Demand: Medium
Cognitive Demand: Medium

Modifications

The evaluation form may also be used partway through a unit of instruction to make midcourse corrections to the instructional methods or activities used. You may consider other data to be correlated with learning gains, such as gender, grade (for example, multigrade classes in high school), class (if not self-contained), and so on.

Caveats

To ensure meaningful results, student responses should be anonymous. Beware of changing the emphasis of the instrument on student "gains" to other purposes such as asking students what they "liked" about the unit. The purpose of this FACT should stay focused on student achievement by emphasizing what students perceive as a gain in their learning.

Use With Other Disciplines

This FACT can also be used in mathematics, social studies, language arts, health, foreign languages, and performing arts.

My Notes

_____

_____

_____

Figure 4.40 *Student Evaluation of Learning Gains* for a Fourth-Grade Unit on Force and Motion

Check off how well each of the following helped you learn during the Force and Motion unit.	Not at all	Only a little bit	Fairly useful	It helped me a lot!
1. The balls and ramps activities				
2. The playground investigation				
3. The marbles activity				
4. Working in pairs				
5. Working in small groups				
6. The class discussions				
7. Working on my project				
8. The class project presentations				
9. The Word Wall				
10. Asking questions in class				
11. Listening to others ask questions				
12. The homework assignments				
13. The computer game				
14. The visit from the engineer				
15. Reading sections from the trade books				
16. The *Sheep in a Jeep* story				
17. The Commit and Toss activity and discussion				
18. Comparing my ideas to the scientist's ideas				

Please share any ideas you have that could help me improve this unit:

#58: SYNECTICS

Description

The word *Synectics* is derived from a Greek term meaning the fitting together of different and apparently irrelevant elements. This FACT uses analogies or metaphors to connect students' ideas with a concept.

How This FACT Promotes Student Learning

Synectics provides a metacognitive opportunity for students to examine abstractly what they know about a concept. It can be used to jump-start their learning and engage students in a creative way to link prior knowledge to new information. Exchanging *Synectics* examples with their peers helps students make new connections, solidify understandings, and improve retention of information.

How This FACT Informs Instruction

Analogies are a type of conceptual model (AAAS, 1988) that can give teachers a glimpse into student thinking. The use of analogies and metaphors in *Synectics* provides an opportunity for the teacher to examine the connections students bring to their learning. It surfaces difficulties students have in thinking about a concept as well as misconceptions and inaccuracies in their content knowledge. It also reveals the depth of thinking students have about an abstract concept. The information is used to modify teaching or plan for additional opportunities to develop conceptual understanding.

Design and Administration

Students are provided with a chart containing four to six boxes. They are given a category, seemingly unrelated to the identified concept, and asked to fill in the four squares with an item from that category. For example, if the category is "things at a fast-food restaurant," students might record *french fries, burgers, drive-thru window,* and *milk shakes.* The students are then given a scientific concept to relate each of the items to using the following completion sentence: A _____ is like a _____ because _____. For example, if the concept given was "chemical reaction," a student might say, "A chemical reaction is like a milk shake because different ingredients are put together and then combined to make something different." After students have filled in their *Synectics* chart, have pairs of students share their analogies or metaphors with each other and then with the class. The teacher and/or class can provide feedback on the aptness of the analogies or metaphors to further guide students' learning. For example, feedback on the milk shake analogy might include mention that the individual ingredients in the milk shake are not combined chemically; they still retain their own character and can be physically separated.

General Implementation Attributes

Ease of Use: High   Time Demand: Low/Medium
Cognitive Demand: Medium

Modifications

Instead of having students list the items, consider choosing unrelated items that would lend themselves to the concept being described. For example, Figure 4.41 shows a four-box *Synectics* developed by the teacher to create metaphors on cell structure and function. *Synectics* can be assigned as a brainstorming activity in small groups, with the students filling in as many completions as they can in an allotted time (Lipton & Wellman, 1998). Each group then chooses the example to share with the class. For younger students, consider using *Visual Synectics*. Give students a set of picture cards and ask them how a _____ is like the picture on the card.

Caveats

Analogies are a type of model. Recognizing when an analogy is not apt is a critical skill in critiquing the usefulness of models (AAAS, 1993). Make sure that students understand the usefulness of analogies and metaphors but recognize that the similarity between a concept and the analogy or metaphor is not always completely accurate.

Figure 4.41   Four-Square *Synectics* for Cell Structure and Function

A cell is like a(n) _____ because _____

shopping mall	a bowl of Jell-O
iPod	brick wall

Use With Other Disciplines

This FACT can also be used in mathematics, social studies, language arts, health, foreign languages, and performing arts.

My Notes

_____

_____

_____

#59: TEN-TWO

Description

Ten-Two is a reflection strategy originally developed by Dr. Mary Budd Rowe. After 10 minutes of instruction that involves a large amount of information, students take two minutes to reflect on and summarize what they have learned thus far.

How This FACT Promotes Student Learning

Ten-Two provides a metacognitive opportunity for students to frequently summarize and reflect on their learning, particularly when large amounts of information, difficult and abstract ideas, or new information is presented either by the teacher or through guest lecture, video, audio, or other media.

How This FACT Informs Instruction

Ten-Two is primarily used as a metacognitive instructional technique. Linking it to formative assessment for the purpose of informing instruction, the teacher asks if the students are ready to move on after they have had an opportunity to summarize; or, when the teacher circulates around the room and examines students' summary notes or discussions with a partner, it may reveal that students are struggling with the information and are not ready to proceed further without help from the teacher. Student feedback on use of this strategy may reinforce the critical need to build in short periods of reflection time throughout any lesson.

Design and Administration

Explain the purpose of the *Ten-Two* to the students. After 10 minutes of instruction, give students two minutes of time to quietly think, summarize, look at their notes, jot down key points or learnings, or discuss what they have learned so far with a partner. Combine this FACT with *Fist to Five* to determine whether students feel they are ready to proceed or need time to discuss their ideas with the class. Resume instruction and repeat again after 10 minutes if needed. Debrief the usefulness of this FACT with students the first time it is used to get their feedback on whether it was helpful to them.

General Implementation Attributes

Ease of Use: High   Time Demand: Low
Cognitive Demand: Medium/High

Modifications

Use any time interval: 5–1, 7–2, 10–3, 15–5, and so on.

Caveats

Break for summarizing only when the flow of the lesson is not compromised. Breaking at 10-minute intervals without considering how the concepts are unfolding may contribute to incoherency. It is also important to recognize the difference between recall and conceptual understanding. Often the latter takes much longer to develop, although recall can provide a starting point to build off of with students' own ideas.

Use With Other Disciplines

This FACT can also be used in mathematics, social studies, language arts, health, foreign languages, and performing arts.

My Notes

_____

_____

_____

#60: THINKING LOG

Description

Thinking Logs are a type of writing journal used during inquiry-based science and conceptual-change instruction in which students react to a series of sentence stems as thinking starters. The purpose is to prompt metacognition during students' investigative and concept development learning experiences (Flick & Tomlinson, 2006).

How This FACT Promotes Student Learning

Thinking Logs promote metacognition and help students see how their prior knowledge, readings, and classroom experiences relate to their science investigations and the development of concept knowledge. Using this FACT helps students become more aware of their own learning and what they can do to self-direct it.

How This FACT Informs Instruction

Thinking Logs help the teacher identify areas where the students are aware of their own learning successes or challenges. The information can be used to provide interventions for individual or groups of students as well as match students with peers who may provide learning support. *Thinking Logs* may also indicate instances where the class as a whole is having difficulty with an investigation or other type of learning experience. It then serves as a signal to the teacher to modify or redirect the experience to meet the learning needs of the class.

Design and Administration

Thinking Logs can be constructed for an individual unit of instruction from five to six sheets of paper folded and center stapled. Students personalize the cover of their *Thinking Log.* Inside the cover of the *Thinking Log,* print, paste, or attach a sticker with the thinking stems you would like students to use. Examples of thinking stems are shown in Figure 4.42.

Composition or spiral notebooks can also be used for *Thinking Logs* that are used throughout the year, rather than for individual units. Use impromptu moments during a learning experience or at the end of a lesson for students to record in their *Thinking Logs.* Students choose the thinking stem that would best describe their thinking at that moment. Provide a few minutes for students to write down their thoughts using the stem. If the purpose of using the *Thinking Log* is to promote student metacognition, there is no need to collect the logs. However, there are times when it is helpful to collect the logs and analyze them to gather information to inform instruction.

General Implementation Attributes

Ease of Use: Medium   Time Demand: Low
Cognitive Demand: Medium

Figure 4.42 *Thinking Log* Stems

I was successful in . . .

I got stuck . . .

I figured out . . .

I got confused when . . . so I . . .

I didn't expect . . .

I think I need to redo . . .

I need to rethink . . .

I first thought . . . but now I realize . . .

I'm not sure . . .

What puzzled me the most was . . .

I was really surprised when . . .

I will understand this better if I . . .

I stopped . . . because . . .

I think tomorrow I would like to try . . .

The hardest part of this was . . .

I figured it out because . . .

Right now I am thinking about . . .

I wish I could . . .

I really feel good about the way . . .

Modifications

As students become used to using the *Thinking Logs*, ask them to generate additional prompts to add to the list of thinking stems. With younger students, it may be helpful to begin by choosing a common thinking stem that everyone responds to, giving examples of how to fill in the stem the first time it is used. *Thinking Logs* can also be incorporated into the Scientists' Notebook strategy used by elementary teachers to combine science and language literacy (Campbell & Fulton, 2003; Rupp, 2007).

Caveats

If *Thinking Logs* are collected by the teacher for analysis, be sure to let students know that the reason you are reading their responses is to help you adjust instruction to meet their needs. Otherwise, students may feel their entries are being read to pass judgment on their abilities or performance, which might change the reflective nature of their entries.

Use With Other Disciplines

This FACT can also be used in mathematics, social studies, language arts, health, foreign languages, and performing arts.

My Notes

_____

_____

_____

#61: THINK-PAIR-SHARE

Description

Think-Pair-Share combines thinking with communication. The teacher poses a question and gives individual students time to think about the question. Students then pair up with a partner to discuss their ideas. After pairs discuss, students share their ideas in a small-group or whole-class discussion.

How This FACT Promotes Student Learning

Think-Pair-Share begins by providing students with an opportunity to activate their own thinking. The pairing strategy allows students to share their ideas and modify them or construct new knowledge as a result of interaction with their peers. When students are asked to share ideas with a larger group, they are more willing to respond after they have had a chance to discuss their ideas with another student. As a result, the quality of their responses improves. This FACT also contributes to students' oral communication skills as they discuss their ideas with one another. *Think-Pair-Share* can also be used as an end-of-unit reflection by asking students to think about and discuss their response to a reflective prompt given by the teacher.

How This FACT Informs Instruction

As students share ideas from their paired discussions, the teacher notes inaccurate ideas or flaws in reasoning that may need to be addressed in targeted instruction. The "share" part of this FACT provides an opportunity for the teacher to probe deeper after students have had an opportunity to surface their ideas with a partner. The whole-class discussion also provides an opportunity for the teacher and class to give feedback on students' ideas. When used as an end-of-unit reflection, the teacher can glean useful information about what students felt was most effective for their learning and use that information the next time the unit is taught or in subsequent units that employ or can employ similar strategies and approaches.

Design and Administration

This FACT can be used during any stage of instruction. It begins by posing an open-ended question and giving students "think time" to activate their own ideas. It can also be administered as a *Think-Ink-Pair-Share* where students are asked to write down their ideas before sharing with a partner. Following "think time," students pair up with a learning partner to share, discuss, clarify, and challenge each others' ideas. The pair then share their thinking with a larger group.

General Implementation Attributes

Ease of Use: High   Time Demand: Low
Cognitive Demand: Medium

Modifications

The "share" part of this FACT can be used with *Partner Speaks*. Not limited to pairs, it can also be used in a triad. The FACT can be modified as a *Think-Pair-Do-Share* in an inquiry-based context. Students think about their own predictions in regard to an investigation, pair up to share their reasons for their prediction, perform the investigation or research, and then share their findings with a larger group, including how their results or findings matched their original prediction.

Caveats

Use different pairing strategies to ensure students have the opportunity to form pairs with students other than the ones who sit next to them in order to avoid having students always interact with the same group of peers.

Use With Other Disciplines

This FACT can also be used in mathematics, social studies, language arts, health, foreign languages, and performing arts.

My Notes

_____

_____

_____

#62: THOUGHT EXPERIMENTS

Description

A *Thought Experiment* involves a prediction about what would happen in a situation that could not be easily carried out as a real-life experiment. Students provide an explanation to support their prediction. For example, asking students to predict how a ball would fall if it were possible to drop a heat-resistant ball through a hole drilled all the way through the Earth, starting and ending on opposite sides of the world, would be considered a *Thought Experiment*. It probes for students' ideas related to gravity and motion. It would be impossible to carry out in a classroom or other real setting, but it is useful for stimulating deep thinking that draws upon students' ideas.

How This FACT Promotes Student Learning

Thought Experiments provide an engaging way for students to activate their thinking and apply their ideas in a novel situation. It generates interest in wanting to learn more about the question posed in order to see if their prediction and explanation are scientifically plausible. As a group activity, *Thought Experiments* promote interesting debate and scientific argument. They can also spark inquiry and connections to other ideas as students think about ways they can test predictions in related contexts or with models.

How This FACT Informs Instruction

Students' predictions and explanations about the *Thought Experiment* provide access to students' thinking. This is particularly helpful in abstract situations where it is not possible to design a hands-on investigation. As students explain their ideas and provide reasons for their prediction, the teacher gains information about student thinking that can be used to design and monitor subsequent learning experiences or provide an opportunity to transfer conceptual understanding to a novel context.

Design and Administration

Thought Experiments can be designed to address students' commonly held ideas. They can be presented through stories, pictures, text, discussion, or any combination of these. They can be used as an individual or group activity. Present students with the *Thought Experiment* and provide time for them to discuss their ideas. Students should be encouraged to draw diagrams to support their ideas. Predicted results of the *Thought Experiment* are used to engage the class in scientific argumentation. Provide time for a scientific discussion of how the students' ideas compare to the way a scientist might explain the hypothetical results.

General Implementation Attributes

Ease of Use: Medium   Time Demand: Medium
Cognitive Demand: High

Modifications

Have students come up with ideas for *Thought Experiments.* Use situations that are less abstract for younger students.

Caveats

Thought Experiments often use hypothetical situations that may not be realistic or involve multiple variables. For example, the ball dropped through the center of Earth would encounter intense heat that would cause it to burn up. In this situation, you would ask students to imagine that the ball does not burn up or melt. Be sure students understand the imaginary nature of the context in order not to convey misconceptions by the context used.

Use With Other Disciplines

This FACT can also be used in mathematics and social studies.

My Notes

_____

_____

_____

#63: THREE-MINUTE PAUSE

Description

The *Three-Minute Pause* provides a break during a block of instruction in order to provide time for students to summarize, clarify, and reflect on their understanding through discussion with a partner or small group. A *Three-Minute Pause* is especially helpful when large amounts of information need to be processed for understanding. Three-minute egg timers are used to keep track of the time. All students end their discussion at the same time, bringing their attention back to the teacher to facilitate the next steps in learning.

How This FACT Promotes Student Learning

This FACT provides a short, metacognitive break during a hands-on activity, video, lecture, reading assignment, and so forth so students can think about what they are doing and learning before going on to the next step or chunk of information. By breaking up an information-heavy lesson or complex activity, students are better able to process and retain the important conceptual understandings from the learning experience. The discussion that occurs between pairs or triads provides an opportunity for students to help resolve difficulties they may be experiencing in understanding the concept, skill, or procedure targeted in the lesson.

How This FACT Informs Instruction

Since this FACT requires students to track their understanding and work together to clarify any difficulties they are having at a given point in time, it allows the teacher to move ahead with instruction without interrupting the flow of a lesson with numerous questions. The responsibility for making sense of the lesson is initially put on the students. The final three-minute pause provides an opportunity for students to list any lingering questions or concepts and ideas they are having difficulty understanding that were not resolved in their peer discussions. This information can then be used by the teacher to clarify parts of the lesson or to design additional experiences to support student understanding.

Design and Administration

Decide when it is a good time to logically break during a lesson or activity. Provide pairs or triads of students with three-minute sand egg timers (these can be purchased inexpensively at a kitchen supply store) or use another timing device. Everyone starts their timers at the same time on cue. Groups discuss the ideas from the lesson or activity for three minutes, helping each other process their thoughts and clarify misunderstandings. When three minutes are up, students stop talking and direct their attention once again to the teacher, video, lesson, or reading they are engaged in, and the lesson resumes seamlessly. It is remarkable how much students can say in three minutes! Anything left unresolved is recorded after the time runs out and saved for the final three-minute pause at the end. The teacher continues with the lesson rather than interrupting the flow with questions. At the end of the lesson, students have three minutes to discuss and resolve any lingering questions. Unresolved questions are then shared with the teacher or the whole class for clarification. The teacher may also choose to collect written lingering questions to address at the beginning of the next lesson.

General Implementation Attributes

Ease of Use: High   Time Demand: Low
Cognitive Demand: Medium

Modifications

For difficult topics, it may be necessary to extend the time for discussion or take time to clarify before resuming.

Caveats

Use this strategy only when there is a need to process large amounts of information; otherwise, it becomes a trivial exercise that can interrupt the flow of learning.

Use With Other Disciplines

This FACT can also be used in mathematics, social studies, language arts, health, foreign languages, and performing arts.

My Notes

_____

_____

_____

#64: THREE-TWO-ONE

Description

Three-Two-One provides a structured way for students to reflect on their learning. Students respond in writing to three reflective prompts; providing six responses (three of the first, two of the second, and one final reflection) that describe what they learned from a lesson or instructional sequence.

How This FACT Promotes Learning

Three-Two-One is a technique that scaffolds students' reflections. The scaffold activates thinking about key learnings (Lipton and Wellman, 1998). This FACT provides students with an opportunity to share their success in learning difficult or new concepts as well as recognize what was challenging for them.

How This FACT Informs Instruction

Three-Two-One provides rich information to the teacher about what students perceive as the key learnings from a lesson or sequence of lessons. The information can be analyzed to see how well the goals of a lesson were met. The FACT also provides information to the teacher about what students are still struggling with so that further instructional opportunities can be provided that target students' learning needs.

Design and Administration

This strategy is best used with difficult concepts or during an instructional sequence when students have learned something new. Figure 4.43 shows an example of a *Three-Two-One* reflection sheet. Provide students with a copy of the reflection sheet and time to complete their reflection. Students can also be paired up to share their *Three-Two-One* reflections with their peers.

General Implementation Attributes

Ease of Use: High   Time Demand: Low
Cognitive Demand: Medium

Modifications

Three-Two-One can also be used when students are learning new inquiry skills or processes. For example, the following can be used with elementary students who are learning how to design their own investigations: **three** ways I can investigate like a scientist, **two** things that I would like to do better when I investigate, and **one** thing I would like help with. If more information is desired for a particular instructional situation, consider a *Five-Three-One*.

Figure 4.43   Example of a *Three-Two-One* Reflection Sheet

Three key ideas I will remember

Two things I am still struggling with

One thing that will help me tomorrow

Caveats

Vary this strategy with other FACTs that encourage reflection and change the prompts periodically or students may quickly tire of this technique.

Use With Other Disciplines

This FACT can also be used in mathematics, social studies, language arts, health, foreign languages, and performing arts.

My Notes

_____

_____

_____

#65: TRAFFIC LIGHT CARDS

Description

Traffic Light Cards are a variation on the popular "traffic lighting" strategy used in the United Kingdom (Black et al., 2003). The traffic light icons—red-, yellow-, and green-colored "lights"—are used to represent levels of student understanding. Students are given three different-colored cards, asked to self-assess their understanding about a concept or skill they are learning, and hold up the card that best matches their understanding: green—"I understand this very well," yellow—"I understand most of it but could use a little help," and red—"Help. I don't get it."

How This FACT Promotes Student Learning

Traffic light icons promote metacognition and help students develop self-assessment skills (Black & Harrison, 2004). Students use the cards to indicate to the teacher when they need additional support for their learning.

How This FACT Informs Instruction

Traffic Light Cards are a monitoring strategy that can be used at any time during instruction to help the teacher gauge the extent of student understanding, which in turn informs the pace of instruction. The colors indicate whether students have full, partial, or minimal understanding. When students are asked to hold up the card that best represents where they are in their current understanding, the teacher can get a quick snapshot of the class as well as individual students' level of understanding. If the majority of students hold up red, this is a clear indication to the teacher that instruction needs to be modified in order to accommodate the needs of the class. Conversely, a majority of greens indicates that most of the class is ready to move on. A mixture of colors indicates the need to provide peer and teacher support before moving on. For example, the yellow card students can be matched up with green card students to help them address difficulties in their understanding. This frees up time for the teacher to work with the red card students who may have more serious learning difficulties.

Design and Administration

Cut red, yellow, and green squares out of card stock. Provide each student with a set to keep in their desk, the inside flap of their notebook, or other accessible area. When the teacher knows the traffic cards will be used in a lesson, students are asked to put them on their desk. When the teacher decides on the right moment to get feedback from students on their understanding, students are asked to hold up the card that represents how well they feel they understand what they have been doing or learning thus far. A traffic light graphic posted in the front of the room can be used to remind students what the colors represent. See the Appendix for a source that explains in detail the use of this strategy.

General Implementation Attributes

Ease of Use: High   Time Demand: Low
Cognitive Demand: Low

Modifications

Traffic Light Cards can also be used with assessment probes to indicate students' confidence level in their commitment to an idea. For example, a green card represents confidence, yellow represents some confidence, and red represents no confidence or a guess. Flip cards for readiness can also be made by gluing a red card to a green card. Students hold up the side that represents how ready they are to proceed with the lesson or next step in a procedure. The green side indicates readiness, and the red side indicates that students are not yet ready.

Caveats

Make sure the green card students who are matched up to help the yellow card students have an accurate grasp of the content or skill targeted by the lesson so that one student's misunderstandings will not be passed on to another. Choose students carefully for peer assistance and, if possible, eavesdrop on the discussions to determine how well students are able to assist others.

Use With Other Disciplines

This FACT can also be used in mathematics, social studies, language arts, health, foreign languages, and performing arts.

My Notes

_____

_____

_____

#66: TRAFFIC LIGHT CUPS

Description

Traffic Light Cups are used during group work and student investigations to signal to the teacher when groups need help or feedback. Red, yellow, and green stackable party cups placed in the center of a group's table or workstation represent whether the group is able to proceed without the need for teacher intervention or whether they need assistance.

How This FACT Promotes Student Learning

Traffic Light Cups promote self-assessment by increasing students' awareness of when they can proceed with a task without assistance or require help or feedback from the teacher.

How This FACT Informs Instruction

During hands-on activities, investigations, and other group activities, the teacher is constantly monitoring groups that need assistance. *Traffic Light Cups* provide a visual signal to the teacher as to when a group may need assistance. It allows the teacher to use time more efficiently to work with groups that have the greatest needs. *Traffic Light Cups* signal to the teacher when a group is proceeding successfully without the need for assistance (green), when a group might like feedback or assistance from the teacher in order to best continue with their work but are still able to proceed in the meantime (yellow), or when a group is stuck and can't go any further without assistance from the teacher (red).

Design and Administration

Obtain green, yellow, and red stackable party cups of the same size from a party store. Give each group a set of cups and ask them to stack them, one inside the other, with the green cup on the outside. The stack of cups is placed in the center of their work area where it can be seen by the teacher. All groups should start with green on the outside. As their needs for instructional support from the teacher increase, students change the outer color to yellow or red. As the teacher scans the room, students with red cups on the outside receive assistance first, followed by yellow cups.

General Implementation Attributes

Ease of Use: High   Time Demand: Low
Cognitive Demand: Low

Modifications

Traffic Light Cups can also be used for individual tasks. They can also be used to signal time on task. Green means the group feels they have plenty of time and will finish on schedule. Yellow signifies the group may need more time but, overall, are close to being on target to finish. Red signifies that they are behind and will need more time to finish.

Caveats

When this strategy is new, students need to be frequently reminded to change their outer cup when their learning needs change. The teacher should check in occasionally with the green cups to keep informed of the groups' progress.

Use With Other Disciplines

This FACT can also be used in mathematics, social studies, language arts, health, foreign languages, and performing arts.

My Notes

_____

_____

_____

#67: TRAFFIC LIGHT DOTS

Description

Traffic Light Dots are used by students to self-assess their work and get feedback from peers or the teacher. Small peel-off colored dots that come in sheets from office supply stores serve as traffic signal icons. Students place the dots in the margins of their work to indicate areas where they feel they successfully completed the task (green), areas where they aren't sure about their work and would like feedback (yellow), and areas where they feel they didn't understand or perform well on the task and need help (red).

How This FACT Promotes Student Learning

Traffic Light Dots provide a way for students to self-assess areas of their work and seek help in developing their understanding. When students exchange a traffic-light-dotted paper with another student, it encourages them to think further about the concepts or ideas in order to provide feedback to other students on their yellow or red areas.

How This FACT Informs Instruction

Student work submitted to the teacher for feedback that has been traffic-light-dotted saves considerable time on the part of the teacher by enabling the teacher to focus on the yellow areas for feedback and the red areas to provide interventions for students who are having difficulty understanding a concept or procedure. A quick scan of a collection of student work from the class that contains a majority of red dots signifies to the teacher that students may not have been ready for the assignment or task and require an adjustment in instruction to help students develop the understanding needed to complete the task. Conversely, papers that have a majority of green dots signify that students were generally able to use their understanding to complete the task. A mixture of dots may indicate the need to have students work in groups to help each other. For example, a student who put a green dot in an area of their work may help a student with yellow or red in the same area.

General Implementation Attributes

Ease of Use: High   Time Demand: Low
Cognitive Demand: Medium

Modifications

Students can also traffic-light-dot other students' papers as a form of peer assessment. Green means the work is acceptable, yellow is partially acceptable, and red means a need for major revision. If peel-and-stick dots are not available, students can create their own icons with red, yellow, and green markers, crayons, or colored pencils.

Caveats

Feedback on yellow dots should be given soon after students have submitted their work in order for the feedback to be useful. Avoid assigning grades to traffic-dotted papers in order to support the use of feedback. Studies have shown that students will pay more attention to feedback if it is not accompanied by a grade (Black et al., 2003).

Use With Other Disciplines

This FACT can also be used in mathematics, social studies, language arts, health, foreign languages, and performing arts.

My Notes

_____

_____

_____

#68: TWO-MINUTE PAPER

Description

The *Two-Minute Paper* is a quick and simple way to collect feedback from students about their learning at the end of an activity, field trip, lecture, video, or other type of learning experience. Students are given two minutes to respond to a predetermined prompt in writing.

How This FACT Promotes Student Learning

The *Two-Minute Paper* requires students to use more than recall in responding to questions about a learning experience. Students must first think about what they have been learning about and determine how well they feel they learned the concept or skill. The FACT also demonstrates to the students the teacher's respect for their feedback, particularly when they see how it is used to make their learning experiences more student centered.

How This FACT Informs Instruction

The *Two-Minute Paper* allows the teacher to collect feedback on student learning with minimal effort and time. Student responses are read, sorted, and analyzed in order to determine how to make adjustments to the lesson the next day.

Design and Administration

Provide a half sheet of paper to students during the last three to five minutes of a lesson. Write two questions on the board or on a chart that you want students to respond to. For example, use some variation of the following:

- What was the most important thing you learned today?
- What did you learn today that you didn't know before class?
- What important question remains unanswered for you?
- What would help you learn better tomorrow?

Give students two minutes to write and then collect their papers. After their responses have been analyzed, share the results with students the next day, letting them know how you are going to use the feedback they shared with you.

General Implementation Attributes

Ease of Use: High   Time Demand: Low
Cognitive Demand: Low/Medium

Modifications

The *Two-Minute Paper* can also be used at the beginning of a day's lesson to reflect on the previous day's lesson, in order to inform the teacher about modifications that may be necessary. It can also be used after completing homework or a class assignment. This technique has also been used as a *One-Minute Paper* with older students (Angelo & Cross, 1993). Extend the time allowed for younger students or students who have difficulty writing in the English language into a *Three-* or *Four-Minute Paper.*

Caveats

Adjust the time according to students' writing ability so that slower writers feel they have had adequate opportunity to give feedback.

Use With Other Disciplines

This FACT can also be used in mathematics, social studies, language arts, health, foreign languages, and performing arts.

My Notes

_____

_____

_____

#69: TWO OR THREE BEFORE ME

Description

Two or Three Before Me provides opportunities for more students to share their ideas during class. It prevents individual students from dominating the responses to the teacher's or other students' questions. The rule is that at least two or three students must have an opportunity to talk before the same person can speak again.

How This FACT Promotes Student Learning

This FACT provides opportunities for a greater number of students in a class to share their thinking, particularly when there are dominant voices in a class. It also provides an opportunity for students who tend to be overly responsive to teacher questioning to listen to the ideas of their peers. Taking the time to listen to the ideas of others before voicing their own thoughts helps dominant students reconsider their own ideas in light of what others think.

How This FACT Informs Instruction

Two or Three Before Me provides a classroom norm teachers can use to ensure that more students in a class have an opportunity for their ideas to be heard. When more student voices are heard, the teacher is better able to determine the extent of understanding and range of ideas in the class that can be used to inform instruction.

Design and Administration

Explain the strategy to students, including the purpose of *Two or Three Before Me*, and practice using it during a class discussion. Eventually students will adopt it as a discussion norm.

General Implementation Attributes

Ease of Use: High   Time Demand: Low
Cognitive Demand: Low

Modifications

The strategy can be changed to any number of students such as *One or Two Before Me* or *Three or Four Before Me*. This FACT can also be applied in reverse to the teacher by encouraging two or three students to speak before the teacher will speak again. It can be used by small groups of four to six students to monitor participation within a group.

Caveats

Make sure to accompany this technique with *Wait Time* strategies.

Use With Other Disciplines

This FACT can also be used in mathematics, social studies, language arts, health, foreign languages, and performing arts.

My Notes

_____

_____

_____

#70: TWO STARS AND A WISH

Description

Two Stars and a Wish is a technique used in "comments-only marking." It is a way to balance positive comments with the need for improvement when providing students with feedback on their work (Black & Harrison, 2004). The first sentence describes two good features of the section of work that is commented on. The second sentence encourages revision or further improvement.

How This FACT Promotes Student Learning

Specific comments, whether positive or comments that indicate the need for improvement, provide students with a better understanding of where their strengths and weaknesses are and how to improve their work. These comments provide the student with better insight into ways to improve their work than comments such as *great job!, nice explanation, needs revision,* or *unclear.* The balance and tone used with *Two Stars and a Wish* encourages students to take action on their work for the purpose of improving their learning. Providing two positive comments for every area of improvement raises the confidence and self-esteem of students who typically feel discouraged and give up when papers are marked wrong and/or given low grades accompanied by comments that only mention what needs to be improved. Because it does not pass judgment by grading and includes positive feedback as well as a suggestion for improvement, students feel success while acknowledging they can do better. This approach is particularly helpful with lower achieving students in improving their desire and ability to succeed. It is also helpful to high-achieving students to indicate that there is always room for improvement.

How This FACT Informs Instruction

Teachers who use this strategy support the culture needed in a classroom to focus on success and the belief that all students can achieve when given feedback that focuses on the learning target. The comments from *Two Stars and a Wish* also provide a stimulus for the student to discuss his or her work with the teacher so that the teacher can individualize improvements for each student.

Design and Administration

Use with assignments that provide an opportunity for students to demonstrate their conceptual understanding through writing and drawing such as essays, open-ended questions, problem solving, explanations of phenomena, and laboratory reports. Instead of marking students' work right or wrong, look for areas throughout the work where you can identify two good features of the students' work and one area for improvement. Place comments on a sticky note or in the margin of their work. The following are examples of feedback given using *Two Stars and a Wish:*

Feedback on a middle school student's lab write-up: *You organized the data nicely in a table and your graph clearly displays the data. Now you need to explain in more detail what the graph shows.*

Feedback on homework questions from a high school lesson on photosynthesis: *Your description of the reactants and products is accurate and your diagram showing where the reactants and products enter, leave, or are found inside the plant is clear and generally accurate. However, you need to show and explain in more detail the role that sunlight has in the process and the organelle involved.*

Feedback on an elementary student's experimental design: *You posed a good question that can be answered through your investigation. You described the procedure in a way that someone else would be able to follow. You should check your materials. Do you think a ruler is the best tool to use to measure the distance around a balloon? What will you use to find out what the balloon weighs after you fill it up with air?*

General Implementation Attributes

Ease of Use: High   Time Demand: Low
Cognitive Demand: Medium

Modifications

This FACT can also be used by students to self-assess their work or peer-assess the work of other students. Students provide two positive statements about their work or the work of their peers and indicate one area that can be improved.

Caveats

This is a comments-only FACT. Research indicates less of a positive effect on student learning when grades are given in addition to comments (Black & Harrison, 2004). Because this strategy reinforces the notion that the teacher wants students to improve their work and that their improvement is being monitored by the teacher, time should be provided in class for students to read and react to the comments. If possible, provide time in class for students to work on their revisions.

Use With Other Disciplines

This FACT can also be used in mathematics, social studies, language arts, health, foreign languages, and performing arts.

My Notes

_____

_____

_____

#71: TWO-THIRDS TESTING

Description

Summative end-of-unit tests often cover a lot of information. This technique provides an opportunity for students to take an ungraded "practice test" two thirds of the way through a unit (Wiliam, 2005). Students are then provided time to get feedback from their peers and the teacher on their responses, gaps in understanding, or difficulties in arriving at their answers.

How This FACT Promotes Student Learning

Two-Thirds Testing provides a metacognitive opportunity for students to identify areas of difficulty or misunderstanding two-thirds of the way through an instructional unit so that interventions and support can be provided to help them learn and be prepared for a final summative assessment. It alleviates the pressure of trying to recall all the ideas and skills learned throughout an instructional unit by providing an opportunity to practice using what they learned in a nonjudgmental way two-thirds of the way through their learning. In addition, working on the test through discussions with a partner or in a small group further develops and solidifies conceptual understanding.

How This FACT Informs Instruction

Examining students' cumulative knowledge and understanding two-thirds of the way through a unit may indicate areas of difficulty for individual students or the class as a whole. The information can be used to differentiate for individuals or revisit difficult concepts with the entire class. This FACT indicates to the teacher whether instruction is on pace in preparation for readiness to take an upcoming summative assessment. It provides an opportunity to give students feedback in the areas that target their learning needs.

Design and Administration

Select an alternative version of a test that will be given at the end of a unit or create a similar test. Check off or make up a new version of questions that were addressed by students' learning experiences two thirds of the way through the instructional unit. Have students work individually or in pairs on the items. Use the results for differentiated feedback or a review through class discussion about items students seem to have difficulty with.

General Implementation Attributes

Ease of Use: Medium   Time Demand: Medium/High
Cognitive Demand: Depends on type of questions

Modifications

Depending on the unit of study, this FACT can be modified as a one-third testing, one-half testing, two-thirds testing, three-quarters testing, and so on. It can also be used as a one-half or two-thirds testing for midterm, semester, or year-end final exams.

Caveats

The use of summative tests with this technique is for formative purposes only. Thus, use comments-only marking, not grades.

Use With Other Disciplines

This FACT can also be used in mathematics, social studies, language arts, health, foreign languages, and performing arts.

My Notes

_____

_____

_____

#72: VOLLEYBALL—NOT PING-PONG!

Description

Volleyball—Not Ping-Pong! describes a technique that changes the nature of the question-and-answer interaction pattern in the classroom from a back-and-forth teacher-to-student exchange to one of teacher to Student A to Student B to Student C, D, or so on . . . then back to the teacher. The ping-pong metaphor represents the typical rapid-fire, back-and-forth cycle of questions and responses that typically take place between the teacher and students. The volleyball metaphor represents the teacher asking a question, a student responding, and other students building off the response until the teacher "serves" another question.

How This FACT Promotes Student Learning

Good questioning techniques that involve all students provide an opportunity for deeper engagement with ideas in science and richer responses to questions. "Volleyball" questioning and responding helps students link, apply, and give reasons for their ideas. It motivates students to consider the ideas of others as they think about how their own ideas may enhance, extend, or challenge other students' thinking. Encouraging several students' to put their ideas forth in the public arena of the classroom rather than accepting one answer and moving on enhances the opportunity for sustained, thoughtful discussions that promote student learning.

How This FACT Informs Instruction

This FACT encourages teachers to change their questioning techniques from simple recall questions that can be answered by one student to more open-ended questions that elicit thoughtful, more detailed responses. A consequence of using this technique is that teachers have a greater opportunity to listen to their students in order to learn more about their understandings, gaps, or misconceptions. The information is used to inform their next instructional moves that will address their students' ideas and needs.

Design and Administration

Share the volleyball and ping-pong metaphor with students before using this strategy. Practice "serving" a question and having several students respond as if they were setting up the ball for the next student and hitting it over the net. When the question becomes exhausted, the "ball" goes back to the teacher for a new "serve." This type of questioning and response takes practice the first few times it is used. It may help to have students sit where they can see each other, such as in a circle, the first time it is used. Encourage students not to look at the teacher when they reply since they are putting their ideas forth to the class, not just to the teacher. They should look at their classmates when they respond. Students should also be encouraged to ask new questions that build off the responses of others that can sustain the volleyball.

General Implementation Attributes

Ease of Use: Medium   Time Demand: Low/Medium
Cognitive Demand: Medium/High

Modifications

Consider setting a minimum number of times the question and responses must go back and forth among students before the next question is asked or a comment is made by the teacher. The first time the strategy is used, it may be helpful to use a physical prop such as a volleyball, beach ball, or other soft ball that can be passed from student to student.

Caveats

This strategy also involves the use of *Wait Time Variations*. It may appear that students are not going to respond when, in fact, they are using wait time to think and formulate their comments. Be patient and don't throw out a new question too soon!

Use With Other Disciplines

This FACT can also be used in mathematics, social studies, language arts, health, foreign languages, and performing arts.

My Notes

_____

_____

_____

#73: WAIT TIME VARIATIONS

Description

Wait Time, also called the "miracle pause," has an extensive body of research behind it (Walsh & Sattes, 2005). Mary Budd Rowe, formerly a science educator at the University of Florida, discovered the value of silence as she conducted research on interactions in K–12 classrooms. Her research found that teachers tend to leave no more than one second of silence before addressing an unanswered question or asking someone to answer it. *Wait Time* is the interval between the time a question is posed and the time either a student or teacher responds to the question. When teachers increase their *Wait Time* to at least three seconds, class participation increases, answers are more detailed, complex thinking increases, and science achievement scores increase significantly (Rowe, 1974). *Wait Time 2* involves the interval between when a student answers a question and the teacher responds.

How This FACT Supports Student Learning

Complex questions require time for students to formulate an answer. *Wait Time* provides the opportunity students need to think. When *Wait Time* of three to five seconds is deliberately practiced, research has found a plethora of different kinds of benefits to students such as (Rowe, 1986; Walsh & Sattes, 2005):

Students give longer, more detailed responses.

Students give evidence for their ideas and conclusions.

Students speculate and hypothesize.

Students ask more questions.

Students talk more to other students.

There are fewer "I don't knows."

Discipline problems decrease as students become more engaged in the lesson.

More students participate in responding.

Students answer with more confidence.

Achievement improves on cognitively complex items.

How This FACT Informs Instruction

In addition to dramatically increasing the participation of students in a class discussion, this FACT also provides information to the teacher about students' understanding and ways of thinking. Since *Wait Time* encourages longer, richer answers, the teacher gains a better sense of what a student knows or the reasoning students use to formulate their ideas. Furthermore, practicing *Wait Time* increases the sample of students from which teachers can gain information about the progress of learning in the class. This information is then used by the teacher to monitor student learning experiences, differentiate for individual students, and adjust instruction accordingly to meet the learning needs of the class. In addition to promoting student thinking and informing instruction, *Wait Time* has been shown to have the following effects on teacher practice:

Teacher responses are more thoughtful and tend to keep the discussion focused and ongoing.

The quality of teacher feedback improves.

Teachers ask fewer questions. The questions they do ask increase in cognitive level.

Teachers expect more from previously nonparticipating students.

Design and Administration

Students are used to rapid-fire questions and answers. Discuss with students what *Wait Time* is and why it is used so they will understand the reason for your long pause. Establish *Wait Time* as a classroom norm practiced by both teachers and students. Practice *Wait Time* by silently counting to at least three seconds (one, one thousand, two, one-thousand, three, one thousand) before calling on a student. Continue to use three- to five-second *Wait Time* after a student answers and before you respond to the students' answer so that the student who replied and the class have time to think about the response. Use lead-ins that encourage the overeager students to wait, such as *"I want everyone to think carefully about their own ideas before we tackle this question"* or *I'm going to wait until everyone has had a chance to think before I ask you to share your thinking."* Teachers can also try deliberately pausing, indicating thinking time, and then asking for no hands to be raised until the teacher gives a signal. Sometimes it helps to give students a chance to jot their own ideas down on paper first before asking for responses. Another way is to have students discuss the proposed question with a partner, using FACTs such as *Think-Pair-Share* before taking responses from the whole class.

The following example shows how *Wait Time* can be used:

"Who can remember why it is important to identify and control variables in a scientific experiment?" Silently count to three seconds before selecting a student to respond. Kerry responds with, "It would be impossible to know what caused the change if you didn't test just one thing at a time." Include a three-second wait time before responding to the student or calling on another student. "Kerry pointed out the need to test just one thing at a time in order to know what caused the change. I want you think about what she said and then I'd like to hear who agrees, disagrees, or would like to add to what Kerry said." Wait time. . . .

General Implementation Attributes

Ease of Use: High   Time Demand: Low
Cognitive Demand: Medium

Modifications

Wait Time between students can also be encouraged and practiced with a variety of FACTs where students interact in pairs or small groups. Remind students to practice pausing before responding to another student or building upon someone else's response so that everyone has a chance to think and process their ideas. Consider using a chart such as the one in Figure 4.44 to help students practice *Wait Time*. See the Appendix for more details on using *Wait Time* and the timeless research that supports it.

Caveats

Three to five seconds of silence can seem agonizingly long! Don't succumb to the silence or students' strategy of waiting out the teacher. Students have learned in the past that if they wait long enough, the teacher will answer his or her own question. Don't give up, and if there are no takers, use the *No-Hands Questioning* strategy. Keep quiet and don't interject comments during wait time such as "Think about it" that distract student thinking.

Figure 4.44   *Wait Time* Classroom Poster

Wait Time
When the teacher asks a question:
• Listen carefully.
• Silently think about your own ideas.
• Don't raise your hand.
• Wait to be called on.
• Answer in a clear voice so everyone can hear.
• Remember that all ideas are important.
• If you are not called on, listen to others' responses.
• Think about how your ideas are similar to or different from the answers you hear.
When a student answers a question and other students can add their ideas:
• Use the silent time to think about your own ideas.
• Be prepared to build off of others' responses.
• Think about what others have said before it is your turn to talk.
• Respect others' ideas when you challenge them.
• Make eye contact with the class, not just the teacher.

SOURCE: Adapted from Walsh and Sattes (2005).

Use With Other Disciplines

This FACT can also be used in mathematics, social studies, language arts, health, foreign languages, and performing arts.

My Notes

_____

_____

_____

#74: WHAT ARE YOU DOING AND WHY?

Description

If a visitor walked into your classroom and asked students what they were doing and why they were doing it, you would hope all students could answer. This FACT helps teachers find out if their students know the goal of an activity-based science lesson and how or why the activity can help them learn. This technique "models" the visitor who walks into the room scenario.

How This FACT Promotes Student Learning

What Are You Doing and Why? activates students' thinking about the purpose of the activity they are engaged in. It asks students to describe what it is they are supposed to be learning about and how the task they have been working on will help them learn. Students are more engaged in their learning when they understand the learning goal and purpose of a learning experience.

How This FACT Informs Instruction

This short, simple monitoring strategy can be quite an eye-opener to teachers, especially if students are highly engaged in an activity yet show they do not know what the purpose of the activity is or how it will help them learn. It encourages teachers to be clear and explicit about the learning targets for the activity and explain to the students how the activity will help them develop skills or understandings. When this question is used as a spot check during an activity, teachers can get a quick read from the class on whether the purpose of the activity is understood by students. If not, teachers can readjust to make sure the activity's purpose and goals are clearly communicated to the students and understood by all. This FACT helps avoid "activitymania" in science where teachers use hands-on activities that are fun and engaging yet students have no understanding of the purpose of the activity and what they will learn from it. As a result, there are no or minimal learning gains.

Design and Administration

At any point partway into an activity, the teacher gets the class's attention and asks a "What are you doing and why are you doing it?" question. Responses can be shared with the class, discussed between partners, or recorded in writing as a *One-Minute Paper* to be passed in to the teacher. The data are analyzed by the teacher to determine if the class understands the purpose of the activity they are involved in.

General Implementation Attributes

Ease of Use: High   Time Demand: Low
Cognitive Demand: Medium

Modifications

This FACT can also be used with non-hands-on learning experiences such as assigned readings, homework, video, Internet searches, and so on. Any instructional task a student is asked to engage in should be clear about the purpose and intended outcomes.

Caveats

Do not substitute this FACT for explicitly addressing the purpose and outcome of a learning activity. Make sure the purpose and outcome are addressed before students start the activity.

Use With Other Disciplines

This FACT can also be used in mathematics, social studies, language arts, health, foreign languages, and performing arts.

My Notes

_____

_____

_____

#75: WHITEBOARDING

Description

Whiteboarding is used in small groups to encourage students to pool their individual thinking and come to a group consensus on an idea that is shared with the teacher and the whole class. The use of whiteboards supports a classroom environment that encourages student-generated ideas. Researchers have found that when students use whiteboards, their discussions are more animated, on task, and draw upon higher-level thinking (Henry, Henry, & Riddoch, 2006). The technique involves using portable 24-by-32-inch large whiteboards and dry erase markers. Students work collaboratively around the whiteboard to draw and record their ideas in response to a prompt given by the teacher. Students use the whiteboard during class discourse to communicate their ideas to their peers and the teacher; thus modeling an essential feature of scientific inquiry—communication supported by evidence and reasoning.

How This FACT Promotes Student Learning

Whiteboarding can be used at the beginning of an instructional unit or throughout a sequence of instruction to elicit students' prior knowledge and current ideas. It activates their thinking and constructing of new understandings through interaction with their peers. As students collaborate on getting their ideas down on a whiteboard and sharing them with the class, they expose their own thinking. They accept, discard, or modify their own ideas based on considering the alternative ideas of others. Unlike writing on chart paper, being able to erase the whiteboards allows students to easily modify their work as new ideas emerge through discussion. The nonpermanent nature of the writing surface encourages students to draw or write something that they may not be sure of, since they know it can be easily changed or modified. *Whiteboarding* can also be used to help students design their investigations as well as analyze data and draw conclusions from investigations.

How This FACT Informs Instruction

The size of the whiteboards allows teachers to quickly see and examine a group's thinking, providing students with feedback when necessary. As students are working on the whiteboards, the teacher is able to circulate through the class, asking questions, probing deeper, and encouraging students to make their thinking visible. The teacher can observe their drawings, writing, and discussions to note areas where additional instructional supports might be needed. As students present their whiteboards to the class, the teacher can help students clarify and solidify their understandings. In addition, the whiteboard presentations provide an opportunity for teachers to give feedback to students on their communication skills such as how to share ideas so that others can understand their reasoning, how to listen carefully to critique others' ideas, how to look for commonalities in thinking, and how to engage in scientific argumentation in a constructive way, including coming to consensus when there are differences in opinions and ideas.

Design and Administration

Whiteboards can be purchased from suppliers, but they are less expensive and a more suitable size when cut from 4-by-8-foot sheets of white economy tile board, available from home building supply stores. Many of these stores will custom cut them for teachers, including cutting handles into the top and rounding off the edges. You will also need low-odor dry erase markers (four colors, preferably black, red, green, and blue), an eraser, and cleaners for dry-erase surfaces. Inexpensive tube socks can be used as erasers and also provide a handy storage receptacle for the markers. Provide students with a prompt that encourages them to work together in pairs or a group of three to four, huddled around the whiteboard, to draw and write about their ideas so that they can use the whiteboard to present their thinking to the class. For example, a prompt for a fourth-grade electricity unit might be as follows:

> *In my hand I have a battery, a flashlight bulb, and a piece of wire. Draw as many ways as you can that show how a battery can light a bulb using one piece of wire.*

Encourage students to use different colors to differentiate parts of their drawing. When groups have finished with their boards, use them to facilitate a whole-class discussion, revealing the variety of ideas in the class. Sometimes it is helpful to line up the whiteboards and allow students an opportunity to do a "walk through" first, silently walking around to look at other groups' work. During whole-class discussion with the whiteboards, it is important to allow the student group to be the center of attention, with other students' eyes on them and their whiteboard. Position students so that everyone can see the whiteboard that is being presented. Encourage the students to interact and exchange ideas, using strategies such as *Volleyball—Not Ping-Pong!* so that the conversation is between the students, with the teacher as listener. After students have had an opportunity to take turns describing and discussing their boards, the teacher may choose to photograph each board for a digital record of students' thinking. If possible, have students test their ideas as drawn on the whiteboard. For example, students can be given a battery, flashlight bulb, and a piece of wire to test their idea and modify their drawing based on their findings.

General Implementation Attributes

Ease of Use: High   Time Demand: Medium/High
Cognitive Demand: Medium/High

Modifications

Smaller individual whiteboards can be used but are not as effective for promoting group thinking as the larger sizes. If whiteboards are not available, shiny-sided freezer paper also works with dry-erase markers and allows the teacher to keep a record of the group's ideas. Depending on the prompt and size of the whiteboard, they can also be divided into four sections, having each student in a group contribute to one of the four sections.

Caveats

As with any new technique, students should be introduced to the use of *Whiteboarding* by modeling it for them the first time they are used for group work and presentation, including ways to use features such as bullets, diagrams, arrows, color, and text size. Make sure there is enough room to accommodate the larger whiteboards either on a table or on the floor, including room for three to four students to simultaneously work on the board together.

Use With Other Disciplines

This FACT can also be used in mathematics.

My Notes

_____

_____

_____

Appendix

Annotated Resources for
Science Formative Assessment

The following resources provide sources of supplementary material to use in designing or informing your use of the FACTs. Each resource lists the FACT numbers that mention use of these annotated resources in the descriptions provided in Chapter 4.

Annenberg Videos. Several of the Annenberg video series show examples of students being interviewed about their ideas in science. These videos are available online as streaming videos at www.learner.org and entering the title of the video series in the search bar. *The Private Universe* videos show examples of individual students participating in a structured interview as well as informal interviews of college graduates. The *Essential Science* series contains video interviews of individual students as well as groups of students in a lab setting. This resource is referenced in FACTs #25 and 35.

Assessment for Learning. This book provides an excellent description of the rationale for formative assessment, the research that supports it, and information on specific techniques teachers have used. This resource is referenced in FACTs #65, 67, and 73.

Black, P., Harrison, C., Lee, C., Marshall, B., & Wiliam, D. (2003). *Assessment for learning*. Berkshire, England: Open University Press.

Concept Cartoons. The Concept Cartoon Web site at www.concept cartoons.com gives examples of concept cartoons and ordering information. The cartoons can be ordered as a book or on a CD. There are also posters and big books that use the concept cartoon format to stimulate discussion. The site also contains selected research studies done in the United Kingdom to examine the impact of concept cartoons on student learning. This resource is referenced in FACTs #9, 19, 21, 35, 43, and 55.

Phenomena and Representations for Instruction of Science in Middle Schools (PRISMS). This Web site (http://prisms.mmsa.org), a project of the Maine Mathematics and Science Alliance, is supported by funding from the National Science Foundation and is included in the National Science Digital Library. It features a collection of reviewed phenomena and representations, aligned to learning goals, that can be used in science instruction. Criteria are included and explained that describe the instructional quality of the phenomena and representations, along with descriptions of common misconceptions. This resource is referenced in FACTs #14 and 51.

Quality Questioning. This book provides a wealth of information on asking good questions. In addition to the FACTs described in Chapter 4, this book provides additional techniques for asking questions, prompting students' responses, and ways to generate, prepare, and process questions. This resource is referenced in FACTs #37 and 73.

Walsh, J., & Sattes, B. (2005). *Quality questioning: Research-based practice to engage every learner.* Thousand Oaks, CA: Corwin Press.

SALG—Student Assessment of Learning Gains. This Web site (www.wcer.wisc.edu/salgains/instructor/default.asp) was developed with funding from the National Science Foundation to help college course instructors evaluate their courses in terms of how well their students think the course components advanced their learning. The site, which can be also used by middle and high school teachers, has an online instrument where teachers can develop their own survey and provide access to students to take the survey online. This resource is referenced in FACT #57.

Science Curriculum Topic Study—Bridging the Gap Between Standards and Practice. This book was funded by a grant from the National Science Foundation awarded to the Maine Mathematics and Science Alliance for the project *Curriculum Topic Study—A Systematic Approach to Utilizing National Standards and Cognitive Research.* It provides a process to use national standards and cognitive research to deeply examine K–12 teaching and learning in 147 science topics. The vetted readings included in the curriculum topic study (CTS) study guides point out areas of the cognitive research where teachers can learn more about students' misconceptions. Chapter 4 includes a process for developing formative assessment probes similar to the ones described in several of the FACTs. The book is available through Corwin Press (www.corwinpress.com) and the NSTA Press (nsta.org). This resource is referenced in FACTs #2, #4, 8, 9, 30, 35, and 50.

Keeley, P. (2005). *Science curriculum topic study: Bridging the gap between standards and practice.* Thousand Oaks, CA: Corwin Press.

Uncovering Student Ideas in Science Series. This multivolume series contains ready-to-use formative assessment probes that can be adapted for use with several of the FACTs described in this book. Each book contains 25 probes along with extensive teacher background notes. The first volume includes an introduction to formative assessment. Volume 2 describes instructional strategies that can be used with the probes. Volume 3 describes ways teachers can use probes for professional development and support professional learning communities. The books are available through NSTA Press at www.nsta.org or through the Maine Mathematics and Science Alliance at www.mmsa.org. This resource is referenced in FACTs #4, 7, 14, 19, 21, 30, 35, 43, 50, 53, and 55.

Keeley, P., Eberle, F., & Farrin, L. (2005). *Uncovering student ideas in science: 25 formative assessment probes* (Vol. 1). Arlington, VA: NSTA Press.
Keeley, P., Eberle, F., & Tugel, J. (2007). *Uncovering student ideas in science: 25 more formative assessment probes* (Vol. 2). Arlington, VA: NSTA Press.
Keeley, P., Eberle, F., & Dorsey, C. (2008). *Uncovering student ideas in science: 25 more formative assessment probes* (Vol. 3). Arlington, VA: NSTA Press.

Workshops and Professional Development on Formative Assessment. The author and her colleagues at the Maine Mathematics and Science Alliance provide professional development on formative assessment and the FACTs described in this book to schools, school districts, organizations, math-science partnership projects, and curriculum developers. Workshops range from half to full-day sessions, two- to three-day conferences, and weeklong leadership institutes. For information on our professional development components or to arrange for speakers or professional development related to formative assessment, please visit the MMSA Web site at www.mmsa.org or contact the author at pkeeley@mmsa.org or Joyce Tugel at jtugel@mmsa.org.

Coming soon: Stay tuned for a mathematics version of this book: *Mathematics Formative Assessment: 50 Practical Strategies for Linking Assessment, Instruction, and Learning.* Anticipated date of publication: 2009.

References

Abell, S., & Volkmann, M. (2006). *Seamless assessment in science: A guide for elementary and middle school teachers.* Portsmouth, NH: Heinemann.

Ainsworth, L., & Viegut, D. (2006). *Common formative assessments.* Thousand Oaks, CA: Corwin Press.

American Association for the Advancement of Science. (1988). *Science for all Americans.* New York: Oxford University Press.

American Association for the Advancement of Science. (1993). *Benchmarks for science literacy.* New York: Oxford University Press.

Angelo, T., & Cross, K. P. (1993). *Classroom assessment techniques: A handbook for college teachers.* San Francisco: Jossey-Bass.

Ausubel, D., Novak, J., & Hanesian, H. (1978). *Educational psychology: A cognitive view* (2nd ed.). New York: Holt, Rinehart, and Winston.

Black, B., & Harrison, C. (2004). *Science inside the black box: Assessment for learning in the science classroom.* London: NFER/Nelson.

Black, P., Harrison, C., Lee, C., Marshall, B., & Wiliam, D. (2003). *Assessment for learning.* Berkshire, England: Open University Press.

Black, P., & Wiliam, D. (1998). Inside the black box: Raising standards through classroom assessment. *Phi Delta Kappan, 80*(2), 139–148.

Bransford, J., Brown, A., & Cocking, R. (1999). *How people learn: Brain, mind, experience, and school.* Washington, DC: National Academy Press.

Buehl, D. (2001). *Classroom strategies for interactive learning.* Newark, DE: International Reading Association.

Bybee, R. (1997). *Achieving scientific literacy.* Portsmouth, NH: Heinemann.

Carey, S. (2000). Science education as conceptual change. *Journal of Applied Developmental Psychology, 21*(1), 13.

Carlson, M., Humphrey, G., & Reinhardt, K. (2003). *Weaving science inquiry and continuous assessment.* Thousand Oaks, CA: Corwin Press.

Campbell, B., & Fulton, L. (2003). *Science notebooks: Writing about inquiry.* Portsmouth, NH: Heinemann.

Carre, C. (1993). Performance in subject-matter knowledge in science. In N. Bennet & C. Carre (Eds.), *Learning to teach* (pp. 18–35). London, UK: Routledge.

Clarke, S. (2005). *Formative assessment in the secondary classroom.* London: Hodder Murray.

Connor, J. V. (1990). Naive conceptions and the school science curriculum. In M. B. Rowe (Ed.), *The process of knowing: What research says to the science teacher* (Vol. 6, pp. 5–18). Washington, DC: NSTA.

Cox-Peterson, A., & Olson, J. (2002). Assessing student learning. In R. Bybee (Ed.), *Learning science and the science of learning* (pp. 105–120). Arlington, VA: NSTA Press.

Donovan, S., & Bransford, J. (2005). *How students learn science in the classroom.* Washington, DC: National Academy Press.

Driver, R., Squires, A., Rushworth, P., & Wood-Robinson, V. (1994). *Making sense of secondary science.* New York: Routledge.

Erickson, L. (1998). *Concept-based curriculum and instruction.* Thousand Oaks, CA: Corwin Press.

Flick, L., & Tomlinson, M. (2006). Helping students understand the minds-on side of learning science. In M. McMahon, P. Simmons, R. Sommers, D. DeBaets, & F. Crawley (Eds.), *Assessment in science: Practical experiences and education research* (pp. 183–196). Arlington, VA: NSTA Press.

Goldberg, F., Bendall, S., Heller, P., & Poel, R. (2006). *Interactions in physical science.* Armonk, NY: It's About Time Publishing.

Hall, K., & Burke, W. (2003). *Making formative assessment work-effective practice in the primary classroom.* Berkshire, England: Open University Press.

Hammer, D., & Van Zee, E. (2006). *Seeing the science in children's thinking.* Portsmouth, NH: Heinemann.

Henry, D., Henry, J., & Riddoch, S. (2006, April). Whiteboarding your way to great student discussions. *Science Scope,* pp. 50-53

Hewson, P. (1992, June). *Conceptual change in science teaching and teacher education.* Paper presented at a meeting on "Research and Curriculum Development in Science Teaching," National Center for Educational Research, Documentation, and Assessment, Ministry for Education and Science, Madrid, Spain.

Keeley, P. (2005). *Science curriculum topic study: Bridging the gap between standards and practice.* Thousand Oaks, CA: Corwin Press.

Keeley, P., Eberle, F., & Farrin, L. (2005). *Uncovering student ideas in science: 25 formative assessment probes* (Vol. 1). Arlington, VA: NSTA Press.

Keeley, P., Eberle, F., & Tugel, J. (2007). *Uncovering student ideas in science: 25 more formative assessment probes* (Vol. 2). Arlington, VA: NSTA Press.

Krajcik, J., Moje, E., Sutherland, L., Meriweather, A., Rucker, S., Sarratt, P., et al. (2006). More emphasis on scientific explanation: developing conceptual understanding and science literacy. In R. Douglas, M. Klentschy, K. Worth, & W. Binder (Eds.), *Exemplary science in Grades 5–8: Standards-based success stories* (pp. 99–113). Arlington, VA: NSTA Press.

Lawson, A. (2002). The learning cycle. In R. Fuller (Ed.), *A love of discovery: Science education—The second career of Robert Karplus* (pp. 51–56). New York: Kluwer Academic/Plenum.

Lipton, L., & Wellman, B. (1998). *Pathways to understanding: Patterns and practices in the learning-focused classroom.* Sherman, CT: Mira Via.

Love, N. (2002). *Using data/getting results: A practical guide for school improvement in mathematics and science.* Norwood, MA: Christopher-Gordon Publishers.

Maine Department of Education. (2007). *Maine's learning results.* Augusta: Maine Department of Education. www.maine.gov/education/lres/review/sci_tech 071107.pdf

National Research Council. (1996). *National science education standards.* Washington, DC: National Academy Press.

National Research Council. (2001). *Classroom assessment and the national science education standards.* Washington, DC: National Academy Press.

National Science Teachers Association (NSTA). (2006). Picturing to learn makes science visual. *NSTA Reports, 18*(2), 20.

Naylor, S., & Keogh, B. (2000). *Concept cartoons in science education.* Cheshire, UK: Millgate House Publisher.

Naylor, S., Keogh, B., & Goldsworthy, A. (2004). *Active assessment: Thinking, learning and assessment in science.* London: David Fulton.

Novak, J. (1998). *Learning, creating, and using knowledge: Concept maps as facilitative tools in schools and corporations.* Mahwah, NJ: Lawrence Erlbaum.

Osborne, R., & Freyberg, P. (1985). *Learning in science: The implications of children's science.* Portsmouth, NH: Heinemann.

Perkins, D. (1992). *Smart schools.* New York: Free Press.

Posner, G., Strike, K., Hewson, P., & Gertzog, W. (1982). Accommodation of a scientific conception: Toward a theory of conceptual change. *Science Education, 66,* 211–227.

Rowe, M. (1974). Wait time and rewards as instructional variables, their influence on language, logic, and fate control. *Journal of Research in Science Teaching, 11,* 81–94.

Rowe, M. (1986). Wait time: Slowing down may be a way of speeding up! *Journal of Teacher Education, 37*(1), 43–50.

Rupp, B. (2007). *Writing in science: How to scaffold instruction to support learning.* Portsmouth, NH: Heinemann.

Sato, M. (2003). Working with teachers in assessment-related professional development. In M. Atkin & J. Coffey (Eds.), *Everyday assessment in the science classroom* (pp. 109–119). Arlington, VA: NSTA Press.

Shapiro, B. (1994). *What children bring to light: A constructivist perspective on children's learning in science.* New York: Teachers College Press.

Stepans, J. (2003). *Targeting students' science misconceptions.* Tampa, FL: Showboard, Inc.

Vygotsky, L. (1978). *Mind in society.* Cambridge, MA: Harvard University Press.

Walsh, J., & Sattes, B. (2005). *Quality questioning: Research-based practice to engage every learner.* Thousand Oaks, CA: Corwin Press.

White, B., & Frederickson, J. (1998). Inquiry, modeling, and metacognition: Making science accessible to all students. *Cognition and Science, 16,* 90–91.

White, R., & Gunstone, R. (1992). *Probing understanding.* London: Falmer.

Wiliam, D. (2005, November 9). *Science assessment: Research and practical approaches for Grades 3–12 teachers and school and district administrators.* Remarks made at the closing Plenary Session, NSTA Assessment Conference, Chicago.

Index

CORWIN PRESS

The Corwin Press logo—a raven striding across an open book—represents the union of courage and learning. Corwin Press is committed to improving education for all learners by publishing books and other professional development resources for those serving the field of PreK–12 education. By providing practical, hands-on materials, Corwin Press continues to carry out the promise of its motto: **"Helping Educators Do Their Work Better."**

National Science Teachers Association

The National Science Teachers Association is the largest professional organization in the world promoting excellence and innovation in science teaching and learning for all. NSTA's membership includes more than 55,000 science teachers, science supervisors, administrators, scientists, business and industry representatives, and others involved in science education.